ALSO BY LOUISE BARNETT

Touched by Fire: The Life, Death,
and Mythic Afterlife of George Armstrong Custer

Authority and Speech: Language, Society,
and Self in the American Novel

Swift's Poetic Worlds

The Ignoble Savage: American Literary Racism, 1790–1890

UNGENTLEMANLY ACTS

UNGENTLEMANLY *Acts*

THE ARMY'S NOTORIOUS
INCEST TRIAL

Louise Barnett

HILL AND WANG

A DIVISION OF FARRAR, STRAUS AND GIROUX

NEW YORK

Hill and Wang
A division of Farrar, Straus and Giroux
19 Union Square West, New York 10003

Library of Congress Cataloging-in-Publication Data
Barnett, Louise K.
    Ungentlemanly acts : the army's notorious incest trial / Louise
Barnett. — 1st ed.
        p.   cm.
    Includes bibliographical references and index
    ISBN 0-8090-7397-8
    1. Geddes, Andrew, 1845?–1921—Trials, litigation, etc.
    2. Orleman, Louis Henry, 1842?–1936—Trials, litigation, etc.
    3. Courts-martial and courts of inquiry—United States.   4. Trials
(Incest)—Texas—San Antonio.   I. Title.
KF7642.G43B37   2000
343.73'0143—dc21   99-42881

Frontispiece: Lillie Orleman, age seventeen. The back of this photo is inscribed "To my dearest mamma, from her daughter." [Courtesy of Paul Orleman]

FOR NICHOLAS STEPHEN BARNETT

CONTENTS

ACKNOWLEDGMENTS

"Acknowledgments" is a pale word for the debts that historians accumulate. Without the generous help of Brian Pohanka, this book would not exist. He brought the 1879 trial of Andrew Geddes to my attention and then provided help and encouragement during every stage of my research. I am more grateful than I can express for his patience and knowledge, both seemingly inexhaustible. Other researchers have also shared their expertise unstintingly and deserve far greater thanks than I can articulate. I would have had to abandon the idea of writing about the Geddes trial had not David Wallace found the missing trial transcript at the National Archives. Other archivists there, Michael Musick and Michael Meier, ran down any number of obscure matters for me, and it was always heartening to find former archivist DeAnn Blanton on duty in the military archives room.

Glenna Matthews, in calling my attention to the Byron-Stowe furor, substantially increased my knowledge of the mid-nineteenth century's attitude toward incest, while Janis Johnson enlightened me on incest in twentieth-century America. For interest and help I am also grateful to Leanna Biles, Historic Fort Stockton; John Slonaker, Military History Institute, Carlisle Barracks; and Susan Lintelmann, United States Military Academy Archive. Dr. Thomas P. Lowry and Beverly Lowry have shared their formidable knowledge of Civil War courts-martial with me and have always provided supportive friendship.

The advice of my editor, Lauren Osborne, has resulted in a stronger book, as has that of my brother, Stephen Kennamer, and my husband, Robert Barnett. As usual, I have relied on my agent, Gerry McCauley, for professionalism that meets the highest standard.

In accessing secondary sources I am indebted to the Shadek-Fackenthal Library of Franklin and Marshall College, particularly the services of Thomas A. Karel and Mary K. Shelly. A year's fellowship at the Rutgers University Center for Historical Analysis aided my research, and I especially thank co-directors Deborah Gray White and Mia Bay for presiding over a richly inspiring intellectual experience.

My thanks to all of these generous people, and to Michael O'Keefe for sharing some Texas family history with me.

In this, as in other endeavors, I have been sustained by my husband, by my sons Rob and Greg, and my daughters-in-law Laura and Sylvia. This book is dedicated with love to my first grandchild, Nicholas Stephen Barnett.

Absolute and perfect obedience to the Constitution of the United States is, and should be, the duty and pride of every good citizen. The fifth, sixth, seventh, and eighth amendments guarantee to the vilest criminal protection till duly convicted, and to no single man or community is given the right to set aside these fundamental principles of eternal justice.

—William Tecumseh Sherman
August 26, 1869

BEGINNINGS

SCANDAL

Today, Americans are accustomed to the image of the court stenographer, clacking away at a machine that will spew forth a printed transcript of a trial almost immediately. But in 1879, transcripts were still copied out in longhand. For army courts-martial, these transcripts were boiled down into bare-bones abstracts, which provided an official printed summary of the proceedings. Each abstract listed the name of the defendant, the accusation, the verdict, and the sentence. Accusations were broken down into two parts: *charges,* which were general ("conduct unbecoming an officer and a gentleman," for example), and *specifications,* which described exactly what was done, where, and when.

In the case of Captain Andrew J. Geddes, whose trial lasted for the extraordinarily long period of three months, an exception was made. Geddes was tried for "conduct unbecoming," but in the space where specifications were usually listed in the printed record appeared the phrase "not fit to be specified."

What abhorrent crime had Geddes committed? What deed so horrifying that the Army's official record could not mention it? In the answer lies the true irony of this case. Geddes had accused a fellow officer, Lieutenant Louis H. Orleman, of an unspeakable offense—but instead of investigating Orleman, the Army tried Geddes for speaking of Orleman's alleged crime. And as it turned out, there would be a great deal in the proceedings against Captain Geddes that would not be fit to be specified.

Nothing in the extensive professional experience of Civil War veteran General E.O.C. Ord, commander of the Department of Texas, could have prepared him for the document that arrived at his San Antonio headquarters in April of 1879. The sworn and notarized deposition of Captain Andrew J. Geddes of the Twenty-fifth U.S. Infantry baldly accused First Lieutenant Louis H. Orleman, an officer of the Tenth U.S. Cavalry, of incest. Both men were stationed at Fort Stockton, a small frontier post in the still wild and sparsely populated region of West Texas. Ord regarded Geddes as one of his best field officers, but his deposition was shocking, even unprecedented. In an army where officers often preferred charges against each other to settle disputes, the matter of Geddes's charge was extraordinary.

Geddes stated that he had spoken out only in self-defense because he had learned that Orleman was bringing charges against him. To defend himself against these charges, he had to expose the relationship of "criminal intimacy" he had accidentally discovered between the thirty-eight-year-old lieutenant and his eighteen-year-old daughter, Lillie:

> I would state that on Sunday March 2nd 1879 . . . I saw Lt. L. H. Orleman, 10th Cavalry, having criminal intercourse with his said

daughter. . . . I heard from the adjoining quarters (the same being of [sic] those of Lt. Orleman, and divided from mine by a partition wall) a voice which I recognized to be that of Miss Lillie Orleman, saying, "Papa, please don't. I'll call Major Geddes,* if you don't quit" and . . . in the most piteous and pleading tone, "Oh, Papa, for God's sake don't. Major Geddes is Officer of the Day and will hear us" and other expressions in which my name occurred. Having had my suspicions aroused before this that something was wrong, I went to the window of said room and looked in, and there saw Lt. Orleman in bed with his said daughter, having criminal intercourse with her.

On the following day, March 3rd 1879, Miss Lillie Orleman confessed to me that her father, Lt. Orleman, had been having sexual intercourse with her for the past five years, or since she was thirteen years of age, and that he had placed a loaded revolver to her head, threatening that he would blow out her brains if she did not consent to his horrible desires. Miss Orleman begged me repeatedly and implored me on bended knee to save her, and take her from this terrible life of shame that she had been leading since she was thirteen years of age. This I consented to do, with the full knowledge and consent of her father; I having told him, at her urgent request (March 12th 1879, I think) that I had discovered his infamous crime, I made full preparations to take her away, either to her home in Austin, or to my wife—in the latter case, with the understanding that she (my wife) should be made aware of my reasons for so doing, and that Miss Orleman should herself tell to my wife her sad story.

Geddes's deposition concluded, aggressively:

I would state that I was not alone in my suspicions that criminal intimacy existed between Lt. Orleman and his daughter. Mr. Joseph

---

*Although Geddes's actual rank was captain, his brevet rank was major. A brevet title is a form of commendation for merit, the brevet title being higher than the ranking for which the officer is paid. As a courtesy, officers are often addressed or referred to by their brevet titles. Geddes, like many officers in the frontier army, held a brevet rank for Civil War exploits.

Friedlander of Fort Stockton and myself, together with Lt. Orleman and his daughter, went from Fort Stockton to Fort Davis and return[ed] in an ambulance and while on the road we saw Lt. Orleman fondling with the breast of his daughter, and heard her appealing to him to desist.

I respectfully submit that if this unfortunate affair is to be brought before a Court (which on account of the young lady, I deprecate beyond measure) that he who is guilty should be tried, and I believe a Court of Inquiry would determine as between Lt. Orleman and myself that he should be the party who ought to be tried.[1]

As departmental commander, General Ord had complete latitude in determining how to proceed, and the unusually sensitive nature of the issue might have given him pause. He could have considered Geddes's deposition a privileged document and handled the matter quietly. Well before the events of Geddes's affidavit, Orleman had applied to retire from active duty for reasons of ill health. He and his daughter would soon be leaving Fort Stockton, and with their departure the scandal surrounding the episode might have been contained. As Geddes intimated, a court proceeding was bound to be agonizing for Lillie Orleman. Vindication of her innocence would be a Pyrrhic victory at best. But Ord chose to order a court-martial, not of Orleman, but of Geddes, on the charges Orleman had preferred. Orleman claimed that Geddes had libelled him with a false accusation of incest as part of his attempted seduction and abduction of Lillie Orleman.

Why did General Ord so quickly conclude that Orleman's charges had merit and Geddes's did not? Before the trial both sides were represented only by competing stories. But acknowledging the possibility of incest by bringing charges against Orleman would have officially validated and magnified a scandal that would have haunted the Army, and the Department of Texas, for years to come. Fortunately for Orleman, this course of action was unthinkable because incest itself was unthinkable in America in

1879. It was far easier for General Ord to believe the familiar kind of wrongdoing set forth in Orleman's accusation: that Geddes's charge was an act of retaliation after his effort to seduce and abduct Lillie Orleman failed.

Ord was the single most powerful figure in the trial—although he had no role in the actual court proceedings. It was up to him to rule that a court-martial would take place, on charges that required no "oath to accompany their filing nor a formal pretrial investigation to test their validity."[2] He chose the officers who composed the court, appointed the judge advocate who prosecuted the case, and reviewed the verdict and sentence, which were merely recommendations to him. Until 1920, the departmental commander had the power to reverse acquittals or return "inadequate" sentences to the court for augmentation.[3] Too many acquittals were considered incompatible with military discipline.

As military historian William Generous writes of that period, "charges could be made almost capriciously," and the verdict of a court-martial would be reviewed "by the very commander who levied the charges, convened the court, and appointed its members and officers."[4] Under these circumstances, command influence was unavoidable. The judge advocate, who presented the Army's case, was also supposed to represent the defendant, but in practice he usually functioned as a prosecutor. The judge advocate had to approve defense applications for witnesses—an enormous power, although his decisions could be overruled by the court—and *he joined in the court's deliberations.*

That giving the judge advocate such a dominant role in the proceedings might lead to abuse seems to be the message of one military authority on court-martial procedure. Stephen Vincent Benét, whose *Treatise on Military Law and the Practice of Courts-Martial* was a widely invoked manual, wrote about the judge advocate in a cautionary tone:

The court is not required to decide points of law and fact according to his advice or opinion. He is a mere *prosecutor,* not a judge; and the members of the court, and *they alone,* are, by their oaths, to *administer justice* according to their consciences, the best of their understandings, and the custom of war in like cases—and not according to the understanding and conscience of the judge advocate.[5]

Benét's phrasing suggests that overactive judge advocates might rather easily usurp the prerogatives of the court.

As late as the 1950s, another military writer recalled a Judge Advocate Basic Officers' Class in which students training to be judge advocates were taught that they were officers first, lawyers second, and their commander was their most important client.[6] A commander could always, if he so desired, "exert great influence over the results of courts-martial."[7]

In general, courts-martial during the frontier army period (roughly the post–Civil War era to 1898) were characterized by the kind of procedure that may be found today in a small-claims court—an assembly-line approach marked by haste and standardized responses. It was always difficult to round up enough officers for a trial session. Continually downsized by Congress, the postwar army was spread too thin to perform any of its duties adequately—to police the still volatile South during the early years of the period, to oversee thousands of miles of frontier, to train adequately, and to conduct courts-martial. Commanders of understrength units were loath to give up their officers to court-martial duty for long periods of time, and, as one anonymous voice indicates, the officers themselves tended to regard this service as a tiresome duty:

> *The worst of our dreary routine*
> *Upon the bleak frontier,*
> *Is to meet in solemn conclave*
> *And these stupid cases hear.*[8]

8

In 1879, the year that Geddes came to trial, there were 2,127 army officers to handle 1,673 courts-martial, at a time when the full strength of the Army was only 26,389.[9] Probably because there were so few officers available, a member of the court or the judge advocate was also allowed to appear as a witness in a court-martial.

Since many offenses now handled by administrative punishments had to go through the court-martial procedure back then, the sheer volume of trials, "often for trivial offenses, was staggering," and the time involved correspondingly great.[10] Given that the overwhelming number of cases resolved themselves into desertion or some form of alcohol-induced offense, the members of an army court often gave in to the temptation to dispose of each case quickly. (Incidentally, having been court-martialled himself did not disqualify an officer from subsequently serving on a court.)

In spite of the rigid hierarchy that automatically conferred presidency of the court on the highest-ranking officer, and the formulaic language, some aspects of court-martial procedure were astonishingly casual. For one thing, few officers knew anything about law, and—it might be said—not by accident. As General of the Army William Tecumseh Sherman wrote,

> It will be a grave error if . . . we permit the Military Law to become emasculated by allowing lawyers to inject into it principles derived from their practice in the civil courts. . . . The objects of the civil law are to secure to everyone all the liberty, security, and happiness consistent with the safety of all. The purpose of military law is to govern armies of strong men, so as to be capable of exercising the largest measure of force at the will of the nation.

Sherman envisioned the contrast between the two systems of jurisprudence in terms of soft and hard, "happiness" versus "force," or peace versus war. As the image of strong men capable of exercising force and the threat of emasculation insinuate, an unstated formulation of Sherman's ruminations might be female versus male. Civil law can concern itself with individual rights, but military law—because of its special mission—must be made of sterner stuff. "Civilian lawyers," Sherman remarked, "are too apt to charge that army discipline is tyranny."[11]*

Another commentator, General Alfred Terry, spoke in favor of legal expertise when he addressed an 1876 congressional hearing on the subject of military judicial reform. "As a rule," General Terry observed disapprovingly, "the officers who are empowered to convene courts are no more versed in the law than the officers who compose them." Terry, a lawyer himself, came to a conclusion opposed to Sherman's:

> In view of the despotic character of all military institutions, of the powers necessarily given to the superior over the inferior in rank, it would seem that a precise and definite construction of the law, an exact and systematic administration of it, would be even the more necessary.[12]

For Terry, the very nature of the military demanded safeguards. For Sherman, this same nature demanded something more coercive than the civilian judicial system.

Geddes was charged with two counts of conduct unbecoming an officer and a gentlemen—one for an attempt to corrupt and abduct Lillie Orleman, the other for accusing her father of incest—and one count of "false swearing to the prejudice of good

---

*The date of Sherman's letter, December 9, suggests that Sherman may well have had in mind the Geddes case, in which he had taken a strong personal interest. The President was the final reviewing authority for a court-martial, and President Hayes's decision on the Geddes trial was dated December 3.

order and military discipline." This charge simply restated the incest accusation charge, focusing on Geddes's affidavit.

According to the first charge Geddes, "a married man, did by persuasion, advice, threats, and other means, endeavor to corrupt Miss Lillie Orleman . . . to his own illicit purposes." He was also accused of plotting to abduct her.

The second charge stated that Geddes

> did, by wilfully and falsely accusing said Lt. Orleman of the heinous crime of incestuous intercourse with his said Orleman's daughter . . . and by threatening to make the same public, attempt to force and coerce said Lt. Orleman into giving his consent to the departure of his daughter . . . with the said Captain Geddes, and did subsequently further attempt to obtain this consent just mentioned by promises, then and there, made to the said Lt. Orleman to keep secret his accusations hereinbefore mentioned if said Lt. Orleman permitted the departure of his said daughter Miss Lillie Orleman with the said Captain Geddes; and all this on the part of the said Captain Geddes with the intent to corrupt the said Miss Lillie Orleman to his own illicit purposes.

Charges in army courts-martial of this period tend to be rhetorically overblown, using a ritualized and excessive language that is often tempered in the court's final written disposition of the case. Having such singularly promising material at hand, the author of the final specification against Geddes (probably the judge advocate, the officer who prosecuted the case for the Army) expressed his moral outrage at some length. Geddes had "wickedly and maliciously" devised and intended "unlawfully and unjustly to aggrieve, oppress, injure, defame and falsely accuse" Lieutenant Orleman. Then the specification repeats the whole sequence of condemnatory words, this time marshalling them against Geddes's behavior toward Lillie Orleman.

Geddes had hoped to have the matter settled without a court-martial by entering a plea in bar,* but this was rejected. He then pleaded not guilty to all charges.

In commenting on the charges at the beginning of court proceedings, Judge Advocate John W. Clous invoked "the great unwritten law of the Army" that any matter that may be considered conduct unbecoming an officer and a gentleman is a proper subject for trial. "Conduct unbecoming" was the military's charge for any misbehavior that did not fall tidily under one of the Articles of War. Such behavior was instead governed by "the custom of the service, a usefully vague concept."[13] In fact, the notion of the proper behavior of an officer and a gentleman embodied an idealistic view of the officer corps. Major General John M. Schofield, in his annual report for 1875, was matter-of-fact in asserting that "it is not necessary even to refer to the generally recognized high standard of honor among military men."[14] This high standard was routinely invoked in courts-martial, where the label "conduct unbecoming" was attached to whatever actions someone believed it applied to.

In his opening statement to the court, Judge Advocate Clous immediately addressed the issue of conduct unbecoming:

> An officer of the Army has higher obligations than the ordinary citizen—he is responsible to a far more comprehensive code than that found in the laws of the United States, the common law or the laws of the several states. He must at all times conduct himself as a gentleman should and whatever is unbecoming a gentleman is of necessity unbecoming an officer.

Trying to abduct a brother officer's daughter, he went on to say, qualified as conduct unbecoming an officer and a gentleman.

As characterized by the prosecution, Geddes was not acting in good faith in bringing an affidavit to departmental headquarters;

---

*A plea in bar is a request to dismiss the case.

instead, he was making "counter accusations of such a frightful and heinous nature, and with such a force as to secure himself the vantage ground of accusor instead of becoming the accused."

The Geddes court-martial would go on for the extraordinary period of three months, with court in session every weekday between the hours of 10:30 and 1:30 or 2:30, May through August, the hottest part of the year in San Antonio. As Major General Irvin McDowell reflected on court-martial custom, the early hour of adjournment was a relic of older times:

> [A] great inconvenience and delay in the administration of military justice . . . [is] the limitation now imposed by law on the hours of session of courts-martial, making it illegal to sit after three o'clock p.m. . . . The restriction has ceased to have any justification; and is simply a relic of the past which is the cause of much inconvenience and delay.[15]

The court met in departmental headquarters, a building erected for the Army by the well-known Maverick family.[16]

When Geddes first entered the courtroom on May 19, 1879, he found himself in a familiar situation. Seven years earlier he had been the defendant in a completely different kind of case, one involving financial transactions. Cleared of intentional fraud by the court, he was nevertheless dismissed, only to be reinstated through the decision of the Army's first Judge Advocate General, Joseph Holt.* In reversing the decision and restoring Geddes to his duties, Holt had written, "It is hoped that he will profit by the lesson of this trial, and that his future career will exhibit the same

---

*The Judge Advocate General is the final reviewer of a court-martial in the Army's judicial system. His recommendation is forwarded to the President.

scrupulous regard for his obligations as an officer of the Army that testimony to his previous reputation seems to show him to have observed in the past."[17]

After the 1872 verdict, but before the Judge Advocate General had ruled, Geddes addressed a plea for clemency to Secretary of War William Belknap. "I am proud of my state and proud of my profession," he wrote. "If I were to be dismissed, it would be as if my whole life were ruined."[18] These were prophetic words.

BYRON AND STOWE

Although the decision to prosecute Captain Geddes rather than Lieutenant Orleman may seem more than a little odd to observers in our day, a publishing event in 1869 reveals attitudes toward incest that explain the Army's action.

Harriet Beecher Stowe, the author of *Uncle Tom's Cabin* and a woman known for her stern sense of moral duty, published a magazine article stating that the celebrated poet Lord Byron had committed incest with his half sister, Augusta Leigh.[19] In response to the outcry that followed, Stowe turned her "True Story of Lady Byron's Life" into a substantial book, *Lady Byron Vindicated: A History of the Byron Controversy from Its Beginning in 1816 to the Present Time.*[20] This famous and widely acclaimed American author had expected that her revelation would provoke a furor, and she hoped it would divert sympathy from Byron to his wife. She never imagined that the episode would destroy her own reputation.[21]

The title of Stowe's book indicates her compelling motive—to defend a woman she first met in 1853 and came to regard as a friend. When she returned to England in 1856 Stowe was summoned to Lady Byron's sickbed, where she found the elderly woman preoccupied by her doctor's pronouncement that she should not live much longer.* During the months that followed, the two women were often together until, on a memorable day in early November, Lady Byron took Stowe aside for an interview lasting many hours in which she confided the secret behind her separation from her husband after a year of marriage: he had committed incest with his half sister Augusta and fathered Augusta's child Medora. The revelation was not proffered as mere scandalous gossip:

> She wanted Harriet's advice. Some publishers were about to bring out a cheap edition of the poet's works and in the promotion meant to revive the old story of Byron's having been driven to exile and death by the cold, mercenary heart of his wife. Should that wife keep silent any longer?[22]

With her characteristic moral fervor, Stowe at first intended to advise immediate publication. Her sister Mary persuaded her otherwise, so that the advice Stowe ultimately gave Lady Byron was to trust "discreet friends" to publish the truth after Lady Byron's death. No one knows what Lady Byron thought of this advice: she neither answered Stowe's letter nor spoke out about her late husband.

Byron had ridiculed his wife publicly during his lifetime, and, after his premature death in Greece in 1824, many of his supporters characterized Lady Byron as a cold and uncongenial wife. Her failure to respond with her own version of their separation had naturally given her husband's side of the story some advantage.

By 1869 both Byrons were dead, but the recent publication of the memoirs of Teresa Guiccioli, Byron's Italian mistress, revived the old complaints about Lady Byron. When no English friends rose to tell the story as Stowe had heard it from Lady Byron

---

*She actually survived another four years, dying in 1860.

herself, Stowe jumped into the fray with her usual zeal for a good cause, in this case defending a blameless and high-minded woman who had been abused by a monster of depravity. "Reverence for pure womanhood is, we think, a national characteristic of the American,"[23] Stowe wrote confidently, failing to realize that, even among the respectable, her portrait of a faultless Lady Byron might be less appealing than the reading public's image of Byron, the flawed yet attractive poet who had died at the age of thirty-six as he prepared to fight for Greek independence.

The accusation of incest produced a firestorm on both sides of the Atlantic. A number of British critics were outraged that an American should meddle in such private English matters: in the *Times* of London Stowe, who had been much admired in England for *Uncle Tom's Cabin,* was described as "a stranger and a foreigner." Others took her to task for having violated Lady Byron's confidence.

When they turned from such issues to the substance of Stowe's accusation, critics generally exonerated Byron and excoriated Lady Byron and Stowe. One writer asked, "Did she [Lady Byron] believe the hideous tale she told? Was she the wilful fabricator of the monstrous calumny, or was she herself the victim of insane delusions?"[24] These appeared to be the only possibilities the press entertained to explain Lady Byron's behavior. In this respect Justin McCarthy's front-page article in *The Independent* was typical:

> I am not defending Byron's moral character. He lived at a time and in a society when morality was rare among men. His temptations were unusually powerful, and he often succumbed to them. But I am sure no one will believe him guilty of the hideous crime of incest, merely because Mrs. Stowe says Lady Byron told her so. I do not think Mrs. Stowe has done much to serve the memory of her friend; and I know she has done much to injure her own fame. She has stooped to

promulgate a foul and filthy scandal; she has helped to pollute American households with a story of worse than Byzantine abomination. *Were it true, its publication would still be inexcusable.*[25] [my emphasis]

Another article remarked that Byron was "guilty of sins enough in his maturer years." But, it concluded, "he was probably not a beast."[26]

Significantly, "pollution" ranked high among the charges levelled at Stowe. The "reverence for pure womanhood" that she had expected to elicit for her side of the controversy was deployed against Stowe herself. *She* was seen as a violator of female purity because *she* spoke out about incest. When Stowe promised to follow up her article with a book on the subject, one periodical expressed the hope that publication could be prevented:

There is no good reason why she or any body else, should be permitted to needlessly poison the public mind, and deprave the public morals. We hope grand juries will interpose to save the world from the polluting influences of this promised deluge of nastiness, if a private sense of decency will not.[27]

There was a sexist bias to this criticism. In the *Spectator*'s opinion, "a woman should not have stained herself with handling the story at all." The *Independent* flatly proclaimed that "an offense against Christian charity is more ungentle in a woman than in a man."[28]

Unlike McCarthy, who was certain that few people believed the story, the anonymous reviewer for the *Saturday Review* did believe it, but still condemned Stowe for publishing the article.[29] True or false, incest was not a fit subject for discussion, particularly among women.

Most negative reactions simply dismissed the accusation out of hand. As J. Paget wrote in *Blackwood's Edinburgh Magazine,* the tale was "so monstrous, so improbable, so contradictory to all the rules that govern the actions of human beings" that it was impossible to believe. Or, as another writer for the *Independent* insisted, "The very fact that it is a crime against nature ought to be *prima facie* evidence against its commission."[30]

The Savannah *Republican* reported that near Stowe's Florida residence people jokingly said they wanted to erect two monuments to "the heroes of her most famous novels—Uncle Tom and Lord Byron."[31] Other critics pointed out that Stowe's efforts, in contrast to her stated purpose, had only made Byron more popular.

The denial that Byron, or indeed *anyone,* could be guilty of a crime like incest, came exclusively from male writers. In his disavowal James Russell Lowell made a nice distinction. "Incest," he wrote with an assumed expertise, "when it does happen (and it is rare enough) is not the fruit of perverted lust but of thwarted animal passion. It occurs in lonely farmhouses and not in cities swarming with public women."[32] How a cultivated man of letters like Lowell could speak so authoritatively is a mystery since at the time virtually nothing was known, let alone published, about incest.

The editor of *Harper's* was a dissenting voice. He described the indignation against Stowe as "evidence of the universal unwillingness to believe any man guilty of so hideous an offense. But for all that," he continued, "the reception of her statement has not been candid. There has been an evident disposition to insist that it is too horrible to be true, and that that is the end of it."[33]

Not surprisingly, the prominent feminist Elizabeth Cady Stanton saw the Byron marriage as part of a universal paradigm: the real issue was the relations existing between men and women. From the response of the press, she wrote, "one would suppose that American editors had lived only in the atmosphere of Paradise, wholly ignorant of the facts of life, of the hideous, disgusting slavery in which the women of every class and clime ever have been and are held to-day." The ignorance, she goes on to say, is willfull: "All alike turn from the mirror that so truly reflects the crimes of our present social system, from which they see no escape."[34]

For Stanton, the controversy was an occasion to preach against "the worst form of slavery, that of woman to man, that has ever cursed the earth." Where men donned the mantle of *natural protectors,* they were in fact enemies of woman's development, who promulgated "the monstrous thought that woman was made for man!—not for herself, for happiness, and heaven"![35]

After her experience of the "many abusive articles" that followed her disclosure, Stowe, too, saw the episode more clearly in terms of a conflict between the sexes: "There are thousands of poor victims suffering in sadness, discouragement, and poverty; heartbroken wives of brutal, drunken husbands; women enduring nameless wrongs and horrors which the delicacy of their sex forbids them to utter." And if these victims are rendered mute by the constraints of their nature, in Stowe's view, their victimizers are not similarly held back. As she describes Byron, hating his wife for knowing his secret, the discovery of which would have brought him "utter ruin, and expulsion from civilized society," he "tried to destroy her character before the world, that she might not have the power to testify against him."[36]

By the time of her book, Stowe was also able to see a particular version of the double standard that had driven the negative reception of her article: "The world may finally forgive the man of genius anything; but for a woman there is no mercy and no redemption."[37] Neither for herself—the messenger—nor for the wronged wife.

More than a century later, it is now widely accepted that Byron did have an incestuous relationship with Augusta. To arrive at this conclusion, twentieth-century researchers have consulted large caches of documents that were unavailable to scholars in the nineteenth century, notably, Lady Byron's voluminous record of events, prepared at first to ensure that her husband would not gain custody of their daughter and continued, it would seem, out of a lifelong obsession with the affair that ended her marriage.[38]

According to a recent biographer, Byron assumed he was the father of Augusta's daughter Medora, who was said to resemble him as a child. The poet referred to her as his daughter, but might have done so without a sense of biological paternity, since he was her godfather. To friends he remarked that Augusta's husband had been away during the time of conception whereas he had been at hand.[39] Shortly after the baby's birth, he wrote to Lady Melbourne, his confidante, a manic letter in which he defended his relationship with Augusta: "Oh! but it is 'worth while.'. . . I have been all my life trying to make some one love me—& never got the sort that I preferred before.—But positively she & I will grow good." He also noted that "the child is *not* an '*Ape*,'" a reference to the superstition that an incestuous relationship would produce a monster. Byron further intimated to Lady Melbourne that the "new situation" (that is, his having fathered Augusta's child) might make her withdraw her support of his proposed marriage to her niece, Annabella Milbanke.[40]

Annabella recalled that after she had married Byron, he was "continually lamenting her [Augusta's] absence, saying no one loved him as she did—no one understood how to make him happy but her." When Augusta came for a visit, Byron tormented his wife by making his preference for his sister's company apparent, even sending Annabella up to bed two hours early

and remaining below with Augusta. Lady Byron would ultimately avow that he had confessed to being Medora's father. In
1841 she would also announce this as a fact to Medora, and later
to her own daughter, Ada, arranging a meeting of the putative
half sisters in Paris. As Medora became increasingly estranged
from her mother, and destitute, Lady Byron stepped in to provide
financial help.[41]

The use of documentary evidence is a telling difference
between the approach of researchers today and that of the critics
who rushed to attack Stowe. For many of the latter, their own
revulsion from the idea was reason enough to cast doubt on
Stowe's account. For others, the denials of those around Lady
Byron were sufficient to negate the accusation. One story featured
Lady Byron's longtime personal maid, Mrs. Minns, who had come
forward to denounce Stowe's book. Her evidence was that Lady
Byron "always spoke well of Mrs. Leigh"![42]*

The Byron scandal, which became displaced onto Harriet
Beecher Stowe, is instructive in the Geddes case although some
particulars differ. For one thing, Stowe's accusation partook of the
gratuitous: the principals were long dead,† she had not been asked
to intervene, and any affair that existed between Byron and his sister was a consensual affair between adults who evidently loved and
respected each other. The incest Geddes accused Orleman of was
an exploitative and coercive relationship in which a powerful
father abused a vulnerable daughter.

---

*This may initially have been part of a strategy that Lady Byron adopted at the suggestion
of her divorce lawyer. But it seems that over the years Lady Byron's continuing preoccupation with her former husband included maintaining good relations with Augusta and her
family.

†Byron had died in 1824. Medora died in 1849, Augusta in 1851, and Lady Byron in
1860.

But there was this common denominator: The easiest attitude for a public that never spoke about such things was to assume that an accusation of incest could not be true. Even if it were, many would maintain, bringing it to light was the greater scandal, a corruption of public discourse.

DRAMATIS PERSONAE

In a military courtroom, two men who were officers and presumed to be gentlemen would contest the truth: Lieutenant Louis Orleman and Captain Andrew Geddes. Each would claim to be a victim of the other's lies. Each would accuse the other of inventing these lies to cover up his own wrongful actions. Through a court-martial, the Army would decide between them.

There was a third figure in this contest, unseen in the courtroom but dominating the proceedings nevertheless. This was the departmental commander, General E.O.C. Ord.

LIEUTENANT ORLEMAN

Louis Henry Orleman was born in Worms, Germany, and came to the United States on the eve of the Civil War. He was twenty-four when he enlisted as a private in the 103rd New York

Infantry Volunteers in 1862. He moved to the 119th New York a few months later as a first lieutenant and finished the war as a captain. His unit, composed mostly of Germans or men of German descent, saw plenty of action—at Chancellorsville, Gettysburg, and Atlanta—and it accompanied Sherman on his march to the sea. It also became part of a sharp controversy in which Orleman played a small but significant role.

The battle of Chancellorsville on May 2, 1863, was one in a series of bitter Union defeats, more bitter because it could have been an impressive victory. The Army of Northern Virginia, commanded by Robert E. Lee, had 60,000 men and 170 guns. It was opposed by a much stronger army of 131,491 men and 400 guns commanded by Joseph Hooker, but because of a series of blunders, the superior Union force was profoundly defeated. As one man in blue wrote about his own side, "Never was an army more completely surprised, more absolutely overwhelmed." While Hooker and his generals ignored intelligence and expected an attack elsewhere, the Eleventh Corps, in which the 119th fought, was "crushed" by Stonewall Jackson's far greater strength.[1] The Eleventh became the scapegoat for the defeat.

After the battle, the graceless Hooker blamed his subordinates, particularly the commanders of the Eleventh, although Theodore Dodge, who fought in the battle and later wrote about it, charges that the fault was Hooker's for allowing the right flank to be held by "an untried corps, composed of the most heterogeneous and untrustworthy elements in the Army of the Potomac." What made the Eleventh "heterogeneous and untrustworthy," according to Dodge, was simply the number of foreign-born it contained: his oblique but readily understood language expresses a native New Englander's prejudice. After the Chancellorsville defeat, the German troops in the Eleventh "were hooted at on all sides and called in derision Dutchmen," or "flying Dutchmen" because they were thought to have run from battle.[2]

Not long after Chancellorsville, the commander of the Third Division of the Eleventh, Major General Carl Schurz, wrote to Secretary of War Edwin Stanton to protest: "It is a very hard thing for soldiers to be universally stigmatized as cowards, and is apt to demoralize them more than a defeat." In his report on the battle Schurz commented that the Eleventh Corps had been "overwhelmed by the army and the press with abuse and insult beyond measure."[3]

Not all of the commanders Hooker castigated were content to be scapegoats. Schurz, himself a German immigrant, requested and received a court of inquiry to determine if Hooker's "strictures" on his conduct were proper. Schurz testified that because he was leading the First Brigade of the Eleventh, he had expected to be followed by the rest of the corps. Instead, he found himself alone: the Second and Third Brigades had halted, "under orders." Several witnesses reported they had been given these orders by Captain Orleman, at that time a staff officer serving under Colonel Wladimir Krzyzanowski of the Second Brigade. One witness added that Orleman had not said where the orders came from.[4]

The court's "Statement of Facts" rejected Hooker's strictures and vindicated Schurz's conduct. "There is nothing in the evidence," they concluded, "to authorize or justify the halting of the Second Brigade at the time and place it did. Orders had been given to and received by its commander to follow the First Brigade. . . . The only evidence on this subject is the hearsay statement of a staff officer of Colonel Hecker, who testifies that he was told by a staff officer of Colonel Krzyzanowski [Orleman] that he (Krzyzanowski) had been ordered to halt."[5]

It was never determined where the mysterious orders, countermanding the orders of the division commander, had come from. Orleman's role, if blameless, was certainly inglorious, one tiny action that exemplified the large-scale disaster it was part of.

The court of inquiry vindicated Schurz, but the bad reputation of the Eleventh remained, no doubt buttressed by the prejudices of people like Dodge who automatically blamed foreigners. Philippe Régis De Trobriand, that thoughtful observer of the American military, noted that the Eleventh Corps "was the object of a general hue and cry, nobody stopping to ask if there were not some extenuating circumstances—so quickly does injustice germinate in adversity."[6] Thus, Orleman would carry into his postwar career in the regular army the stigma of having served in a unit accused of cowardice and blamed for defeat.

In any case the battle of Chancellorsville was not his entire Civil War. From September 4, 1864, he served as a topographical engineer under the direction of Brevet Brigadier General O. M. Poe at the headquarters of General Sherman.

When the Army administered qualifying tests to its officers after the war, Orleman did extremely well. He answered every mathematical question correctly—in keeping with his training in engineering—but was similarly proficient in defining latitude and longitude, naming the number of states and the country's principal rivers, and discussing the republic's early history.[7]

On the frontier he was commended twice for his participation in encounters with warring Plains Indians. When Captain Louis Carpenter made a fierce dash over unfamiliar territory to save his former commander, George Forsyth—under siege from a large body of Cheyenne—"the task of laying out and running the course to be followed was intrusted to Lieutenant Orleman."* Orleman was commended for that rescue and for an action at Beaver Creek pitting eighty men against some six hundred Indians. In a general field order General Sheridan thanked the men involved.[8]

---

*In this famous clash, known as the Battle of Beecher's Island, Major George A. Forsyth and a group of fifty experienced plainsmen held off six or seven hundred Sioux and Cheyenne for a week until Captain Carpenter and his soldiers arrived.

Orleman wrote up for the St. Louis *Daily Democrat* one of his frontier experiences, an attempt to find desperately needed forage in a howling blizzard and ice storm. Seven of the eight men with him became frostbitten. Horses began to bleed from ice cuts. On the second night out, "without food for the men, or forage for the stock, we passed the night without shelter, and exposed to a keen north wind."[9] A member of the frontier army might receive a medal or a commendation for fighting Indians, but the more constant and equally deadly enemy on the Great Plains was the weather. Extreme and capricious, it ultimately disabled more men than the Indians did.

In another fierce storm Orleman contracted the ailment that would eventually end his active duty, a severe case of conjunctivitis that claimed most of the sight of his left eye and seriously weakened the right. His eyes became painfully sensitive to light, forcing him to wear dark glasses out of doors.[10]

Carpenter's H Company of the Tenth Cavalry, which rescued Forsyth's scouting party, also escorted General Sherman from Fort Sill to Fort Gibson in 1871. Carpenter, Orleman, Sherman, and Sherman's aides constituted a small band of officers: during this trip Orleman surely would have mentioned to Sherman that he had been attached to Sherman's Civil War headquarters, and reminisced with the general about the Atlanta campaign. When the Geddes court-martial came to his attention eight years later, Sherman might well have remembered Orleman.

CAPTAIN GEDDES

As a child Andrew Geddes had been transplanted from Canada to the little town of Vinton, Iowa, but his parents had come from Scotland, where an elder brother had been born. Geddes had joined the Union volunteer army in 1861 at the age of sixteen.[11] His Civil War record appears to have been exemplary. For most of the war he served as a captain in the Eighth Iowa but was mustered out as a lieutenant colonel of volunteers, possibly the youngest man to hold that rank. Describing a battle outside Memphis, Lieutenant Colonel William B. Bell reports that when his regiment became inadvertently divided, he left Captain Geddes in command while he rode off to find the missing units. Geddes was nineteen at the time.[12] Of the action at Spanish Fort, New Orleans, Brigadier General Eugene A. Carr wrote, "I cannot commend too highly the conduct of the officers and soldiers of my division during this trying, dangerous, and laborious siege."[13] He included Andrew Geddes in his list of officers to be specifically commended.

In 1868 Geddes received brevets of captain and major for "gallant and meritorious service" in the siege of Vicksburg and the capture of Spanish Fort. In recommending these brevets, Nelson Miles, who would attain the Army's highest rank, described Geddes as "a gentleman of high culture, an officer of fine ability and excellent character." In 1867 Geddes sought an appointment in the regular army, buttressed by the usual letters of recommendation. N. B. Baker, the Adjutant General of Iowa, wrote to Secretary of War Stanton that Geddes was "brave, capable, prompt and of the strictest integrity."[14] His congressional representative extolled him as "a brave and gallant soldier . . . a man of correct habits and good moral character . . . [who] has all the qualities and the capacity for a good officer."[15] Geddes became a first lieutenant in the Fortieth U.S. Infantry on September 15, 1868.

In 1872, Geddes found himself facing court-martial charges for breaking an archaic and universally violated regulation.[16] He had made several transfers of advance pay to two post traders at Fort Clark, accompanying each transfer with a signed certificate that enabled it to be cashed when it fell due on the last day of the month. The traders then advanced Geddes the specified amounts, minus their fees. On one occasion Geddes had attempted to cash one month's pay in two different places, intending to cancel one before it matured, but when one of these checks failed to clear, he wrote to the holder of the account and "made prompt amends." This practice of anticipating one's pay happened to be illegal. It was also widespread. The Army argued that certificates signed in advance were false because the money would not be available until the end of the month.

J. P. Alexander, a post trader, testified that he had known Geddes for five years and always had pleasant relations with him. He said that it was customary for officers to transfer their accounts to him before they were due, and that he would not accept them without a signed certificate since otherwise they could not be cashed. Two other post traders stated that they followed the same practice.

Captain J. W. French, Twenty-fifth Infantry, Geddes's company and post commander, gave Geddes a character reference. He related that Geddes had served as adjutant and quartermaster. He knew "nothing derogatory to his character as an officer and a gentleman."

Geddes did not deny the transactions; he did disclaim any intent to commit fraud. In his closing statement to the court he hoped that "in a spirit of liberality" it would rule that he had made "an error of judgment only." Nevertheless, he was found guilty and sentenced to be cashiered (dismissed dishonorably).

Reviewing the case, Judge Advocate General Joseph Holt noted that officers in Texas "habitually transferred their pay accounts before they were due. . . . That such a custom has grown up in the service is notorious, and that the paragraph of the army regulations forbidding it has come to be looked upon as a dead letter cannot be questioned." Rather than upholding the letter of the law, however dead, the Judge Advocate General surprisingly concluded that "prevailing custom affords a moral if not a legal defense."[17]

Moreover, to judge officers culpable for signing certificates before the last day of the month "would probably render nearly every officer of the army answerable to trial." There were many circumstances in the uncertain life of a frontier army officer that might make the signing of a certificate in advance prudent. If a married officer were to go on field duty, where he might remain away for a lengthy and indeterminate period, it would only be common sense to leave a signed certificate with his wife so that she could collect his pay in his absence.

In short, Judge Advocate General Holt found a number of reasons for leniency:

> The absence of any wrongful intention on the part of the accused, . . . the unsullied record his career as a soldier presents, together with the manifest feeling of humiliation at his position, affords, it is believed, ample basis for the conclusion that the mortification inflicted by his trial and conviction may be safely accepted as a sufficient expiation for his conduct.

While Holt was reviewing the case, some of Geddes's old friends were not idle. The Iowa state treasurer, who had served with Geddes during the Civil War, wrote on his behalf: "A better and braver soldier was not to be found. I cannot think that his present offense was committed with any criminal intent."[18] Another supporter asked the Secretary of War for clemency, adding that if Geddes had any fault, "it is a reckless use of money."[19] Influence was always useful, but the commonsense opinion of the Judge Advocate General was probably more telling. The verdict was thrown out and Geddes reinstated.

After the verdict, but before the Judge Advocate General had ruled, Geddes addressed a plea for clemency to Secretary of War

William Belknap: "I give you my word of honor that I am innocent of any intention of wrong or evil in what I did," he wrote. "My conduct was careless and I regret it more than I am able to express."[20]

On the frontier, Geddes's most notable exploit was an 1875 march that quickly became legendary. Accounts of the Texas frontier army always refer to it, but perhaps no one has described this saga with more gusto than that chronicler of West Texas, James Evetts Haley. Lieutenant Colonel William R. Shafter, a rugged non–West Pointer, was given command of a field expedition out of Fort Concho in 1875. On October 23, near Cedar Lake, he "detached Lieutenant Andrew Geddes with two companies of cavalry and Seminole scouts, ordering him 'to follow the trail [of the Indians] as long as possible.'" Geddes, Haley writes admiringly, "was one of those remarkably determined individuals, badly out of the [sic] place in the world today, in that he took the English language literally and believed in following orders."[21]

Geddes rode south on the trail of the Indians. At a place called Howard's Wells he dispatched his provision wagons to Fort Clark with orders to replenish supplies and rejoin them on the way back. He crossed the Pecos and continued south toward the Rio Grande. "This day's march was a very hard one," Lieutenant Hans J. Gasman wrote in his diary, "over very mountainous country and completely covered with Bear and Dagger grass, causing the lameness of several horses and mules."[22]

Two days later Geddes found the Indians he had been pursuing, "killing the only brave there and capturing four squaws and a little boy." He was told that the other Indians had left. Now weary, with horses going lame and suffering from lack of food, the force turned back, finally meeting up with a provisions wagon on the San Antonio road. Due to an error, provisions for only one day had been sent.[23]

When Geddes arrived at Fort Concho on November 27, he had "marched 650 miles over trying terrain following the trail as far 'as possible' within the territorial bounds of the United States, and had wound up with only one scalp." As Haley concludes, regretfully, "Had less than an impartial providence watched over the affairs of warriors—both red and white—he would have got back with a tow sack full."[24] It was, then, a typical frontier army foray: the Indians eluded pursuit; the soldiers demonstrated their ability to endure the rigors of a harsh terrain.

If Geddes did not slaughter a large number of Indians, he did perform valuable service by finding water holes and camping places that would be useful to future expeditions southwest of Fort Concho. And his arduous trek earned him the respect of Shafter, who would continue to be his firm supporter in the days ahead, and of Ord, who would not.

For Geddes himself, when proof of his military virtue was called for, his youthful service in the Civil War and his 1875 march for Shafter remained examples of performance to be flourished like battle-worn flags, tattered but still proud, even in a losing fight.

One more entry needs to be added to the résumé of Andrew Geddes. The Geddes supporter who wrote to the Secretary of War that Geddes's one fault was recklessness with money may not have known otherwise, but his assertion was inaccurate. Geddes did indeed have another fault: he was a persistent, perhaps even compulsive, womanizer who had had a number of liaisons with married women, some of which produced scandalous repercussions (including at least one child). Although these episodes never found their way into the 1879 court-martial, they were widely known in the Department of Texas.

The Army eventually learned of a number of specific incidents when it set out to investigate Geddes after the 1879 trial. In 1869

Geddes had been the groom in a shotgun wedding to a young woman of Montgomery, Alabama, whom he had seduced.[*] He lived apart from his wife and evidently pursued other women regardless of their marital status.

The earliest instance of adulterous behavior the army investigator reported linked a then unmarried Geddes with Mrs. Baily, "wife of Surgeon Baily of the Army, whose trial a few years ago brought great scandal on the service."[25] The court-martial of army surgeon Elisha J. Baily in 1870 had been a strange and embarrassing affair from the beginning. Baily was charged with conduct unbecoming an officer and a gentleman because he had abandoned his wife "without cause" and refused to support her. For his part, Baily asked if the court would, "on mere rumor, step in and force the accused to defend himself and lay bare his domestic difficulties," although the matter had "nothing whatever to do with the military service."[26] The Army did step in and lived to regret it.

The Bailys had never been happily married, largely because of Mrs. Baily's flirtatious and independent ways. In fact, as the court-martial would reveal, the trusting husband had been badly and repeatedly deceived. He eventually obtained an act of divorce from the legislature of his home state and refused to support the woman whom he began to refer to as his "so-called wife."

Andrew Geddes made a brief appearance at the end of this marital debacle. Once her husband had renounced her, Cornelia Baily travelled to Pensacola, Florida, where her lover, Captain William Cuyler (son of one of her husband's oldest friends), had

---

[*]His wife, who is not named in the army report, was Florence Towers. However, Geddes gave the date of his marriage as October of 1868 in his trial testimony.

been transferred. She hoped that Cuyler would agree to support her, but "he refused to have anything to do with her, in any form."[27]

Cornelia did manage to find consolation for Cuyler's disdain, at least temporarily. Geddes had accompanied her to Florida, and there was compelling testimony that the two had shared a room with one bed. In an extremely long concluding statement at Baily's court-martial, Baily's attorney heaped scorn upon Geddes for his part in the affair:

> The philanthropy of the Officer of the 25th Infantry in thus coming to Pensacola with this lone woman according to Captain Burbank's testimony—when he had nothing else to call him there—and his willingness to give her the "temporary" protection of his name in a marital capacity, cannot be too highly commended for the instruction and imitation of such officers *"still* in the Army" as have an idea that it is a very proper or convenient thing to do thus toward those who may in any way have been connected with the families of Brother Officers.[28]

After hearing a mountain of evidence about Mrs. Baily's activities and Baily's long forbearance, the Army acquitted the doctor, wisely deciding that this was a civil matter, after all.[29]

Cornelia Baily was from Wilmington, Delaware, and had spent the past three years in Massachusetts. Geddes was stationed in New Orleans at the time of the Pensacola trip. How the two met and came to an understanding is unclear. It seems unlikely that they could have had a long acquaintance. Whatever brought them together, they were two of a kind, people who sought sexual adventure whenever an opportunity presented itself.

Cornelia Baily was only the first of Geddes's many sexual improprieties discovered by the Army. In the more recent past, according to the army investigator, Assistant Inspector General

Absalom Baird, Geddes's intimacy with a citizen's wife at Fort Davis had led to a dramatic confrontation. The outraged husband discharged a shotgun at Geddes, but a bystander "threw up the muzzle of the gun," thus deflecting the bullet intended for the captain. Since the Army's report has no other details, and attributes the account to no definite source, we can assume that this story came to Baird in hearsay form.

A Fort Stockton episode involved a Mexican servant girl named Josephine. The deposition of Private Robert Jones affirmed that he had delivered notes back and forth between Geddes and Josephine, who worked for the post trader. Jones was able to describe in detail a pair of slippers Geddes supposedly gave Josephine: "They were a small pair of ladies slippers, they had open spaces across the toes, with blue color in the open spaces between the leather." According to Jones, Geddes had enjoined secrecy: "The general impression was, and is, that improper relations did or had existed between them for some time." Around Christmas of 1878, Josephine was "sick at her stomach avomiting the way ladies do when they are in delicate health" (a euphemism for pregnancy).[30]

Unfortunately for the Army's desire to build a case against Geddes, a man named John Burton also gave a sworn statement asserting that Josephine had been treated for constipation, a recurring ailment. She had never had an abortion or miscarriage nor been pregnant. Since she subsequently married a soldier, the army investigator reluctantly advised that this charge not be pursued.[31]

Geddes also appeared to have been active at the other end of the social scale, notoriously with Fannie McLaughlen, the wife of Fort Stockton's commanding officer, Napoleon Bonaparte McLaughlen. Mrs. McLaughlen was a cultivated lady from a socially prominent New York family, "no longer in the bloom of youth, formerly rather restrained and prudish in her intercourse with gentlemen." In August of 1878, when the affair with Geddes was either incipient or already under way, Lieutenant John Bigelow, Jr., described Mrs. McLaughlen in his diary as "very well dressed" and a good dancer, but "no longer handsome."[32]

Presumably under the influence of Geddes, Fannie McLaughlen's character changed completely, and she was soon running with a fast crowd that included another adulterous couple, Geddes's friend Joseph Friedlander and Rachel Beck, the wife of Lieutenant William Beck. Finally, after giving birth to a child who was repudiated by her husband, Mrs. McLaughlen was sent back to her wealthy family in New York.

When McLaughlen was questioned about his wishes in the matter, his mood was much like that of the ghost of Hamlet's father, willing to leave his wife to heaven's justice but eager to see her lover prosecuted. McLaughlen claimed that his wife had not denied that Geddes had fathered her child.

Lieutenant Bigelow, a young officer in the Tenth Cavalry, observed Geddes's romantic overtures with disgust and condemned him in the pages of his diary. The cosmopolitan Bigelow, a graduate of West Point, had been educated in Europe when his father was United States ambassador to France.* He had decided opinions and disliked most of his fellow officers (including a fellow diarist, Captain George Armes), but he was a careful observer, not only recording his own actions and thoughts but commenting insightfully on aspects of the military and the world around him. Fond of transcribing passages from writers he admired, Bigelow on one occasion copied into his diary the maxim "Nothing but an adherence to principle conduces to a quiet conscience."[33] Like the high-

---

*John Bigelow, Sr., had handled much of the delicate negotiation with the French over their position in Mexico.

minded Victorian American he was, Bigelow gave much thought to the moral dimension of action. His distaste for gossip suits his character but has deprived posterity of details of the Fort Stockton scandals that a less scrupulous diarist might have set down.

Lieutenant Bigelow's diary records an episode concerning Geddes that evidently never progressed beyond flirtation and thus does not turn up in the Army's report. The entry of August 18, 1878, notes that a Miss Candelaria Garza was considered the belle of an officers' ball that had taken place that evening. A week later Bigelow told his diary that Geddes and a local trader, M. F. Corbett, were "at swords' point": Corbett had forbidden Geddes to enter his house because of his bad character. Bigelow went on to note that in spite of being married, Geddes had been "very attentive to Miss Garza," who, in her innocence, had given ear to his "seductive speeches." Bigelow and another officer, "determined to protect female virtue against a man's infamous designs," enlightened Miss Garza about Geddes's marital status.[34]

When Bigelow first heard about the Geddes-Orleman affair, he saw it as a repetition of Geddes's designs on Candelaria Garza, believing that Geddes had "used his devilish arts with such success as to have blinded her [Lillie Orleman] to the danger of his company."[35]

Much of the Army's investigation of Geddes was unsubstantiated allegation, but by the time he first met Lillie Orleman the thirty-four-year-old captain had a well-established reputation as a philanderer.

GENERAL ORD

The man who had total power over the military disposition of the Geddes-Orleman affair was Edward Otho Cresap Ord, who was, at sixty-one, in his fortieth year of military service and within a few years of an unwelcome retirement. He had already commanded four other military departments and had hoped for a last service assignment to California, but in 1875 President Grant, bypassing consultation with the military hierarchy, had dispatched Ord to Texas, where a violent frontier situation was complicated by a troublesome international border.

Mexico had received its independence from Spain in 1821, but as a new nation it remained vulnerable to European powers, especially because the fledgling liberal government that came to power there in 1861 could not pay its foreign debts. President Benito Juárez was forced to declare a two-year moratorium on repayment. When the United States was preoccupied with the Civil War, England, Spain, and France used the issue of nonpayment of foreign debts as an excuse for invading Mexico. Early in 1862 England and Spain agreed to withdraw their forces and negotiate; France, obeying the imperial prescription of Napoleon III, pressed on, while publicly proclaiming that it had no territorial ambitions. Privately, France expected the Civil War to weaken, if not completely destroy, the United States and thus render American opposition ineffectual. The French established a provisional Mexican government whose hand-picked assembly immediately voted for monarchy and then obligingly offered the crown to Napoleon's candidate, Maximilian of Austria.[36]

The United States steadfastly refused to recognize Maximilian's government, and as the Civil War drew to an end, with Confederates talking of continuing to fight from Mexico, federal military units were dispatched to Texas for a show of force. At the time it seemed possible that the French-Mexican empire would destabilize the border, but the threat quickly evaporated. Confederate holdouts surrendered, and France agreed to withdraw its troops from Mexico. Only a few months later, in June of 1867, the Juárez government defeated and executed Maximilian.

The Monroe Doctrine triumphed,* but Mexico remained unstable and the border on both sides of the Rio Grande was a lawless area. Indian raids steadily bled West Texas of settlers and livestock because the raiders had no trouble escaping into Mexico. This was the situation Ord inherited when he arrived in Texas. Calibrating a correct response to Indian and outlaw incursions from Mexico was a delicate assignment, and Ord was more suited by temperament and talent to direct military action. His aggressive response to the problems of Texas caused consternation in Washington and in Mexico but made him immensely popular in the state.

Ord's very first posting out of West Point in 1839 had been to the Seminole Indian War, a typical governmental action against Indians whose presence inhibited white settlement. Tracking down these Indians in the Everglades, Ord acquired a reputation for enduring dangers and hardships. He seemed to have an aptitude, or even an actual preference, for such physical challenges. General Sherman once told a congressional committee that as a young officer Ord "would swim rivers with ice floating in them when he might have bridged them, and he would go over the tops of mountains when he might have gone around."[37]

Even at the end of his life—when he became a railroad representative in Mexico—Ord made field trips into rough country, sleeping on the floor of huts and eating, as he wrote to one of his sons, "what you never had to."[38] The linking of father and son in

---

*President James Monroe's address of 1823 warned European powers that the United States would view with hostility any attempt to colonize in the Americas.

this remark suggests both Ord's straightforward satisfaction that he had been able to provide well for his son and the more oblique pride that he had had to face more challenges than his son, give more proofs of manhood. Could a son read such words from his father without a measure of guilt or inadequacy?

Ord, the product of a Catholic education, saw himself as a moral man: "God Almighty & Pa," he once wrote his brother Pacificus, "have made us too honorable."[39] As Ulysses S. Grant would one day describe him, Ord was "honest, but unsteady and fond of change."[40] The comment that Ord was "fond of change" referred to a career-long habit of requesting new postings, sometimes simply because Ord felt he had exhausted the possibilities of a job or a place, other times because of personality conflicts with other officers.

Ord had favored the annexation of Texas in 1845, "as it may give us something to do."[41] When war against Mexico was declared—supposedly because Americans had died, but actually because the United States wanted to acquire new territory—he sought action but was routed to California by way of Cape Horn. He arrived—after a six-month sea voyage during which he shared a cabin with fellow lieutenant William Tecumseh Sherman—only to find the fighting over.

Ord next saw action as the commander of an artillery company in Washington Territory during the Yakima War (1855–59). When the first expedition of that war failed, Ord preferred charges of incompetency against its commander, Major Gabriel Rains. Army authorities transferred Rains elsewhere rather than calling a court-martial. In a later action Ord achieved what the San Francisco *Daily Herald* lauded as "the first regular defeat of the Indians" in the war and "the first time the whites had charged the Indians after being attacked by them."[42] Another battlefield success followed and then the Indians' surrender. Ord returned to San

Francisco, but a recurrence of the Yakima War in 1858 brought him back for another rigorous field campaign in Washington Territory. This, too, ended in Indian surrender, and Ord was transferred to Fort Monroe, Virginia, a congenial posting outside Washington, D.C. He was positioned, at the age of forty, to make his mark in the coming Civil War.

The qualities of eccentricity and individualism attributed to Ord were apt to go against the grain of a hierarchical institution like the Army. During the Civil War he protested serving under General Irwin McDowell because he felt McDowell was "not fit for his command."[43] He was also prepared to resign rather than serve under General John K. McClernand; when President Lincoln brought McClernand back for political reasons, Ord bypassed the military chain of command to write to Lincoln directly. In his letter he resigned command of the Thirteenth Corps, one of the largest in the Army.[44]

But along with his contentiousness Ord had powerful strengths. Before the war was over, when Grant replaced McClernand with Ord, Grant wrote to a friend, "The change is better than 10,000 reinforcements."[45] Ord finished the war as commander of the fifty-thousand-man Army of the James, outranked only by Grant and General George G. Meade, commander of the Army of the Potomac.

By the time Ord came to San Antonio to run the vast Department of Texas, he had had ample experience, not only on the battlefield but in all areas of command. He had fought the rebels with distinction and done his share of politicking in the intensely political atmosphere of the Union military and the Reconstruction South. In Texas, ironically, he would inherit troops he had done his best to avoid, the four black regiments of the Army—troops he regarded as inferior. Some of these were units removed from Virginia at Ord's instigation immediately after the Civil

War. These black soldiers were assigned to the Twenty-fifth Infantry and sent to Texas, where Ord encountered them ten years later.

Ord had been brought up in Cumberland, Maryland, as a Southerner and a believer in slavery, a cultural background reinforced by his marriage to a Virginia relation of Confederate general Jubal Early. Although he fought for the Union, a number of Ord's family members were Confederate sympathizers. Writing to his friend Sherman in 1863, Ord admitted, "I was in 49 & until 54, a pro slavery man, and I am not quite such a radical now as to think we can turn all these black people loose among the whites, any more than we could so many tame Indians, with advantage to either race."[46] Not surprisingly, he was a strong opponent of black suffrage.

Ord continued to believe that black soldiers were inferior to white soldiers: he would have preferred their elimination from the postwar military altogether. As commander of the Department of Texas, he constantly requested their removal from his area, on one occasion even offering to trade two black regiments for one white one.[47]

Ord had had some experiences with the military judicial system at the top—where generals are investigated for actions in battle. He was a witness at the court of inquiry investigating the Crater disaster, for which General Meade held General Ambrose E. Burnside responsible. On July 30, 1864, the Union forces outside Petersburg, Virginia, had set off a charge of explosives in a tunnel they had constructed into the Confederate camp. They rushed into the large hole created by the blast, but found themselves cornered and destroyed there since no one had properly planned out the operation beyond the moment of explosion. Union losses were 4,000 dead to 1,500 for the Confederates. Although several of his subordinates were censured, Burnside was removed but not court-martialed.[48]

More significant, in November of 1862, Ord served with four other generals on a military commission charged with evaluating

General Don Carlos Buell's prosecution of the war in Kentucky and Tennessee. Buell had not pursued Confederate general Braxton Bragg aggressively enough to suit his superiors and was relieved of his command. Apparently, Secretary of War Edwin Stanton had intended for a kangaroo court to uphold Buell's removal, but when the judge advocate voiced this assumption, he received—among other expressions of indignation—a dressing-down from Ord.

Perhaps because he had himself felt pressure from above while serving on a military court, Ord was sensitive to such influence in the system of military justice. He believed that enlisted men of the same grade as the accused should be allowed to serve on courts-martial. Having only officers on the courts, he wrote to the House Subcommittee on Military Affairs, is "a little like the Republicans having the right to select the juries to try the Democrats."[49] This view was expressed slightly more than a year before the Geddes deposition crossed his desk.

Like Louis Orleman, Edward Ord had a large family of sons and daughters, and like Orleman his oldest child was a daughter, a beautiful and accomplished young woman only a few years older than Lillie Orleman. A picture of the Ords taken in 1865 shows the handsome general and his wife sitting opposite each other with the pretty child leaning against her father, her arm on his shoulder, their heads touching, his arm around her waist in intimate physical proximity. The positioning of the figures divides the overall composition into a 2:1 arrangement, with father and daughter forming one unit slightly apart from Mrs. Ord. Nine-year-old Roberta (Bertie) wears an off-the-shoulder dress: her skin in the black-and-white photograph seems startlingly white and vulnerable. Ord, sitting with his legs crossed, is still fairly straight and stiff-looking while Bertie's posture is yielding, clinging.

Would Ord have prolonged a position of such physical contact when Bertie was eighteen? He might have seen nothing wrong with her leaning against him to sleep during a long journey in an army ambulance (as Orleman was to do with Lillie). He was a devoted father in a culture in which "daughters' idealization of fathers was encouraged and the affection of fathers for daughters given fairly free rein."[50] When Bertie later married a Mexican counterpart of her father, a general much older than herself, Ord gave her an elaborate wedding.

This was the man who, more than any other, would determine Andrew Geddes's fate.

FORT STOCKTON AND
THE WEST TEXAS FRONTIER

Fort Stockton was established in 1859 on the trail that the Comanches took on their periodic raids down through Texas from the north and into Mexico. The fort was designed to control Indian depredations in West Texas, but a few years after it was built federal troops withdrew to fight the Civil War. When the fort was reopened, it was staffed entirely by black regiments—part of the Army's effort to keep such troops away from populated areas that might resent their presence. No one at the time saw any irony in one unwanted minority group being used to check another.

Looking backward from the safety of the 1980s, historian Glenda Riley characterized the conflicts between Indians and whites in mid-nineteenth-century Texas as a "tragic misunderstanding."[1] There was undoubtedly misunderstanding enough between two radically different cultures that perceived each other through the experience of armed confrontation, but this was secondary to the central issue, which was tragic without being a misunderstanding: the opposed cultures were contesting the land, and however well they came to understand each other, nothing could have made it possible for them to share it peaceably.

In 1871 General Sherman made a tour of inspection of military posts in Texas, accompanied by Inspector General Randolph B. Marcy. The Inspector General, a talented observer and writer, kept a journal of the trip, in which he noted that "this rich and beautiful section does not contain today [May 17, 1871] as many white people as it did when I visited it eighteen years ago, and if the Indian marauders are not punished, the whole country seems to be in a fair way of becoming totally depopulated."[2]

Two days later General Sherman received a delegation from Jack and Parker Counties.* Marcy described their message in language redolent of the views of nineteenth-century white settlers:

> [They] represented the exact condition of affairs, growing out of the infamous and suicidal government policy of rewarding these savage brutes for murdering the whites, and assured him that unless decisive action was taken, and the Indians put down, that Northwest Texas would soon become depopulated, the labor and industry and accumulations of years would be lost, families scattered, important interests sacrificed, society ruined, and a delightful and improving country given over to the blight of these demons.

For Marcy, the issue came down to this: "The border settlers of Texas must all be annihilated, or the Indian chastised and disarmed."[3]

The apocalyptic language reflects the way Texans talked about the warlike southern Plains Indians, whose way of life was based on raiding. They struck at will, running off horses and cattle, killing settlers, taking women and children captive, and eluding pursuers. Indians discovered, in fact, that it was far more prof-

---

*These two counties are slightly to the west of the Dallas–Fort Worth area.

itable to capture a woman or a child than several horses or mules.[4] Herman Lehmann, who spent his teenage years in the 1870s as a captive of the Mescalero Apaches and then as a willing member of a Comanche tribe, noted that "nearly every band had white and Mexican captive children . . . there were hundreds of captives in the various tribes." In particular, he added, "there were many white children and women captured in South and West Texas."[5]

In the Indians' view Texas had been their land from time immemorial, and they were accustomed to ranging freely over its vast territory and on into Mexico. In 1853, when Frederick Law Olmsted and his brother travelled across Texas, they observed that the Indians were already in a lamentable condition, "permanently on the verge of starvation. Having been forced back, step by step, from the hunting-grounds and the fertile soil of Lower Texas to the bare and arid plains, it is no wonder they are driven to violence and angry depredations."[6]

Although government policy was to relocate Indian tribes to reservations and persuade them to exchange their nomadic culture for a sedentary, agriculture-based life, as early as 1858 an officer in Texas, Brevet Major Earl Van Dorn, complained that one such reservation was too small. "It cannot reasonably be expected," he wrote to his superiors, "that they, as wild and as free as the eagle, would voluntarily shut themselves up in such a coop, or that they would be driven there without a violent struggle." He added, with the kind of empathy rarely found on the frontier: "Who would?"[7]

Major Van Dorn was prescient: the final defeat of the various Indian tribes in the region—the Comanche, Kiowa, Apache, Lipan, and Kickapoo—would not be accomplished without another quarter century of violence and bloodshed. Speaking, grimly, to his state legislature in 1875, Texas Governor Richard Coke described how official government policy and the unofficial actions of surreptitious traders conjoined to encourage Indian violence:

Under the present Indian policy of the general government the Texas frontier has suffered more than it ever did before and the country near the reservations has suffered worst. Permits are granted the Indians to leave the reservations sometimes to hunt; sometimes on one pretext then on another, and they invariably come into Texas, steal horses, drive off cattle, and very frequently kill and scalp men, women, and children, and when they return, it is a fact that can be substantiated with abundant proof, that white men, on or near the reservation, are always ready with guns and ammunition, blankets, and other things desired by the Indians to trade for stolen stock and other plunder gotten from Texas.[8]

Settlers on the frontier had little use for "Mr. Lo," a designation derived from Alexander Pope, who had written in his poem *An Essay on Man,* "Lo, the poor Indian." Pope had intended *lo* as an interjection meaning "behold," but on the frontier it became an ironic noun. Colonel John A. Wilcox, who fought Indians in Texas, wrote some verses titled "Owed (Ode) to Lo! The Poor Indian" that express the common feeling:

> *Bedecked with paint, they go to war, with frantic, hideous yell,*
> *Remorseless, cruel, vengeful, they are merciless as hell.*
> *You'll never find upon this earth wherever you may go,*
> *A meaner, dirtier, murdering thief, than you will find in Lo!*[9]

To members of the U.S. military there was a meaningful distinction between a "civilized enemy," like the British in the War of 1812 or the Confederates in the Civil War, and Indians. The civilized enemy fought the way you did but in a different uniform. You and he shared a common culture, the Judeo-Christian tradition and a European intellectual heritage that went back to ancient Greece. Indians were Other—hence uncivilized, inferior, fiendish. History might hold examples of whites who had all the characteristics Colonel Wilcox attributed to Lo, and it might produce examples of oppressive white rulers, but these would be considered aberrations.

48

Whites observed that it was not one warrior who exhibited merci-less cruelty; it was the Indian way of warfare. It had to be eradicated, or instead of expansion, the great mantra of the nineteenth century, Texas would experience the often invoked "depopulation"—the very opposite of what Americans regarded as progress.

Although the Indians could usually elude pursuing troops, they could not at the same time hunt enough to stay alive. In 1874, Colonel Ranald Mackenzie surprised a large group of Comanche in Palo Duro Canyon in northern Texas. The Indians got away but lost an enormous horse herd: Mackenzie slaughtered some two thousand ponies and destroyed large quantities of Indian goods. Such losses could be remedied less easily as time passed and the once plentiful buffalo became virtually extinct. The Indians would learn, as General Sherman once said, "that when the Government commands, they must obey."[10]

By 1879, General Ord could note with satisfaction in his annual report for the Department of Texas that in the Pecos District "all Indians penetrating the country have been so hotly pressed by the troops as to prevent their doing much damage— only three murders, by marauders, during the year. Last year there were seventeen in the region referred to."[11] Ord's rejoicing was a little premature: in the early 1880s there would be one more big campaign against the stubborn Apaches, but the trend was unmis-takable. Even the wild country of West Texas and the volatile bor-der were settling down.

Supposedly, General Sherman once remarked that if he owned hell and Texas, he would live in hell and rent out Texas. The remark, perhaps made soon after he narrowly escaped being killed by Indi-ans in Texas, expressed a widely held sentiment, even if a patriotic Texas editor retorted that the general was just standing up for his own country.[12] Another Texas patriot, the writer Larry McMurtry, contrasts the nation's romantic image of the South with its view of his home state: "Texas is only scenery, and poor scenery at that."[13] West Texas in particular, with its lawless desert expanses, was not regarded as a desirable military posting: when Colonel Benjamin Grierson, commanding officer of the Tenth Cavalry, was sent there from Indian Territory in 1875, he felt both disappointed and slighted. His brother pronounced it "the most God-forsaken part of Uncle Sam's Dominions."[14]

Army wives who penned their memoirs held similar views. When Lydia Spencer Lane received the "dreadful news" that her husband was being transferred from Missouri to West Texas, she had to summon all of her personal resources—trust in Providence, her commitment to the life of a soldier, and the fatalistic realization that "there was no escape." She and her husband travelled to their destination "through a dreary, desolate country, where nothing lived but Indians, snakes, and other venomous reptiles." Indeed, she never went to bed "without making a thorough search for a snake, tarantula, or centipede." At Fort McIntosh, twelve days' journey from San Antonio, the litany continues: "Not a green thing was to be seen but a few ragged mesquite-trees. . . . Back of our quarters was quite a large yard, but there was not a living thing in it, except tarantulas, scorpions, and centipedes, with an occasional rattlesnake for variety."[15]

If this seems like the overreaction of a complaining wife, here is the dispassionate report of Assistant Surgeons W. M. Notson and W. F. Buchanan,* made in 1875:

---

*Army doctors were either surgeons, receiving the pay and emoluments of cavalry majors, or assistant surgeons, receiving during their first five years of service the pay and emoluments of first lieutenants in the cavalry, after which they were promoted to the rank of captain. See Appendix A for a list of commissioned officer ranks.

Tarantulas and lesser spiders lurk under every cactus shrub, and the centipede brings forth its interesting brood in every pile of chips or lumber about one's quarters. Small scorpions, from two to three inches in length, are found, though less frequently than either the centipede or the tarantula. Indians, believed to be chiefly Comanches and Kiowas, commit frequent depredations in the vicinity.[16]

The casual coupling of Indians with noxious vermin by the army doctors and Mrs. Lane was a commonplace of frontier writing.

In 1872, Major Zenas R. Bliss accompanied some officers and their families from Fort Clark to Fort Stockton. "When the ladies first got a sight of the Post that some of them were to live in," he wrote, "the sight caused many sad hearts. The post looked in the distance like a camp of Mexican carts," in other words, a stark collection of boxlike structures. Moreover, "there was not a tree to be seen. . . . There was little if any grass, and the whole landscape had a grayish appearance." Once they became accustomed to the fort, Major Bliss admitted, they came to think of it as "a very desirable station."[17]

In fact, compared to other frontier posts, Fort Stockton had some advantages, notably, a flourishing garden that one proud officer pronounced "inestimable" in value, "not only the best garden on this frontier but it would compare favorably with any in the States." It produced a variety of sorely needed fresh vegetables: onions, carrots, beets, turnips, pumpkins, squash, yams, peas, radishes, cucumbers, beans, corn, lettuce, cabbage, watermelons, and cantaloupes. The creek that bordered the post on one side furnished "an inexhaustible supply of water-cresses . . . invaluable" for counteracting scurvy. During the fall and winter numerous water fowl populated first the marshes of Comanche Creek and then the tables of the fort.[18]

The bounty of nature could be disrupted by the violence of weather. On May 30, 1875, a severe hailstorm completely destroyed that year's garden as well as breaking ten window lights in the hospital and stripping the post's roofs of shingles. Many of the hailstones were "as large as a man's closed hands." They averaged eight to the pound and covered the parade ground to a depth of three inches.[19]

Any frontier fort, newspaper reporter Randolph Keim thought, suggested a ship at sea, "isolation within and desolation without." The landscape of West Texas, so flat and dusty that riders could be seen approaching from miles away, eloquently defined desolation. San Antonio, the hub of the military Department of Texas, was almost 392 miles away. The nearest military post, Fort Davis, was 70 miles, or a day's journey by stage. As for the isolation within, an army chaplain at Fort Davis remarked that it "tends to superinduce a restive spirit, and creates a cheerless atmosphere—which render temptations to intemperance very strong."[20]

No army post was immune to the twinned evils of alcohol and gambling, and few were so removed that they eluded opportunities to acquire venereal disease. Commenting on an increase in such ailments among the troops, a Fort Stockton doctor recommended that a Mexican prostitute named Maria "be induced to leave the vicinity." (He didn't suggest what form this inducement might take.) Beyond these communal effects of isolation lay the kind that Joseph Conrad wrote about in *The Heart of Darkness*, the darkness within that could unmoor a man, casting him adrift on an uncharted inner sea that mirrored the "appallingly wide-open world called West Texas."[21]

The officers of Fort Stockton, and whatever family they had with them, constituted the society of the post, a handful of people who saw each other constantly. Shared hardships and dangers—the desolation without—united them, creating, as one frontier army officer wrote in his memoirs, "a bond that is never loosened." Yet at times the isolation within bred deep hatreds that fed on these same hardships and dangers. Commenting on a case of two feuding officers, historian Shirley Leckie observes:

> Such filings of charges and countercharges were only too common in this period and absorbed a great deal of the time and energy of commanding officers. Many of the accusations stemmed from the frustration brought on by the lack of promotion opportunities and the relatively low army pay.

The fort's small social group also knew, for good or for ill, "the intimate details of one another's lives." As one army wife remarked of such frontier posts, "Gossip, malicious and otherwise, throve."[22]

The 1870 census had found a population of 582 in the Fort Stockton region, 429 of whom were civilians, Anglos and Mexicans. The area might have seemed lacking in promise to all but the hardiest adventurer: attacks of Indians and outlaw gangs, aided by the convenience of retreat across the border into Mexico, made agriculture a venture that was "one half planting and plowing and one half killing Indians"—or being killed by them, the chronicler might have added. "No man removed more than his coat or brush jacket when he lay down to sleep," cowboy James Cook writes of his experience herding cattle in the region: "There was danger on all sides and from many sources." This was just the kind of place to appeal to General Ord, who clearly took some pleasure in warning away the faint-hearted: "Educated Englishmen, or men to whom English home comforts are necessary, farmers accustomed to good neighbors and to certain security for life and property and unable to cope with the wild rough border people or . . . occasional torrid heat in summer had better stay away from West Texas."[23]

Nevertheless, Fort Stockton was on the move. In 1875 Pecos County was carved out of the immensity of Presidio County, and Saint Gall, the little town that had grown up around the fort, became the county seat and eventually the town of Fort Stockton. By 1877, eight thousand acres were under cultivation, and by 1880, because of promising developments like irrigation, the waning of Indian attacks, and the imminent arrival of railroads, Pecos County had almost four times as many civilians as in 1870—1,689. (Texas during this decade almost doubled its population.) The fort itself had a total of 254 army personnel in 1879.[24]

Fort Stockton was located at Comanche Springs, a major source of water on the north–south Comanche War Trail sweeping down from North Texas and Oklahoma into Mexico. On an east-west axis, the post straddled the road between El Paso and San Antonio, taking its place as part of a string of forts intended to establish a military presence in the sparsely populated immensities of West Texas.[25]

With the eruption of the Civil War two years after its founding, Fort Stockton was evacuated by the United States Army, then briefly occupied, abandoned, and burned by the Confederates. When Federal troops reclaimed it in 1867, the post had to be entirely rebuilt—of adobe, a common building material of the treeless area. (Lumber had to be hauled 160 miles and was thus prohibitively expensive for the construction of a military base.) The fort would ultimately consist of twenty-six buildings, all of adobe except the stone guardhouse and magazine. The 960 acres of land, which was owned by a San Antonio landowner rather than the government, was described as worth about ten cents an acre, not a great deal at a time when a quarter would buy a full meal, but a reasonable valuation of the unpromising land.[26]

Fort Stockton in 1879 might not have resembled a group of Mexican carts, as Major Bliss imagined, but it was an unimpressive square of buildings arranged around a central parade ground, the typical unfortified* military post with a few other civilian buildings nearby and a group of "miserable little mud houses often without fireplace or windows" in which Mexicans lived.[27] Since the surrounding land was flat and treeless, there was nothing to give the place particular character.

Life at a frontier fort was structured and routine, or, as an article in *The Army and Navy Journal* put it, "the rule is monotony and stagnation." There were three daily roll calls: reveille early in the morning was balanced by tattoo at around nine at night, with retreat at sunset. For cavalry there were morning and afternoon stable calls to care for horses. Dinner was at noon, while "lunch" was the evening meal. In between these fixed occurrences the men might drill or go on fatigue details, that is, work constructing roads or post buildings. This practice was so widespread at the time that a citizen charged the Army with requiring "unsoldierly and penitentiary-like work" from enlisted men. He asked the military affairs committees of both houses of Congress to investigate.[28]

At times units would be sent into the field to pursue marauding Indians. They rarely found them. Although there was little possibility of success, there was great chance of danger, and even greater chance of suffering long periods of monotonous field duty and cruel deprivation. There was always more at stake in Indian fighting because the Indians took no prisoners and might torture those who fell into their hands. As one experienced Indian fighter observed,

> The life of a soldier in time of war has scarcely a compensating feature; but he ordinarily expects palatable food whenever obtainable, and good warm quarters during the winter season. In campaigning

---

*Fortification wasn't necessary because any approach created a noticeable cloud of dust.

against the Indians, if anxious to gain success, he must lay aside every idea of good food and comfortable lodgings, and make up his mind to undergo with cheerfulness privations from which other soldiers would shrink back dismayed.

The Army logged thousands of miles over the unfriendly terrain of West Texas, killing an Indian here and there, but rarely matching the Indians' record for killing settlers. As Olmsted remarked, "The inefficiency of regular troops for Indian warfare needs no evidence. Wherever posted, they are the standing butt of the frontiersmen."[29]

Conditions at Fort Stockton were recorded in monthly sanitary reports that covered health, diet, sanitation, and the state of the buildings. From these it appears that hovels near the fort occupied by Mexicans were a health hazard and that unspecified "inducements" were offered to these Mexicans to get free smallpox vaccinations. The soldiers had been vaccinated to good effect although some cases of smallpox were reported on outlying ranches.[30]

A recurring problem was the condition of the outside lavatories, or "sinks," as they were known in army parlance. Neither the officers' quarters nor the enlisted men's barracks had indoor facilities, and both sets of sinks needed applications of dry earth from time to time. In the report of October 31, 1878, Assistant Surgeon John Hall wrote at some length about the condition of the sinks, which he found highly unsatisfactory: "Some of the boxes are broken and leaky and all look unclean. The ground beneath and around the boxes is soaked with decomposed excrementitious matter, and likewise the seat and sides of the privy are in some places stained and foul." Like his predecessors in the writing of sanitary reports, he recommended the application of dry earth on a regular basis. He also noted that two sinks for four companies was inadequate, and conjectured, wistfully, that if a minimum of one sink per company were provided, "the companies would be likely to vie with each other in cleanliness, and to take pride in keeping each privy in good condition."[31]

The only women officially recognized as part of an army post were laundresses, who received "housing, a daily ration, fuel, and the services of the post surgeon in addition to their pay for doing the company wash." Laundresses could always find a clientele if they wished to supplement their pay by baking pies, and they often became the wives of enlisted men. Whatever their marital status, they traditionally inhabited a part of the post called Laundress Row. References to this area in sanitary reports suggest squalor. In 1875 "defects of light and ventilation in these quarters" are characterized as "beyond remedy"; six months later the buildings are described as "gradually becoming uninhabitable from rapid dilapidation of the quarters." An 1878 report judged the complete absence of sinks a "very great defect" in need of immediate remediation—this almost ten years after the post had been rebuilt. However planners had imagined the needs of the laundresses and their children should be met, "the occupants of some of these houses are in the habit of urinating in the corners made by the chimneys on the outside of the houses, thus creating a stench." Once again urging action, the medical officer, Dr. Benjamin Pope, concludes feelingly, "There is no more potent agent for evil than emanations from human excrement."[32]

Fort Stockton shared with a few other Texas military posts the distinction of quartering the Army's only black soldiers, commanded by white officers.* These officers were not necessarily pleased about their postings. On the eve of the Spanish-American War, John Bigelow, Jr., by that time a captain,

---

*These units, created after the Civil War, were the Ninth and Tenth Regiments of Cavalry and the Twenty-fourth and Twenty-fifth Regiments of Infantry.

described himself as having labored for over twenty years "under the disadvantage of serving in a colored regiment." Bigelow did not elaborate on the "disadvantage," but he might have had any number of things in mind. One was an enforced sojourn in places like West Texas. Given the majority feeling that armed black men were potentially dangerous to whites, or at least unwelcome, the black regiments did not experience the rotation that most white regiments enjoyed between frontier posts and more desirable locations. Responding to the constant lobbying of the regiments to have their units brought "closer to civilization," in 1880 the Army finally moved the two black infantry regiments to the Department of Dakota.[33] (Not everyone would have regarded this move as bringing the regiments much closer to "civilization.")

Before the Dakota move, four companies drawn from the Tenth Cavalry and the Twenty-fifth Infantry were billeted at Fort Stockton while their other companies, along with the Ninth Cavalry and the Twenty-fourth Infantry, were distributed among other Texas posts. The four regiments represented ten percent of the Army's effective strength. Their men received the same pay as white soldiers, $13 a month on enlistment with $1 per month increase annually and a bonus for reenlistment after five years.[34]

Equal pay was a hard-won measure, granted to black soldiers during the Civil War only after bitter protests, including at least two executions of black servicemen who had refused to serve for lesser pay. As one private wrote home, "Why are we not worth as much as white soldiers? We do the same work they do, and do what they cannot. We fight as well as they do." When a bill to equalize pay was first introduced in December of 1863, the *New York World* deemed it "unjust in every way to the white soldier to put him on a level with the black." Its passage in June of 1864 concluded what historian James McPherson calls "one of the sorriest episodes of the Civil War."[35]

At the time of the Geddes trial Frederick Douglass's optimistic prediction that wearing the uniform of the United States Army was bound to produce equal treatment for blacks was far from being realized in Texas. The departmental commander, General Ord, was known to—as Sherman characterized him—"lean against the Nigger" and be correspondingly soft on the old Confederacy. Black soldiers would get only grudging recognition from him.[36]

In Indian Territory, where the regiments had first served, the men of the black regiments became known as "buffalo soldiers," supposedly because their hair reminded the Indians of the hair of their sacred animal, the buffalo. Whatever its origin, the name was taken as a compliment: the Tenth Cavalry promptly enshrined the image of the buffalo on the regimental crest.[37]

The officers who led the buffalo soldiers into battle knew that their men were not only good soldiers but less given to intemperance and desertion than their white counterparts. Nevertheless, the prejudices of time and place often held sway. The same Dr. Notson who enumerated the noxious creatures to be found in the West Texas desert also wrote, referring to himself in the third person, that "the impracticability of making intelligent soldiers out of the mass of the negroes, is growing more evident to the Post Surgeon every day, and his opinion is concurred in by their own officers when speaking in confidence."[38]

Some of the commentary that Notson refers to may simply have been the acknowledgment that illiterate men whose life experience had been slavery presented additional problems to the military—and additional work for officers. When Lieutenant Colonel James Carleton inspected the Twenty-fifth Infantry on its arrival in Texas in 1870, he recommended that a clerk be hired to do the bookkeeping and teach the soldiers to read and write:

> In this way too the negroes who serve in the army will become intel-
> ligent and be so much better fitted to take their places as the political

equals of white men, which they have become, under the Constitution. This is a matter of grave importance, and in my judgment should be called to the attention of the highest authority.[39]

For the fair-minded Carleton, the black soldiers' problems were not caused by innate inferiority: they could and should be remedied.

Given the prevailing belief of the time that the white race was superior to any other, though, most people were more sympathetic to Notson's conclusion than to Carleton's. It was a given of nineteenth-century "science" that, left to their own devices, blacks would make no progress. In their huge book on the subject of race, Dr. J. C. Nott and George R. Gliddon laid down a number of prescriptions, among them that "amalgamations," then the scientific term for people of mixed race, "have deteriorated the white element in direct proportion that they are said to have *improved* the black." Mere association with whites was also thought to be helpful to blacks. As Nott and Gliddon observed, "Wild horses, cattle, asses, and other brutes are greatly improved in like manner by domestication." Lieutenant Bigelow's orderly, a man "black as ink," told Bigelow that officers "often appointed men to offices of trust & honor in proportion to the extent to which their blood had been mixed with the white but he did not think it just & right."[40]

Such prejudices extended to other races as well. In his medical history of Fort Stockton, written in 1870 or 1871, the post surgeon described local residents as "chiefly Mexicans," and then went on to define Mexican as "a cross between the Spanish and Indian by which both races are deteriorated, rendering them lazy and immoral and treacherous. Though they are often grateful for kindnesses, they are vindictive for real or supposed injuries." Mexicans, according to Nott and Gliddon, belonged to the "semicivilized races," while American Indians were "unintellectual and uncivilizable."[41]

Fewer graduates of West Point chose to join black regiments, and thirty-six of the original hundred officers of the black regiments eventually transferred out, while only thirteen transferred in. Most officers probably took positions with these regiments not because of a genuine desire to command black soldiers, but in order to obtain a berth in the severely downsized postwar army. There would clearly be more prestige accorded officers of white regiments.[42]

The wives who joined their husbands at frontier military posts might be expected to feel even less enthusiasm for the presence of large groups of armed black men who could find few women of their own race in the vicinity. Women already had reason to fear Indians: every year the Comanches followed their war trail into Mexico and returned with captive women and children; white settlers along the way were not spared. Added to this constant anxiety about Indians, a modern historian observes, "there was always lurking under the surface of the routine garrison life the fear of assault and rape—a fear of the soldiers themselves."[43]

In 1872 an incident occurred at Fort Davis in which a corporal was shot dead by an officer's wife one night as he attempted to break in during her husband's absence. No one could know if the soldier had simply been drunk or bent on robbery: it was assumed that his intention was rape. Colonel George Andrews, commanding officer of the Twenty-fifth Regiment, wrote up the matter as if it were a common occurrence:

> It is now seventeen months since I commenced my services with Colored Troops and during that time, attempts similar to the one related above have been made upon the officers' quarters at Fort Duncan, Stockton, and Davis, and I think McKavett and Concho. While stationed at Fort Clark, five such attempts were reported to me.

Andrews went on to say that married officers *and* enlisted men were "reluctant to leave their families for any purpose after dark and that detached service becomes a positive cruelty."[44]

The conjured image of potential rapists omnipresent in frontier posts reflects a predisposition to view black soldiers as a sexual threat to white women. In reality, the black regiments were more sinned against than sinning, constantly discriminated against and even attacked by civilians who suffered no penalty. In one notorious instance in 1870, John "Humpy" Jackson, an early settler and Indian fighter in the Fort McKavett area, discovered a "love note" written to his fourteen-year-old daughter by one of the black soldiers at the army post. The next morning he shot and killed the first soldier he saw. A fugitive for three years, during which time he killed two other black soldiers, Jackson was regarded in the community as a local hero: "No matter at what ranch house he called he would be welcomed, given the best horse available and all the food he needed." When he was finally arrested, a grand jury refused to indict him.[45]

In Texas another element contributed to the explosive mix—the hostility of the Mexican population to the black soldiers. In his annual report for 1876, General Ord cautioned that "the use of colored soldiers to cross the river after raiding Indians, is in my opinion, impolitic, not because they have shown any want of bravery, but because their employment is much more offensive to Mexican inhabitants than white soldiers."[46]

If this was true of Mexico, chronic flare-ups would prove that it was equally true of the Mexican residents of Texas. As Colonel Cyrus Roberts reported, when he investigated an incident at Fort Ringgold, "They [local Mexicans] consider themselves . . . superiors [of the black troops], whereas with whites they accept their inferiority." This hierarchy of disadvantage receives another formulation when the two groups in question are blacks and Indians. One historian believes that the presence of an Indian reservation near black troops made the white community treat the black soldiers better.[47]

During the various postings of black troops to Texas later in the century the situation never improved. After an outbreak at Laredo in 1899, the head of the Department of Texas, General P. B. McKibbin, wrote that "the trouble at Laredo is due, primarily, to race prejudice between the Mexican residents and the soldiers, and the association of these soldiers with Mexican women."[48]

Conditions in the frontier army tended to be bad in all respects—housing was substandard, food was poor, the pay was low, disease and danger took large tolls. But for the buffalo soldiers, the wretchedness of these basic aspects of life was compounded by prejudice, not only from local civilians but from the Army itself: they were denied enlistment in the more elite units of artillery, engineers, ordnance, and signal corps; they were given inferior horses; and they drew—because of the policy of keeping them away from settled areas—the most isolated frontier posts. Before the Spanish-American War, not a single black enlisted man had risen from the ranks to become a commissioned officer.[49]

Generally speaking, the court-martial offenses of black soldiers were treated more harshly than those of whites. But at Fort Stockton, at least, military punishment was "almost exclusively confined to hard labor under charge of the guard and stoppage of pay." The labor was simply what the soldiers ordinarily did, and in the mind of the thoughtful Dr. Pope, could "only be called *hard* in a Pickwickian sense":

> The hours of labor are short, the intervals of relaxation long; and no more is accomplished by three men than could be well done by one during the same time. Where there is no other incentive to work than a sentence of a Court Martial, or the loose supervision of a sentinel, who has an undoubted sympathy for the man with whom he may change places tomorrow, but little earnest labor can be expected.[50]

The buffalo soldiers usually endured the rigors of military life without losing heart, but on one occasion, the most serious in the frontier army period, the soldiers at Fort Stockton protested. In 1873 Private John Taylor reported sick to the post surgeon, Dr. Peter A. Cleary, and was treated but not excused from duty. Taylor reported sick a second time. When he reappeared a third time, Cleary accused him of malingering and had him placed in the post guardhouse.

Although Dr. Pope had recommended replacing the guardhouse because "its defects of heating and ventilation appear to me to be radical and not susceptible of remedy," it stands today, one of the few remaining buildings of old Fort Stockton. As Dr. Cleary had written not long before the Taylor incident, "the cells have neither ventilation, heat, nor light, and yet such is its crowded condition that prisoners are of necessity obliged to sleep in those cells. If punishment be the object of a guardhouse, it is admirably adapted for the purpose, being little if at all inferior to the celebrated 'black hole of Calcutta.'"[51]

Taylor died the following day. Neither Cleary nor a visiting surgeon could determine a cause of death.

Word quickly spread among the soldiers that the doctor had been responsible for Taylor's death, and someone got up a petition accusing Cleary of negligence.* Their officers demanded that the soldiers withdraw their names from the petition or face charges, but the majority refused. Court-martial proceedings were ordered for those who had refused to withdraw their names, and on August 26, 1873, twenty-one men were tried for mutiny in one court-martial and given sentences of one to two years, to be followed by dismissal. In their final statement to the court, the

---

*It may be significant that in the post medical record book all the pages for 1872 have been ripped out.

accused men wrote that they believed the withdrawal of their names would have been "equivalent to an acknowledgment that the statements therein made were false."[52]

Was Cleary to blame for Taylor's death? When he took the Army's medical examination to qualify for serving in the frontier army, he squeaked through with a score of 795. The minimum passing score was 790; the maximum possible score, 1,070. Cleary achieved the minimum in anatomy, physiology, surgery, and the practice of medicine but failed general pathology and pathological anatomy (one category) and chemistry.[53]

Although Cleary was quickly removed from Fort Stockton as a result of the upheaval, his career as an army doctor continued without pause. He was thirty-three at the time of the Taylor incident and an assistant surgeon. In 1883 he was promoted to full surgeon with the rank of major. He retired in 1903 as a brigadier general and chief surgeon for the Department of Texas.[54]

By 1879 six years had passed since the protest that had ended the military careers of twenty-one enlisted men. This time, the events that would make Fort Stockton notorious throughout the Department of Texas were taking place among the post's officers.

Two

COURT-MARTIAL

THE PROSECUTION

Two of the major figures in the Geddes court-martial came from Germany: Louis Henry Orleman and John Clous, the judge advocate. Was there a particular bond between Clous, the man responsible for presenting the Army's case, and his plaintiff because of their common origin? Possibly, but the Army at the time was full of German immigrants.

John Walter Clous came to the United States when he was eighteen and trained as a lawyer. His picture reveals an earnest countenance and a more carefully shaped mustache and goatee than many men of his era wore. At the time of the Geddes trial he was forty-two.

Army personnel files often contain just an outline of a career: postings and promotions, requests for leave, and so on. For his forty-four-year service Clous's large file reveals "aggressive ambition," and more than a touch of the operator. An early recommendation described him accurately as "zealous and efficient in the performance of his duties—energetic, prompt, and capable in all trust confided to him, ambitious in his profession."[1] The words "zealous" and "efficient" often came to mind when superiors considered John Clous.

His desire to manipulate circumstances for the purpose of advancement also appears early on. In 1867 five officers of the Sixth Cavalry wrote a letter protesting Clous's attempt to transfer back into the Sixth, which he had left in order to gain a promotion to captain in the Thirty-eighth Infantry. The letter complained that "[i]f he should succeed in getting back to this regiment by the proposed arrangement, he would not only rank all the Lieutenants who formerly ranked him, but would set them all back some two or three years in promotion."[2]

Clous wasn't allowed to transfer back in, but neither was he deterred from further efforts at self-aggrandizement. In 1881 he wrote to the Adjutant General to say that his name should appear on the list of Captains of Infantry *above* that of Captain DeWitt Clinton Poole. According to Clous's reckoning, he had served four years, one month, and twenty-three days to Poole's four years, one month, and twenty-one days. Evidently he had counted his own time of service too generously, and his petition was rejected. Similarly, his 1898 attempt to get the Medal of Honor for an Indian engagement in 1872 was turned down.[3]

Clous was prominent on the enemies list of Captain George Armes, an officer whose diary of his army career was eventually published as a book, *Ups and Downs of an Army Officer.* An easily offended and trouble-prone man, Armes was the object of numerous courts-martial and was finally expelled from the army.[4] His description of life in the Tenth is full of contemptuous evaluations of his numerous enemies and elaborate accounts of his many difficulties with the military judicial system. This clear propensity to not get along with his colleagues did not mean, of course, that he was invariably mistaken in his judgments.

"In regard to the Dutchman," Armes wrote, using his favorite epithet for Clous and one often applied to Germans, "he has always had the 'cheek' of a brass band and has succeeded in gulling many and making them believe that he is an individual of some importance." The patrician Armes had instinctively disliked Clous from the first, responding negatively to his obvious ambition. Armes's diary entry for May 11, 1869, at Fort Dodge, Kansas, records that Major Page visited, bringing "a Dutch Captain by the name of Clous with him . . . who seems to have cheek enough to take him anywhere." Their paths crossed again when both men were transferred to Texas, where Clous became a judge advocate and Armes was frequently brought up on charges, circumstances under which his dislike of Clous could only deepen.[5]

Clous's opponent in the Geddes court-martial was defense counsel George Washington Paschal, a local boy whose family was among the early residents of San Antonio. Three years before, he had returned from law school in Washington, D.C., to form a law partnership with John Mason. At the age of thirty-one, he was at the beginning of his career. After his baptism by fire in the Geddes case, he would become well known for his work in military trials and his knowledge of military law.

What happened on the first day of the trial was representative of much that followed. All defendants in court-martial proceedings have a right to challenge members of the court, and unless a challenge appears to be completely frivolous, it is usually upheld. Geddes objected to a member of his court, Captain J. H. Patterson, as prejudiced against him, and Patterson's response to this accusation was less than reassuring. Scuttlebutt was already circulating, Patterson recounted, that a medical report had shown "such a thing [incest] could not have been possible. If such medical testimony is introduced, and if such line of defense be adopted, the charge of incest could not be sustained in the face of the medical experts. I believe that to be so, and I may have expressed myself so." Patterson remained a member of the court, an indication of how future defense requests would be treated.

The trial would be studded with rejected defense objections and other kinds of setbacks for Captain Geddes. Applications for defense witnesses had to be approved by the judge advocate, but he consistently turned down the proposed defense witnesses as "not material to the ends of justice." Usually he got his way. The court's interventions also tended to be in the interest of the prosecution.

Beyond the central matter of whether or not a father and daughter had committed incest, defense and prosecution testimony differed substantially on a number of relevant points. Literature was invoked by both sides to assess Geddes's character and his relationship with Lillie Orleman. The judge advocate told the court that he expected to show that "the accused furnished the daughter of the witness highly sensational novels improper for young girls to read and that the same were discovered by the father and by him returned to the accused." Geddes promptly objected that the only way of judging if the novels were improper would be for the court to admit them into evidence and judge for itself. His objection was not sustained.

The Orleman-Geddes quarters also came in for detailed examination because of Geddes's claim that he had heard the Orlemans' sexual activity and intelligible speech through the wall separating his rooms from the Orlemans'.

Key events received repeated scrutiny. The trip to Fort Davis that the principals had made together in February of 1879 was a locus of dispute, as well as March 2, when Geddes claimed to have both seen and heard the Orlemans engaged in "criminal intimacy," and March 12, when the projected departure of Geddes and Lillie Orleman brought things to a head.

LILLIE ORLEMAN

Lillie Orleman was the first prosecution witness. She testified that she had met Andrew Geddes at a post dance or hop where he had squeezed her hand meaningfully. Their acquaintance developed. He came to her father's quarters almost every day in the afternoon when her father was at Stables.* He told her that he was unhappy, that he had not lived with his wife for many years, had never loved her or anyone as he loved Lillie: "He wished I was his, and that I must be his."

After the first day of the trial, the defense complained that Lillie had testified with her back to Geddes in violation of Article 6 of the Constitution that requires that the accuser confront the accused. Judge Advocate Clous told Paschal that he misinterpreted the meaning of *confront,* and the court overruled the defense objection.

Paschal had cited a standard reference, Stephen Vincent Benét's *Treatise on Military Law and the Practice of Courts-Martial,* to support his objection. As Benét describes the positioning of the various parties in the courtroom, the defendant and his counsel are "on the right hand of the judge advocate, and the witness is seated near the judge advocate, and usually on his left."[6] In other words, in an ordinary court-martial proceeding a witness would not testify as Lillie Orleman did, with her back to the accused. This arrangement was undoubtedly contrived to spare her embarrassment.

---

*"Stables" is the term for both morning and afternoon care of horses in a cavalry regiment. The trial refers to afternoon Stables, beginning around 3:30.

On March 2, Lillie testified, Geddes came to the Orlemans' quarters as usual while her father was at Stables: "He attempted to take liberties with me several times, and also make propositions to me. He asked me to sit on his lap and would kiss and hug me."

> Q: Please state to the Court the nature of the liberties he attempted to take?
> A: He began first by trying to force his hand down the neck of my dress which was rather low. I then pushed his hand away, he then got down on his knees and begged and implored me to allow him to kiss my breast. He also attempted to put his hand under my clothes. He was so rude that it took all my strength to repel him.

Yet Lillie had continued to see Geddes alone. On another occasion, she testified, he asked to wash and also comb her hair and see her undressed. By her own admission, Lillie had not repulsed the captain entirely: "Believing Captain Geddes to be a gentleman I inferred from all his actions that he would get a divorce and make me his wife."

Of the night when Geddes had supposedly surprised the father and daughter in "criminal incest," Lillie testified that she went to bed between nine and ten and slept until morning: the outside shutters and the bedroom window were closed and the curtains drawn. Before this, her father had come into the bedroom and spoken harshly of finding Geddes in their quarters, warning Lillie not to let it happen again on pain of being turned out of the house. She noted that it was only possible to hear "dim sound" from Geddes's adjacent room.

Lillie further testified that when Geddes came over the next day, he asked her to sit on his lap—which she did—and said that he had heard everything the night before. He said he would tell Fort Stockton's commanding officer, Lieutenant Colonel Matthew Blunt, " 'that your father is not treating you right' ":

I was terrified and afraid that my relations towards Captain Geddes
would become known to my father, and I told him that he was right
and that my father had treated me cruelly and meanly, which was
really not so. I told him that to enlist his sympathy in order to take
me home. I then asked him not to tell Colonel Blunt as he had
before said he would.

According to Lillie's account of the March 3 meeting, Geddes
appeared to love her and she returned his love. Further, in her version of the story, the relationship had to be concealed from her
father, who had begun to suspect it. Most significant, Lillie said
that when Geddes accused her father of not "treating her right,"
she agreed for the purpose of winning Geddes's sympathy so that
he would take her to her Austin home *and* renounce his plan of
exposing Orleman to the commanding officer of Fort Stockton.
She testified that when Geddes characterized her father as "not
treating her right," she took it as a reference to her father's having
reprimanded her for her relationship with Geddes.

In their court-martial testimony Orleman, Lillie, and Geddes
all agreed that Geddes told Lillie on March 3 that her father was
not treating her right and that Geddes based his accusation on
what he had discovered the night before. They disagreed about
what Geddes had meant when he said that Lillie's father was not
"treating her right."

Lillie noted that she could not have told Geddes, as he had
alleged, that her father had begun abusing her at the age of thirteen since she had been in a convent until she was fifteen. But she
admitted that she had seen her family at holidays during the convent years.

Regarding the week that followed the scene of March 3, Lillie
stated that she and Geddes were seemingly in harmony. They cor-
responded, and she gave him her thimble and gold cross. They

made plans to leave Fort Stockton together: he wanted her to go to his home with him; she said she had to go to her own home in Austin.

Then, on March 12, Lillie's father told her at breakfast that Geddes had accused him of being too intimate with her; that Geddes professed to have discovered this at their bedroom window where he had stood listening: "I then asked my father what Captain Geddes meant by accusing him of being too intimate with me—he replied that he did not know and would demand an explanation from Captain Geddes."

Lillie said that her father first went to Geddes's room, then both men came over to the Orleman quarters and confronted Lillie together. Geddes said, "'Miss Lillie, you know that your father is not treating you right.'" As she told the court, "Captain Geddes sitting opposite me terrified me with his looks under which I felt guilty and I answered him, 'Captain, you should not ask me such questions. You know all.'"

Geddes asked Lillie if she was going to leave in the stage with him that evening, and she said yes. Then, Lillie continued, he told her father, "'Orleman, if you will consent to let your daughter go down in the stage this evening I will keep the whole matter a secret.' My father then answered, 'Seeing what conspiracy exists between you and my daughter, she can do in the future what she pleases.'" But he also vowed not to let the matter rest.

In what would be only one of many flagrant errors made in trial procedure, Lillie was then allowed to give hearsay testimony—to enter what was actually third-hand gossip into the trial record. The defense objected, but, as was usually the case, was overruled. Lillie's hearsay evidence was that "a lady" had told her that "her husband had seen Mrs. Hart in Captain Geddes's arms on the sofa in her [Mrs. Hart's] parlor." This lady also told Lillie that Captain Geddes had been seen with Mrs. McLaughlen "after Tattoo, to run up the back steps of the Hospital." Both Mrs. Hart and Mrs. McLaughlen were the wives of officers stationed at Fort Stockton.[7] More than that, Mrs. McLaughlen's husband was then commander of the post.

Lillie testified that when she asked Geddes about the two women, he told her that Mrs. Hart was not a lady: "In regard to Mrs. McLaughlen he denied having done any such thing." The court would not allow the defense to ask the identity of the gossiping lady.*

Queried about her feelings toward Geddes, Lillie responded, "Whenever I was in Captain Geddes's presence I was completely mesmerized and consequently he could make me say and do as he pleased." About her father, she stated, "My father has always treated me very kindly and tried to make me as happy and content in his circumstances, having to support such a large family as ours."

When Paschal cross-examined her, Lillie denied all of his suggestions—that she had told Geddes she had the experience of a woman of forty, that she had a great secret, that she would never be happy. She did admit to telling Geddes that if she was unhappy, it "was a matter concerning only herself." Paschal did not press her on what she might have meant by this: had he done so, a member of the court probably would have objected, as happened on other occasions when the questioning became aggressive or personal. Lillie also denied that she had solicited Geddes's visits or encouraged his expressions of love, although she did say that she had "kissed him in return." The defense was able to establish that Geddes's visits to the Orleman quarters were not confined to the times Lillie had described, that is, when her father was absent. In fact, he often visited when her father was there.

About the evening of March 2, Lillie testified that Geddes once again visited while her father was at Stables. When he got up

---

*It later became clear, however, that it was the wife of First Lieutenant Owen Sweet. Both Sweets were described by Lieutenant Bigelow as notorious gossips.

to leave, Lillie detained him by asking him to stay until her father returned. But when Lieutenant Orleman arrived, he found the door locked, "which," Lillie related, "had been accidently done by me without my knowledge." Her father was angry, assuming that the door had been intentionally locked to enable an assignation.

One of the events on which the prosecution and defense offered wildly different accounts was a trip between Fort Stockton and Fort Davis that the Orlemans, Geddes, and Joseph Friedlander took on February 21, 1879. Friedlander, the Fort Stockton postmaster and a local merchant, was a bachelor of thirty-eight and Geddes's close friend. Fort Davis was seventy miles southwest of Fort Stockton, a long day's journey: the party left around 6 a.m. in an army ambulance, a horse-drawn carriage, and arrived at 8 p.m. Only a few months before, in the fall of 1878, the road between the two forts had been considered unsafe for small parties because of recent Indian activity.[8]

What happened during the trip was disputed. Each side accused the other of impropriety within the confines of the vehicle in which the father and daughter faced the officer and his friend, with Lillie sitting directly across from Geddes. This seating arrangement was material to the accusations made. According to Lillie's version of the trip Geddes pressed her legs between his under cover of an army cape.

Beginning with the ambulance ride, Paschal's cross-examination was designed to elicit Lillie's feelings toward Geddes. He drew from her the admission that she did not protest her knees being pressed between Geddes's—nor did she mind.

Q: You have stated the accused would ask you to sit on his lap and kiss and hug you. Now please state if you would comply with these requests upon the part of the accused.
A: Sometimes.

Paschal also asked upon what basis Lillie believed Geddes to be a gentleman. She replied: "I cannot say. I believed that he was a gentleman. I never consented to any of his ungentlemanly acts or propositions so that I never gave them a serious consideration or thought." This confusing answer suggests that Lillie wanted to believe that Geddes was a gentleman as opposed to a sexual predator so that she could pin romantic hopes on him, but to do so she had to ignore or acquiesce to some of his behavior.

Paschal's line of questioning next turned to the explosive subject of Lillie's life with her father in the cramped officers' quarters that they shared, the other half of the one-story house where Geddes lived. He established that the two slept in the same room, without any screen between their beds, but the next defense question was disallowed: "Did your father and yourself dress and undress in the presence of each other?" This was clearly a pertinent question: when the Judge Advocate General later reviewed the court-martial, he expressed surprise that the objection to it had been sustained.

The defense now raised the most powerful evidence against the Orlemans, the letters Lillie had written to Geddes and instructed him to burn. From the first letter, Paschal quoted to her the passage "never let on to my father by your words or actions that I have given you the secret of my life" and asked her to explain what "the secret of my life" referred to. She replied that it was her infatuation with Geddes and their plan to leave Fort Stockton together.

When Paschal asked Lillie what she meant by writing "I could not help telling you all," Lillie replied that she meant "the conversation I had with Captain Geddes on the third of March, 1879," instead of giving an explanation of what *all* referred to. As for what it was Lillie asked Geddes not to tell Colonel Blunt, she said: "I had told him that my father had treated me cruelly and meanly—this was really not so, but I said it to enlist his sympathy, to take me home as I was afraid that my relations with Captain Geddes would become known to my father."

When pressed about her statement that if they knew, people would shun her father and honor Geddes, Lillie replied, "I meant the manner in which my father had spoken to me that night and that if the people knew of such conduct that they would shun him while they would honor Captain Geddes for trying to take my part." Yet in admonishing his daughter to break off a relationship with a married man of dubious reputation, Orleman was only doing what most people of the time would not only approve but expect. That he might be "shunned" for even a heated chastisement under the circumstances, or Geddes "honored" for rescuing her from a fatherly lecture, seems implausible.

Lillie's exegesis of her note to Geddes elides the nebulous expression that everyone agreed he had used. In saying "not treating you right," Geddes avoided specifying the act that few Victorian-era Americans would willingly name. Therefore Lillie could claim that she interpreted "not treating you right" to mean her father's harsh words to her and meant "you already know all" to similarly refer to paternal scoldings.

After Paschal concluded his cross-examination, the court posed questions. Lillie denied that there had been any instances of incestuous behavior with her father. She had been on the witness stand for fourteen days.

Lillie's testimony is open to two interpretations. Either she had turned to Geddes because she wanted his help in ending an unnatural relationship with her father, something she had no power to bring to an end by herself, and was then prevailed upon by her father to recant; or she was an innocent young girl who had been the object of a seduction plot and now understood herself to have been betrayed by the man she loved and hoped to marry. Either way, she had been victimized and must have felt wretched.

Most likely, the court adopted the view of Lillie that a fellow officer had expressed in a letter to Lieutenant Bigelow:

> She is so entirely unsophisticated that she ought not to hear a word spoken unless it's meant. I feel sorry, sometimes, for girls of her character, when I think of the awakening from their delusions, that must come sooner or later and is never a *pleasant* experience.[9]

The very fact that Lillie's plan to leave Fort Stockton with Geddes was described in the court-martial charge as his attempt to abduct her confirms this view of her innocence. Lillie had testified that she and Geddes secretly plotted to leave the post together, she possessed by a romantic vision of love and future marriage that she imagined he shared. That this flight was regarded as an abduction rather than as consensual is a reflection of the then prevailing view that women were at all times the passive recipients of male action. At eighteen, the convent-educated Lillie was regarded as properly subservient to and in need of her father's ruling hand.

LOUIS ORLEMAN

Next to his daughter, Lieutenant Louis Orleman was the most important prosecution witness, the man who had initiated the court-martial charges. He was noticeably better prepared than she had been to address the issues raised, such as his and Lillie's sleeping arrangements. Volunteering an answer to the question the defense had not been allowed to ask, he created a scenario that left no opportunity for the two to dress or undress in the same room at the same time: "My daughter would retire first and I would retire after I knew her to be in bed. In the morning I got up upon the first call of reveille every morning. My daughter usually got up while I was at Stables."

Orleman corroborated Lillie's account of Geddes's actions on the February trip to Fort Davis. He recounted that he had discovered Geddes pressing his daughter's knees when he searched the floor of the ambulance for a corkscrew he had dropped. His reaction to this discovery seems curious: rather than addressing the captain or Lillie, he said that he had simply moved her legs.

Geddes's deposition had stated that Orleman had fondled his daughter's breasts on the trip to Fort Davis. Orleman met this accusation with a strong denial: "I did not, and it would have been impossible for me to do it, as she was wrapt up in a heavy lined overcoat, her arms inside of the coat and not in the sleeves of the coat; the coat was a double breasted one and buttoned down to her waist." He did admit that at one time during the journey, while his daughter had leaned against him and slept, he had had his arms around her.

Orleman's description of the evening of March 2 echoed the testimony his daughter had given. He sat on Lillie's bed and upbraided her for her conduct that day, that is, locking the door while she was alone with Geddes:

> I told my daughter what reputation Captain Geddes bore amongst the officers of his Regiment that I had spoken to about it and that she should never let me find him in the house again, except in my presence. I also told her that on account of his bad reputation no lady could afford to meet Captain Geddes in such a way without having her reputation ruined.

Orleman described the furnishings of the bedroom in minute detail and asserted that "little sound penetrated" from his set of rooms to Geddes's.

In Orleman's account of his confrontation with Geddes on March 12, Geddes said to him, "Lieutenant, you are too intimate with your daughter and you are not treating her right. I heard everything that happened on Sunday night March 2, 1879." Orleman then asked the captain what he had heard and how he had heard it: "At first he would not say. Finally he said that he had heard it at my bedroom window where he had listened. . . . He said that what he heard made him feel so bad that he could not go to sleep."

According to his version of events, Orleman did not respond to this revelation with the shock or outrage that a father falsely accused of incest might be expected to display. Instead, he asked Geddes if he thought such eavesdropping was the action of a gentleman. Orleman testified that he thought Geddes's announcement was simply an attempt to coerce him into granting permission for Geddes and Lillie to leave Fort Stockton together. Knowing Geddes's reputation as a libertine, he assumed that his daughter was already ruined and in need of removal to cover her shame.

What kind of man was Louis Orleman? At thirty-eight he was the father of eight children, five of whom were daughters. The family remained in Austin because the children were in school there. Lillie, the oldest child, had been living with him at Fort Stockton since November of 1878, and before that, alone with him at Fort Clark and Fort Duncan from the fall of 1876 to the spring of 1877.

Colonel Benjamin Grierson, a well-known frontier army officer and commander of the Tenth Cavalry, was asked to testify as a character witness for the prosecution about Orleman's "truth and veracity." When the defense objected, on the grounds that Orleman was not on trial, the judge advocate justified the question by noting that the defense implied "that Lieutenant Orleman is so depraved and steeped in crime that virtually he is not in possession of any moral or other attributes that make up the character of man, thus virtually attempting to assail his character in every particular."

This rhetorical overkill was a useful strategy since it developed the expectation that a man who appeared less than a depraved monster could hardly be guilty of such a terrible offense. As usual, the defense objection to this testimony was overruled.

The tactic of calling character witnesses is always an appeal to the human desire to believe in the consistency of character and, with it, the predictability of behavior. Hence those rueful blurtings of the neighbors who discover a vicious killer in their midst: we never suspected—he was always quiet and polite, attended church, kept his lawn mowed. If a crime is "monstrous," presumably it is committed by a monster rather than an ordinary person. And if someone is a monster, it should be evident not only in the crime but through and through—in outward appearance, in social habits, in the simple act of saying "good morning." Those criminals whose behavior always seemed suspect in some way are the most satisfying since they reinforce our need to feel equipped to recognize and make ourselves safe from predators.

This desire has led to a number of schemes for identifying traits of a criminal predisposition. As an extension of the preoccupation with categorizing race through cranial measurements, Cesare Lombroso began in 1870 to identify criminals by the shapes of their skulls and other physical characteristics. To Lombroso, the "born criminal" was a throwback: "Thus were explained anatomically the enormous jaws, high cheek-bones, prominent superciliary arches . . . handle-shaped or sessile ears found in criminals, savages, and apes."[10] Lombroso also contended that "there is everywhere a preponderance of crime in the districts dominated by dolichocephaly [long skulls]." He wanted to make a similar broad link between crime and dark hair, but was restrained by the consideration that the warm climate of the dark-haired "races" he studied might also be a factor.[11] This may seem like a caricature of racial profiling today, but Lombroso was enormously popular at the end of the nineteenth century and the beginning of the twentieth.[12] In more recent times, researchers have pursued a relationship between criminal tendencies and chromosomal abnormality, correlating a propensity for criminality with an extra Y chromosome.[13] An age that gave considerable credence to phrenology* might well be susceptible to judicial arguments that correlated proper appearance in public with good behavior in private, especially when the issue in question was morally unthinkable.[14] Did Orleman appear neat and well-groomed? Had he ever gone to church? Then he could hardly be guilty of incest!

Colonel Grierson claimed to know the lieutenant and his family "very well." He testified that Orleman had a reputation for veracity and discharged his duties satisfactorily. More than that,

> He [Orleman] was kind and affectionate towards his family and never so far as I know had any trouble whatever officially or personally with anyone. He and his family stood high in the estimation of the officers, were liked by all including their families. The general character of Lieutenant Orleman and his family as to integrity, veracity and morality was excellent always since I have known them. . . . The family was frank, unassuming, industrious, and economical, and from what I know of them I have entertained and do now at this moment entertain the highest regard for Lieutenant Orleman and his family.

In Colonel Grierson's glowing testimonial, the Orlemans were a model family and Orleman himself a paragon.

Although Lillie had admitted to sitting on the lap of a married man when the two were alone and letting him press her legs between his during a day's journey by stage, Clous continued his examination of Grierson by brazenly eliciting a character reference for her, relying on the court to stifle any objection or pressing cross-examination. He asked his high-ranking witness, "What

---

*Phrenology, formulated by F. J. Gall at the beginning of the century, was a system of determining abilities and personality by examining the skull.

was the general demeanor and general behavior of Miss Lillie Orleman as to modesty while you have known her?" and received the gratifying answer, "It has always been very good indeed, very modest and well behaved." Geddes did predictably object to the question as irrelevant, but as usual the court found for the judge advocate.

One small anecdote that does not appear in Grierson's testimony: Orleman makes a fleeting appearance in a letter that Grierson's eleven-year-old son, Charlie, wrote to his mother from Fort Sill on November 5, 1872. A group of ladies had visited the encampment:

> The next day Major Schofield rigged a government wagon up with blankets and buffalo robes for them. Lt. Orlaman [sic] was drunk and he went to put Mrs. Myers into the wagon and he turned her heels up and her head down. Mrs. Myers said I'm afraid you can't put me in. He said *oh yes I put you in.*[15]

Charlie's innocent narrative simply records the facts of the incident, the only thing that he remembered or wrote about the ladies' visit. It isn't much out of Orleman's thirteen years of social interaction at frontier army posts. Still, it is suggestive. Here's a man who assumes the stance of courteously aiding a lady and then, instead of following through, turns her upside down. An experienced army wife, Mrs. Myers was apparently equal to the contretemps. She didn't shriek or exclaim; she made a polite response designed to extricate herself. But Orleman wasn't willing to let her go. He was determined: *"oh yes I put you in."**

---

*Charlie's letter was not available to the defense, of course, or to anyone else outside the Grierson family until the twentieth century, when the Grierson correspondence was collected in four different repositories. A selection of letters, including Charlie's, was published in 1989 (see note 15).

Grierson also overlooked several matters that had already come before the court. When he pronounced Orleman completely free from trouble with fellow officers, he either dismissed as unimportant or was ignorant of Orleman's difficulties with other officers who had already testified (ironically, as witnesses for the prosecution).

Captain C. C. Hood of the Twenty-fourth Infantry was at Fort Duncan when Orleman was there and testified that he had heard "nothing negative" about him. But the following exchange occurred when Hood was cross-examined by the defense:

Q: Did you ever express yourself to the effect that Lieutenant Orleman was a dishonorable man and that you had no respect for him? This while you were at Fort Duncan?

A: I think it very likely I did.

On re-cross Hood said that this pronouncement was the result of an altercation between himself and Orleman over the hiring of a servant.

Another character witness for the prosecution also backfired. Captain Louis H. Carpenter of the Tenth Cavalry was a distinguished soldier who would be awarded a Medal of Honor for the already legendary rescue of Forsyth's scouts from Beecher's Island in September of 1868.[16] Orleman had been one of two officers with him on that mission. Carpenter testified that Orleman had served seven years under him, and that he had never known a more affectionate father or known of any domestic trouble that he ever had: "He and his family lived together in perfect accord." The very phrase "perfect accord" somehow rings false as a description of the life of a large family living on a lieutenant's pay, or indeed, any family, but it was probably the result of an innocuous desire to make the testimonial more effective. A person accused of a monstrous act may need something more than ordinary goodness, as if the lurking shadow of the monster can be obliterated only by the creation of a saint. Under cross-examination a more shaded picture of Orleman emerged:

> Q: Did you not sometime during the year 1870 or 1871 at Leavenworth, Kansas, say in effect and publicly that Lieutenant Orleman's conduct was dishonorable and that he had intentionally lied, and that you would not believe him on oath or words to that effect—this in reference to Lieutenant Orleman's conduct in the case of Captain Graham late of the Tenth Cavalry?*
>
> A: I was very much surprised and disappointed in this [that Orleman did not testify for the prosecution in the Graham case] and made some remarks against the conduct of Lieutenant Orleman in the matter, but I have never had a full explanation of the whole matter.

Carpenter admitted that he had said that Orleman "had not spoken the truth in the matter." He then remarked that "during the last five years he had seen them [the Orleman family] on a number of occasions," adding disingenuously, "particularly Lieutenant Orleman and Miss Lillie, his daughter. I have seen them more frequently than his wife and the rest of the family."

This observation had the effect of strengthening the defense contention that Lillie and her father were isolated from the rest of the family—and thus free to have an unnatural relationship. When Geddes's attorney wanted to drive the point home by asking for specifics of these encounters—a reasonable enough question—a member of the court intervened, complaining that Carpenter was being asked to join in "a game of quibbles." The

---

*Captain George Graham was dismissed from the Army for selling government property (horses) for personal gain.[17]

commenting member continued, "He has stated what he knows and should be excused from irritating and annoying questions."

Paschal was not indulging in a "game of quibbles" nor was he attempting to badger the witness. He wanted to make a point that clinical research on incest would make a hundred years later: that the separation of the father and daughter from the rest of the family was suspicious, a possible sign of an incestuous relationship.*

In all instances during the trial the objection of a member of the court, always unidentified in the record, was sustained, perhaps because the other members did not want to rebuff one of their number.

The parade of character witnesses for Orleman continued. J. C. De Gress, the mayor of Austin, testified to the good repute of the family there, although he admitted that they had lived in Austin only a year and a half. A teacher, Professor Jacob Bickler, also gave the family a good character, which mostly consisted of applying the rubric *gentleman* to Orleman twice in the same sentence and indicating that he had "always moved in the best of society, German as well as American."

ABDUCTION

After the Orlemans' testimony, several minor witnesses were called by the prosecution to confirm Geddes's motive for abducting Lillie Orleman. If Geddes had made such a serious false accusation as incest against the Orlemans, he must have had some motive, hence the seduction-abduction plot the prosecution invoked.

---

*Usually this separation is more symbolic than physical: the daughter is singled out for special attention by the father.

The first charge against Geddes consisted of two counts, the "endeavor to corrupt" Lillie Orleman and the "attempt to abduct her from her home and family." Evidence for the first was Lillie's direct testimony about his advances and the hearsay testimony about Geddes's reputation that Clous had introduced over defense objections. The correspondence between the two suggested more ardor on her part than on his. Two of her notes began "Darling Andrew."

The seduction portion of the case was classic "he said, she said." Lillie's testimony told of persistent attentions on the part of her next-door neighbor in the period following their initial encounter at the hop. But even in answering friendly questions, she did not deny allowing some of these attentions. Certainly if Geddes's advances had been unwelcome, she need not have opened her door to the captain after the first occurrence of inappropriate behavior. Instead, she frankly confessed, she became infatuated with him. She believed he would get a divorce and marry her.

Orleman's testimony on his daughter's departure from Fort Stockton began with Geddes informing him that he had heard that the cavalry would be sent into the field that summer. In that case, Orleman had replied, he would have to send Lillie home to Austin. At eighteen, Lillie was as old as many married women, yet, as an unmarried daughter, when her father went on field duty, she could not continue in his quarters alone. Geddes had volunteered that he was going to apply for a leave and would be willing to escort her away from the post. A concerned father would ordinarily welcome such an offer since it was inadvisable in that still unsettled country for a young woman to make a long stage trip alone. But Orleman said he demurred, preferring to send Lillie with the paymaster. A few days later, Geddes told Orleman that he had two stage passes and that Lillie could use one of them. Orleman still demurred. To Lillie he said that she could never travel with a man of Geddes's dubious reputation. In Orleman's version of events, he had consistently opposed Geddes's accompanying Lillie in spite of the captain's blandishments.

Lillie's account agreed with her father's, but it also included the behind-the-scenes machinations of Geddes and herself to contrive their passage together. "What if I tell him I have two passes?" she reported Geddes as saying. Her response: "I would go with you if I could do so." They made secret arrangements to leave together on March 12, but on the morning of the twelfth her father announced that he had learned of Geddes's departure on the stage that evening. He asked her if she had known that Geddes was going. She denied it. He then forbade her to go on the same stage as Geddes.

Around 11 a.m. on March 12, Orleman testified, Geddes told him that if he refused to let Lillie go with him that evening, he would "publish me for having criminal intercourse with my daughter, that I had better make up my mind to let her go, and that he would keep the whole matter secret and say nothing about it to anybody." On reexamination Orleman emphasized this point: "I thought that the accused had impressed my daughter with the belief that to make this terrible accusation against me was the only means by which the accused could obtain my consent to her going with him."

On cross-examination Orleman was asked if it was not generally known and reported as a fact in and about Fort Stockton that his daughter was to take the same stage as Geddes when he went on leave. Orleman staunchly denied it: "It was not known to me until the day he was to go, March 12th, 1879. I heard it from Lt. Quimby, 25th Infantry, on that morning that the accused was to go."

Orleman claimed to have asked Lieutenant Henry P. Ritzius to take charge of Lillie on the stage, but the time of their conversation was in dispute. John Michael Gandy, a bookkeeper at the stage agent's store, confirmed that Orleman had sent a telegram to

Lieutenant Ritzius that morning, but there was no answer because Ritzius had already left Fort Davis for Fort Stockton. Orleman said he had spoken with Ritzius about the time of afternoon Stables, 3:30 p.m., but Ritzius testified that he had only arrived at Stockton at four, and that he had been approached by Orleman "within an hour" after his arrival. He agreed to escort Lillie, but Ritzius had come to Stockton to travel with Geddes, so it was understood that Geddes was going too.

In cross-examination the defense failed to bring out a point that buttressed Geddes's version of events—namely, that Geddes's prearranged plans to travel with Ritzius ran counter to an abduction scheme.

Gandy testified for the prosecution that Orleman had inquired on the twelfth about the fare to Austin. At the time Gandy assumed that Orleman had come for information only, since he did not reserve a seat for his daughter.

The rest of Gandy's testimony was actually more valuable to the defense than to the prosecution. He stated that Geddes had paid $84 for fares for himself *and* Lillie Orleman to San Antonio (the first stop on the way to Austin). Later in the day Gandy received a message that they were not going and sent back the money. On cross-examination he was asked: "When the accused paid you the stage fare of himself and Miss Orleman, did he act as though he was trying to conceal the fact that Miss Orleman was going with him?" He answered, "No sir."

Gandy also mentioned in passing a detail that would reverberate: when Orleman sent the telegram to Ritzius at Fort Davis, he charged it because he was "short of funds." Orleman flatly denied that he had lacked money at the time, but Joseph Friedlander testified that on March 12 at Friedlander's store Orleman asked Geddes to pay for Lillie's passage and that Geddes had agreed. Geddes had drawn $84 from Friedlander to pay for the two fares. Lillie's

trunk was subsequently delivered to the store, which was the stage
stop for Fort Stockton.

INTERLUDE

In the last week of May 1879, Lieutenant John Bigelow, Jr., made
the long stage trip from Fort Stockton to San Antonio at the sum-
mons of the court. He would spend most of the next three months
simply waiting to testify—and confiding to his diary what he
observed.

On May 27 Bigelow met Lillie and her father on their way to a
well-known boardinghouse. Later in the day, the proprietor told
Bigelow that she had at first agreed to rent them rooms, but then
withdrew the offer when she heard that they were involved in a
scandal. She asked Bigelow's opinion, and he was glad for an
opportunity to defend his friends:

> I told her that Miss Orleman was an unfortunate young lady who
> had been most outrageously slandered and that there were persons
> in the city who employed every means in their power to make the
> slander as public as possible.

Bigelow's pointed comment could have been a reference to Geddes's friend, Joe Friedlander, since Bigelow had heard from
another officer that Friedlander might have hired a detective to
spy on the Orlemans in San Antonio. After his conversation at the
boardinghouse, Bigelow went looking for the Orlemans and
learned that they had removed to Hord's Hotel—a decision that
displeased him:

> I was in hope that I would be able to dissuade him [Orleman] from
> going there. Neither he nor Miss Lilly seems to have the delicacy

that would prompt them to avoid publicity. They go every evening
to Fests Bier Garden. When the Lieut knew of my having arrived
here, he wanted Miss Lilly to go with him to call on me at the hotel.
She had sense of propriety enough to tell the Lieut that if I wanted
to see her, I could call on her and that she was not going to call
on me.[18]

Although he did not always approve of their actions, Bigelow
never questioned his friends' version of the Geddes matter. Shortly
before leaving Fort Stockton he had discovered that Lillie had lied
about her relationship with Geddes. But his reaction was to
bypass the lying and focus instead on the relationship itself:

The Chaplain informed me yesterday that Miss Orleman had equiv-
ocated in pretending not to have had any correspondence with Maj.
Geddes.* She afterwards acknowledged the equivocation. How, as a
respectable young woman, she could have engaged in a clandestine
correspondence with a man about whom she knew or surmised as
much as she did about Maj. Geddes, I cannot understand. She
showed herself lacking in moral perception.

Above the line at the end of this passage Bigelow wrote "female
delicacy," without crossing out "moral perception."

Bigelow had had a friendly relationship with Lieutenant Orleman and his daughter, often riding with Lillie in the vicinity of
the post. But his partisanship in the Geddes trial was not merely a
matter of friendship for the Orlemans. Geddes's past behavior as a
womanizer, and especially his attempt to seduce the young girl
Candelaria Garza, had condemned Geddes in Bigelow's eyes. In
his diary Bigelow refers to Geddes as a villain and a fiend who
must have used "his devilish arts with such success as to have

---

*Bigelow follows the army custom of referring to officers by their brevet titles. Geddes
was only a captain. Evidently, Lillie had at first hoped that Geddes had destroyed her letters to him, in which case it would have been her word against his.

blinded her [Lillie] to the danger of his company." In Bigelow's judgment Lillie had behaved imprudently, but she was still "this guiltless girl," whose happiness had been destroyed by a man who should be "kicked out of the army."[19]

Bigelow's distaste for Geddes was so strong that it overrode the rules of military protocol. On the streets of San Antonio Bigelow gave no acknowledgment of acquaintance when he saw Geddes. A fellow officer had to remind him that Geddes's "rank entitled him to a military salute."[20]

Bigelow had appeared briefly at the beginning of the trial to present the diagrams he had made of the Geddes-Orleman quarters, but he was told by Judge Advocate Clous that he would be called again during rebuttal testimony. As the trial dragged on through the hottest months of the year, Bigelow began to question the Army's custom of keeping witnesses like himself in idleness. He wrote with some exasperation, "Since I have been away from my company, which I left over a month ago, I have not done two good days work for the government."[21]

Instead, he developed his own routine. After breakfast every morning he went to the nearby army headquarters building to get his mail. While out, he attended to whatever shopping or other business he needed to do, then came back to his room in the Menger Hotel.* He usually got back at 10:30 and read until 1 or 2 p.m., dinnertime. After dinner, like breakfast a meal taken at the hotel, he went back to headquarters to check for mail, and read in his room for the rest of the afternoon.

> At about 6 oclock I fix up a little and then wander aimlessly forth from the hotel, alternately thinking of deciding upon someone to call on, and hoping to meet with something or somebody of interest

---

*The Menger, located next to the Alamo, was San Antonio's first modern hotel and a popular gathering place. Geddes was staying there, too.

in the course of my walk. I usually stay out until 8 oclock and then go to supper. Supper over, I am again at a loss what to do with myself. Generally if I have no engagement, I make one or two calls during the evening.

With a lively mind and much time on his hands, Bigelow read through Shakespeare's plays but bogged down in Sir Walter Scott's *Waverly,* finally telling his diary, "I got so sick of Scott's Waverly that I decided to-day upon exchanging it for another book. I have now J. G. Holland's Lessons in Life, which I like much better." His main diversion, however, was one that would have attracted an unattached young man anywhere: the calls that he made were often upon eligible young women, well-brought-up middle-class girls who were by definition virgins.[22]

VIRGINITY

The prosecution's most valuable witness was the doctor who had examined Lillie Orleman to determine whether or not she was a virgin. Although the court had a strong aversion to hearing anything about incest, it showed an excessive and prurient interest in virginity. Obviously, Lillie Orleman's virginity was a central issue in the case because Geddes had accused her father of having criminal intercourse with her. But more than that, "purity" was the totemic ideal of the nineteenth-century American woman, a condition resting upon lack of sexual experience in the unmarried and sexual fidelity in the married. Widely proclaimed to be woman's chief virtue, purity implied a separation from the male sphere and its multitudinous activities.[23] "In women's fiction," literary critic Nina Baym writes, "it was so taken for granted that it was ignored."[24]

The idea of an absolute distinction between the pure and the sexually experienced woman, a dividing line that was emphatically inscribed on the genitalia, was a natural medical corollary of cultural beliefs about virginity. The physical evidence was intended to be the unshakable cornerstone of prosecution testimony about Lillie Orleman. As one of the officers sitting in judgment on Andrew Geddes had remarked before hearing any evidence whatsoever, if Lillie were found to be a virgin, Geddes would unquestionably be guilty. Although the court devoted a great deal of attention to the question of virginity, it never considered whether sexual activities short of full intercourse would constitute "criminal intimacy" between a father and a daughter.

But as the trial progressed, with doctor after doctor taking the stand to expatiate on virginity, the line between the sexually pure and impure became increasingly blurred rather than more sharply delineated. Soon, the purported subject, Lillie Orleman, was left behind. Only one doctor had examined her genitalia; the others spoke generally.

Almost six weeks into the trial, at what would turn out to be the halfway point, M. K. Taylor, an army assistant surgeon and a practicing physician for twenty-eight years, began testimony for the prosecution. To the question "What experience have you had in the examination of the sexual organs of females?" he answered carefully, if not very precisely, "I have had considerable experience *professionally* [my emphasis]." Dr. Taylor had examined Lillie not once, but three times—an odd circumstance in and of itself if, as he intended to convey, the state of her virginity was such an open-and-shut matter.

The first "evidence" Dr. Taylor referred to was "the general appearance of the person." Presumably, a demure manner, modest attire, and an air of respectability could weigh in favor of virginity. In turning to the more pertinent condition of the genitalia,

Taylor was an ideal witness for the prosecution. Lillie was not only as virginal as might be expected for an eighteen-year-old, he testified; the immaturity of her genital organs suggested a twelve- or fourteen-year-old. Although physical descriptions of Lillie indicated that she was fully developed and more likely to be thought older rather than younger, Dr. Taylor found everything pertaining to her virginity to be *under*developed, including her nipples. He produced a litany of negatives: not only had she never been penetrated; she had not had "incomplete or vulval intercourse"; she had not even masturbated.

According to Dr. Taylor, these other forms of deviant behavior, like sexual promiscuity, changed the appearance of the genitalia. Lillie, however, "had the same delicate tints to the mucus [sic] membrane that are commonly observed in children or young females." Such medical observation supported the cultural view that "self-abuse," as Dr. Taylor called it, and whoring, might well be lumped together under a general heading of illicit and harmful behavior. Furthermore, they would leave physical signs that could distinguish the pure from the polluted.

The judge advocate had a number of questions about the hymen: Was it found in its "proper place"? What about its "tensity"? Was it hard and resisting or in the opposite condition? Such questions seemed to belabor the point since Dr. Taylor had already testified that the hymen was well enough developed "to show clearly that she never had had sexual intercourse."

Yet on cross-examination Dr. Taylor was forced to retreat a bit from his emphatic position. Asked outright if Lillie had ever had sexual intercourse, his "clearly never" became the waffling "I think not, sir, in the full meaning of that term." When pressed by counsel for the defense to answer yes or no, Taylor refused until instructed to do so by the court. He then produced this belabored reply: "I could not say that she had not had vulval intercourse in a single instance within a year or two because that would leave no trace, but as I understand the question it has reference to a full and complete intercourse, which I emphatically answer 'no.'"

The closed door was now slightly ajar. Although Dr. Taylor had no intention of cracking it more than the tiniest bit, a speculative person might have wondered: if only a single instance of vulval intercourse would leave no trace, what about several? What about ten? Actually, the cracking of the door was more than enough to destroy the absolute distinction between purity and experience. As far as this case was concerned, a single instance of vulval intercourse on the part of Orleman and his daughter would have been sufficient to confirm criminal intimacy and validate Geddes's accusation.

On July 17 Dr. Taylor would be recalled as a hostile witness for the defense—a necessary strategy since he was the only person who had physically examined Lillie. He was then asked to distinguish between a "complete hymen" and a "perfect hymen," and between full and partial intercourse. He was also asked to define sexual intercourse, which he did impressionistically, as

> those peculiar instinctive movements which take place between the male and female for the propagation of the species, generally contributing very much to the personal gratification of both parties to the act, temporarily, which gratifications are more easily felt than described.

Lillie's breasts also became the subject of defense questions. Even among practicing physicians, gynecological information was not widely disseminated, so it is not surprising that Paschal's attempt to undermine Dr. Taylor's testimony on breasts was itself somewhat misguided. He posed the question, "Is it not a fact that the breasts of many widows and mothers may compare with undoubted virgins in size, color, and shape to such an extent that it cannot be told from the breasts whether they are virgins or not?" Taylor replied that if the nipples were included, the answer was "no." The distinction the defense attorney was groping for was between virgins and married women who had never been pregnant: the breasts of a young widow who had had no pregnancy would have been indistinguishable from those of a young woman without sexual experience.

After the judge advocate declined to cross-examine, the court asked, irrelevantly, "May not sexual intercourse be incomplete as to penetration and yet be followed by impregnation"? As testimony on virginity proceeded, questions asked by the court sharply increased.

The defense was attempting to set up Dr. Taylor's testimony so that it could be assailed by the defense's own expert witnesses. Dr. George Cupples, described as having "an extensive practice in female diseases," immediately disputed Taylor's definition of virginity. When asked to state its "anatomical signs," he invoked both "the highest authorities" and the "general opinion of the profession" to assert that there were none that could be regarded as conclusive: "In other words, that any one of the signs alone is fallacious."[25] He was happy to expand upon his iconoclastic views at length, testifying that the clitorises of prostitutes may be of an exaggerated size *or* abnormally small. No doubt he had the military experience of the court in mind in giving another answer:

Q: Is it possible for a crescentic shaped hymen to entirely close the orifice of the vagina?
A: No. It bears absolutely to the vagina the same relation that a wad would with a piece cut out of it, with the bore of a barrell of a gun.

The judge advocate made a weak effort to cross-examine Cupples by demanding the names of some of the "highest authorities" the doctor had referred to. These being readily provided, he asked no further questions. Not so the court, which was obviously intrigued by the possibilities opened up by this witness's testimony. Members asked Cupples question after question, including the key question that Paschal had attempted in his cross-examination of Dr. Taylor:

> Have you ever been called upon to examine lewd women, or those you had reason to believe were not virtuous, but who had never had children, and if so, have you or have you not found any differences in the genitals of such and those girls you had reason to believe to be entirely virtuous?

If Dr. Taylor had insinuated that it was *always* possible to make this distinction and absolutely separate virtue from vice, Dr. Cupples predictably implied that it was rarely possible to do so.

Paschal's strategy in calling a number of other "medical experts" was undoubtedly based on his awareness that popular predisposition favored Dr. Taylor's view: it would take a number of opposing doctors to counteract not only Taylor's description of the (almost) black-and-white nature of virginity, but his repeated examinations of Lillie Orleman.

The next defense witness was even more extreme than Dr. Cupples. Dr. Thomas R. Chew maintained that it was "the current opinion of the profession that the anatomical signs taken singly or collectively have no value in establishing virginity or the contrary." This nihilism was too much for the judge advocate, who forced Chew's admission that "repeated intercourse would make a change."

When Dr. John J. Gaenslen also affirmed that there were *no* anatomical signs of virginity, Clous was not prepared to let him get off as lightly as Cupples and Chew had. He asked Dr. Gaenslen to suppose that the vagina was "so tightly closed that it is difficult to insert a little finger to the first joint," essentially what Dr. Taylor had said of his examination of Lillie. Unfazed, Gaenslen replied that this would determine "the question of penetration, not of chastity," once again raising the unwelcome larger issue of a sexual intimacy that did not involve full intercourse. To further queries he declared that an "imperforate hymen bulging with menstrual fluid" would be positive evidence of lack of penetration and virginity. This was of little help to the prosecution since no one had suggested that Lillie's menstrual discharge had been held back by her hymen.

Clous might have wished that he had let well enough alone when Gaenslen went on to recall a case where the hymen of a married woman was so dense that penetration did not take place: "She had been copulating for six years through the urethra."

The court was still preoccupied with the question it had posed to Dr. Cupples, how to distinguish virtue from vice in the female genitalia. If, it pursued, the presence of a hymen was no evidence of chastity, nor its absence proof of illicit sexual activity, was it not, however, "extremely improbable that the hymen would remain unruptured after frequent intercourse with an ordinarily well developed male"? Gaenslen refused to satisfy the court, telling them that the hymen "frequently has to be incised before childbirth." One may question the meaning of "frequent" in both examples as well as speculate on the dimensions of the "ordinarily well developed male" so casually referred to. No one had suggested an examination of Lieutenant Orleman to furnish any particulars about *his* sexual organs.

Modern-day gynecology would support defense testimony that any one indication of virginity in a given individual could be misleading, but Dr. Taylor's testimony about Lillie Orleman was extremely thorough. Nevertheless, it was governed by a presupposition that may well have undermined its accuracy. Lillie's breasts, for example, were described as virginal because the nipples were both small and light in color, yet change in the nipples occurs, in the form of flaccidity and darker pigmentation, as the result of pregnancy rather than sexual experience. Women who have breast-fed infants exhibit these characteristics more markedly.

Gynecology was still a new field of specialization in the 1870s, and young women were not likely to have a genital examination unless they had severe problems. In spite of his long professional experience, it may well have been that Dr. Taylor was primarily familiar with women who had had children rather than those who had had some sexual experience without pregnancy and childbirth.

Similarly, the "delicate tints" of the genitalia that he observed could have been due to the unpleasant nature of the occasion for his patient. What changes the appearance of the external female genitalia from pale to more vivid coloration is sexual arousal, a condition Lillie was unlikely to have experienced while submitting to such a gross violation of her person.[26]

In his examination of the external genitals, Dr. Taylor described his difficulty in "introducing more than the end of his little finger." Certainly that tightness could have been evidence in favor of virginity, but it might well have indicated Lillie's extreme psychological discomfort with this attempted penetration or a calculated response on her part to produce the proper verdict. Or she may have had a very small opening. Examining a girl he was already convinced was a virgin, under the embarrassing circumstances of the trial, Dr. Taylor was unlikely to have forced this penetration further if Lillie had cried out in pain. Or simulated pain: the stakes were high for both the Orlemans. As Dr. Judith Herman was to write a century later,

> Within the medical profession, denial persists even in the presence of incontrovertible physical evidence, such as venereal disease in children. Rather than acknowledge the possibility of sexual abuse,

physicians have been known to assert that children can contract venereal disease from clothing, towels, or toilet seats, an idea that transcends the limits of biological possibility.[27]

In an essay on the "taboo" of virginity in certain tribal societies, Freud noted that "the high value which her suitor places on a woman's virginity seems to us so firmly rooted, so much a matter of course, that we find ourselves almost at a loss if we have to give reasons for this opinion." The reasons he found for the practice of assigning defloration to someone other than the husband in certain tribes, primarily a primitive fear of blood and of women, clearly struck Freud as inferior to the reasoning of his own culture on the subject. As he wrote, the requirement of virginity is "a logical continuation of the right to exclusive possession of a woman, which forms the essence of monogamy . . . Some such measure of sexual bondage is, indeed, indispensable to the maintenance of civilized marriage."[28]

Virginia Woolf found a similar rationale for virginity in St. Paul, that is,

> a very strong and natural desire that the woman's mind and body shall be reserved for the use of one man and one only. Such a conception when supported by the Angels, nature, law, custom and the Church, and enforced by a sex with a strong personal interest to enforce it, and the economic means, was of undoubted power.[29]

In Woolf, a sober assessment of the institutions arrayed on the side of this "sexual bondage" replaces Freud's palpable satisfaction with these cultural arrangements.

Sex outside marriage, whatever the degree of the woman's culpability, was regarded as ruining her beyond redemption. In 1840, the thirty-three-year-old governor of South Carolina, James Henry Hammond, and his four teenage nieces, daughters of Wade

Hampton, drifted into a reciprocal relationship of physical intimacy, which he recorded in his diary:

> All of them rushing on every occasion into my arms and covering me with kisses—lolling in my lap—pressing their bodies almost into mine, wreathing their limbs with mine, encountering warmly every part of my frame, and permitting my hands to stray unchecked over every part of theirs and to rest without the slightest shrinking from it, on the most secret and sacred regions.[30]

In spite of "prescribed rigid standards of purity for ladies of their social position," Hammond's biographer conjectures that the girls were innocent because they had lacked close supervision after their mother's death. Hammond clearly did know better, yet when the relationship was exposed, the culpable uncle rode out the storm of negative public opinion and was later elected to the United States Senate. His four nieces were unable to find husbands. A "state legislator remarked that 'after all the fuss made no man who valued his standing could marry one of the Hampton girls.'"[31] This was an instructive story for any young lady whose purity might be open to question.

There were closer object lessons at hand in West Texas. As was clear from recent history, the region was particularly notorious for Indian captivity, and most of the residents there were familiar with shocking stories of what captured white women could expect; some were probably acquainted with actual victims. They knew that the Comanches and Kiowa raped captive women, who were considered by white society to have suffered "a fate worse than death," an experience that was so far beyond remedy that only a few years before the Geddes trial, General Philip Sheridan had refused to ransom a woman believed to be held by Indians on the grounds that after her presumed rape, there was nothing left worth reclaiming.[32]

The nineteenth-century ideal of pure womanhood imposed a new burden on women:

> In the past, as long as she repented, the woman who once sinned—like a male transgressor—could be reintegrated into the community. Now, however, because woman allegedly occupied a higher moral plane than man, her fall was so great that it tainted her for life.[33]

Whatever the reality of Lillie's situation—and she need not have experienced actual or repeated penetration to have had a "criminal intimacy" with her father—Lillie could not claim the identity of a respectable middle-class woman if she was found to be other than virginal. But more than her personal fate was at stake. If she was judged to be impure, the trial would almost inevitably conclude with Geddes's acquittal and her father's condemnation. In turn, the entire Orleman family would suffer a peculiarly horrific form of disgrace entailing both social ostracism and the loss of occupation for their breadwinner.

QUARTERS

In most frontier army posts, Officers' Row consisted of a line of double-occupancy houses, except for the commanding officer's.* In the quarters divided between Lieutenant Orleman and Captain Geddes, the lieutenant and his daughter occupied the left side of the structure and the captain the right. One room in back, attached to Geddes's side, was claimed by Lieutenant Bigelow, who, as a second lieutenant, was lower in rank than the other occupants.* A great deal of investigation and trial testimony con-

---

*Some double-occupancies could be turned into something resembling a rooming house if space was at a premium and there were a number of unmarried junior officers.

cerned the probability of Geddes's having overheard from one of his rooms the incriminating speech of the Orlemans in their adjacent bedroom. As usual, prosecution and defense witnesses gave differing testimony.

Second Lieutenant Edwin F. Glenn of the Twenty-fifth Infantry was asked if he had ever been able to overhear talking in Orleman's quarters when he was in Geddes's. He replied that he had, and added that even if windows and doors were closed, "conversation could probably be heard because of the canvas ceiling." Frederick W. Ruoff, the forage master at Fort Stockton, went to Geddes's quarters frequently at night. He indicated that he had heard noises from Orleman's quarters: "It sounded as though it was a pot in the chamber, down on the floor and sounded as though it had been struck—as though it had struck the leg of a chair—it sounded that way—I could hear sounds as though persons were walking across the room—if I remember rightly I could hear voices as though persons were talking but I could not distinguish anything." At that time, of course, Ruoff was not trying to hear the conversation in the Orlemans' quarters. Ruoff had occupied the Orleman quarters in July and said he was able to hear voices from Geddes's quarters there.

On cross-examination Clous attempted to discredit the contention that voices could be heard from one set of quarters to the other by suggesting that the conversation Ruoff had heard had come through the open door. Ruoff replied, "I think if the door had been closed, I [would have] heard it plainer."

On reexamination Paschal asked Ruoff to explain this surprising statement. He told the court that after the Orleman-Geddes affair had become public at Fort Stockton, he had conducted an experiment to satisfy his curiosity: "I closed the door and windows one morning when the Sergeant of B Company brought his

---

*Orleman was a first lieutenant.

morning report. I cannot state exactly the exact words that I heard, but I could hear Lieutenant McMartin say, 'What is this for Sergeant . . .' something of that kind."

Post trader F. W. Young was called by the prosecution because he had lived in the Orleman quarters for five months. He denied the possibility of hearing anything: "There was a solid wall. I never heard anything, a person cannot—the only thing I ever heard was when Lieutenant Nordstrom was living there. He drove a nail in the wall." Cross-examination established that Young had lived in the quarters in 1875 when the ceiling was different.[34]

Orleman, recalled by the prosecution, testified that the floor covering in his bedroom consisted of a heavy layer of hay and a carpet stretched over it.

Four of the seven original buildings on Officers' Row at Fort Stockton remain standing today, but they have clearly been altered over time. Present-day examination cannot settle the question of how much sound might travel through the partition wall. In the one unit open to visitors—not the unit Orleman and Geddes lived in—the partition wall is two feet thick, but it is not adobe and appears to be hollow. With the door closed it is possible in one set of quarters to hear talking in the other.

Several details in the court-martial testimony on this matter raise questions that were not pursued in the trial. The mysterious difference between the thickness of the partition wall in the quarterly building reports and in the diagram created by Bigelow for the trial—one foot versus two feet—requires that one measurement be grossly inaccurate. The quarterly building reports were presumably disinterested documents; on the other hand, they may have been done in the perfunctory manner of routine reports. An error in the original set could easily have been perpetuated down through the years since no one would think to remeasure the post's buildings every quarter. It seems like a strange mistake, nonetheless. For one thing, a foot would be a more customary width for an internal wall of an officer's quarters; for another, a mistake of a foot would be a significant error.

As for Lieutenant Bigelow's diagrams, he was a fervent partisan of the Orlemans, but he was also a punctilious and principled man, unlikely to cook the measurements, especially when he would have to attest to their accuracy under oath. On May 13, he wrote in his diary that he had been summoned to San Antonio as a witness in the trial. He had been instructed "to verify the drawings and surveys that are to be used as evidence . . . I infer from the telegram that I shall have to certify under oath to the accuracy of the documentary evidence; I must therefore make all the measurements myself." On May 17, however, Clous sent another telegram to the commanding officer of Fort Stockton:

> Drawing Geddes Orleman quarters received but found defective. Let Lieut Bigelow thoroughly post himself on matter contained in my letter: height of partition walls, whether going up to roof or not; character of material of which built—height of ceiling and of what material made, paths, if any, inside of enclosure to be delinated [sic], the nature of ground and character of obstructions if any between Lieut Bigelow's quarters and the kitchens and outhouses in same inclosure to be thoroughly examined and described. All these are matters of the utmost importance, and Lieut Bigelow should be well posted.[35]

It would be useful to know in what way the original diagrams were "defective." Most likely, given the second telegram's list of particulars, they were simply not as comprehensive as Clous wanted. Bigelow never did testify about his carefully detailed diagrams, but they were introduced into evidence, and the defense did not challenge the width of the partition wall. It did object to the labelling of the rooms, stating that Geddes's sitting room and bedroom were reversed. Given that Bigelow lived in the same house, this, too, is an odd mistake.

Ruoff's personal experiment—which in a modern court would have been ordered—seems the closest we can come to an objective assessment. He was able to make out some words, just as Geddes testified to doing. We can assume that Geddes was actively eaves-dropping because he confessed to having already had suspicions about the Orlemans. He may have become curious when he began to hear noises and snatches of conversation, especially when he heard his own name mentioned. The buildings on frontier army posts were notorious for poor construction, and the likelihood of noise travelling from one half of the house to the other would be increased by the canvas ceiling. Moreover, the cushioning under-foot in the Orlemans' bedroom would have done little to absorb voices.

LITERATURE AND ITS DISCONTENTS

Lieutenant Orleman testified that Geddes had given his daughter a "scandalous novel" entitled *Infelice,* which he—Orleman—had thrown into the fire after finding his daughter crying over it. Wit-nesses friendly to Geddes countered that he had a perfectly respect-able library although each defined respectability in terms of somewhat different genres of literature. Two of Geddes's friends invoked the safe rubric of "standard works," but for Joseph Fried-lander, respectability was most demonstrated by poetry, while for First Lieutenant Henry Landon, the preferred genres were history and biography. Friedlander said that he had "examined" Geddes's library and that it contained "standard works, English and Scot-tish poems—and most all the poets' works." When asked if there were any sensational works, he replied that he had never seen any.

Landon, a friend of Geddes stationed at Fort Davis, told the court that Geddes's library consisted of "biographies, histories and standard works." He, too, denied finding any highly sensational novels in the collection.

Another officer of the Twenty-fifth Infantry stationed at Fort Davis, First Lieutenant Walter Scott, said that Lieutenant Reade of Fort Davis had borrowed the novel *Infelice* from Geddes and Scott had returned it to Geddes on a trip to Fort Stockton. In speaking of the book with Lillie Orleman, Scott had praised it, and Lillie had expressed a desire to read it. He arranged for its loan to her. Scott further remarked that he did not think *Infelice* was "sensationalistic or improper for a young lady to read."

Geddes had suggested that the members of the court read *Infelice* and decide for themselves, but they had failed to embrace this idea. When Geddes took the stand, he testified that he had indeed lent Lillie some books, but that none was "highly sensational or sensational in any sense of the term." He denied having given her *Infelice*. What he recalled her borrowing were the works of the proper neoclassical poet Oliver Goldsmith, as well as a religious tract sent to him by his sister: "The other books were all returned to me except this tract which Miss Orleman informed me her father had thrown in the fire, saying that that trash would do for me to read but that he did not want any such in his house."

So Orleman destroyed either a novel that he regarded as trashy and sensationalistic or a religious tract that he mistook for a scandalous novel. In this matter Geddes's desire to protect himself from the accusation of furnishing improper reading material to Lillie produced a weak story, for even in a rage it seems improbable that Orleman would have confused a novel with a religious tract— unless the tract was a book rather than a pamphlet, and he simply pitched the suspect volume into the fire without first examining it. If he was expressing his anger over his daughter's relationship with the philandering captain, destroying anything associated with Geddes and labelling it "trash" would have made the point.

Geddes's denying that he gave *Infelice* to Lillie may have been literal without being accurate; that is, an intermediary arranged the loan, but the book belonged to Geddes: if he did not hand it to Lillie directly, he certainly acquiesced in making it available to her. Lieutenant Scott had already said as much, and he was a witness for the defense. What would have been more natural at the time when Geddes and Lillie were on friendly terms than for Lillie, who had already borrowed a number of books from Geddes, to ask to borrow the novel? By characterizing the work as suitable for a young girl, Scott had pointed the way to the strongest defense on the matter—that *Infelice* was a highly moral work in a respectable genre and Geddes's loan a token of high-mindedness.

Making such an argument might have been difficult: the substitution of a religious tract for a novel in Geddes's account shows his own awareness of the lingering American belief that fiction was inherently frivolous or even dangerous. Although it made his story implausible, the religious tract could not be assailed on grounds of impropriety.

Orleman might well have confiscated the novel had he assumed, as many people still did, that *all* novels were improper reading material for unmarried young women. In a book called *Ladies Guide in Health and Disease, Girlhood, Maidenhood, Wifehood, Motherhood,* John Kellogg, the man who revolutionized the American breakfast, wrote that the emotional stimulation that accompanied novel reading tended "to develop the passions prematurely and to turn the thoughts into a channel which led in the direction of the formation of vicious habits." He concluded that the physician should oppose novel reading as "one of the greatest causes of uterine disease in young women."[36]

Another contemporary writer went further. Orson Fowler, a well-known phrenologist, proclaimed that novel reading could directly affect the reproductive system, "producing or increasing a tendency to uterine congestion, which may in turn give rise to a great variety of maladies, including all the different forms of displacement [of the uterus], the presence of which is indicated by weak backs, painful menstruation, and leukorrhea."[37] Such ideas exemplified the widely accepted principle that "the brain and ovary could not develop at the same time."[38]

Nevertheless, many "proper American girls . . . voraciously devoured novels," causing a certain amount of anxiety among the guardians of public morality.[39] In 1881 the American Library Association Cooperation Committee sent a questionnaire to seventy major public libraries to determine which authors were objectionable. Ten writers of "women's fiction"—themselves women—made the list, including the author of *Infelice*.[40] In addition to whatever occurred between the covers of their books, many people were undoubtedly made uneasy by the spectacle of popular women authors making large sums of money.

There was a more specific reason for Geddes to avoid all association with *Infelice* other than not wanting to be guilty of recommending a novel to a young woman. Had any members of the court bothered to read the novel—and there is no evidence they did—they would have discovered that Mr. Palma, the man who wishes to marry the heroine, Regina Orme, tells her that in private he will always call her by his own name for her—Lily. Had Geddes admitted giving the book to Lillie, it would have suggested that he did indeed have designs on her, improper designs, since, unlike Palma, he was a married man. The novel would have invited—undoubtedly *did* invite—Lillie to identify the all-powerful rescuer of Regina with the possible rescuer whose copy of the novel was in her hands.

That Lillie was moved by the book appears in Friedlander's testimony. He recounted a conversation with her on March 2 in which she remarked "what a fine character Palma was." Lillie had been crying, Friedlander said, because her father had scolded her for making an error in some army reports she had helped him examine—not, as in Lieutenant Orleman's version, because the novel had upset her.

The work in question is a typical example of a popular nineteenth-century literary genre written by that group of authors whom Nathaniel Hawthorne characterized as a "d———d mob of scribbling women." Hawthorne resented the success of these writers but he also disliked the formulaic nature of their fiction and the unfailingly happy endings: "Worse they could not be, and better they need not be, when they sell by the 100,000."[41] The fame of his remark has perhaps led modern readers to an assessment of this genre as fiction written exclusively for women, but at least three young officers stationed in West Texas evidently read *Infelice* with pleasure.

Augusta Evans Wilson published *Infelice* in 1875, eight years after her triumph with *St. Elmo* (1867). *St. Elmo* sold a million copies, making it possibly the single most successful example of nineteenth-century women's fiction and one of the most successful books of the nineteenth century.[42] Wilson was the oldest of eight children born into an affluent Georgia family that had lost its money by the time she was ten. The Evanses moved first to Texas and then to Mobile, Alabama, but only recovered their fortunes through Augusta's first best-seller, *Beulah,* published in 1859 when she was twenty-four. After breaking off an engagement to a Yankee because of the Civil War, Evans remained single until the age of thirty-three, when she married Colonel Wilson, a neighboring widower with grown children. Adding his name to her own, she continued to be a popular writer, but published at long intervals.

Beginning with the title itself, there is much in *Infelice* that bears upon the circumstances that produced the Geddes court-martial. *Infelice* is Italian for "unhappy," or "the unhappy one," a general rubric that can be applied to the heroines of the plot and subplot. In the novel's conclusion we learn of the more specific meaning of *Infelice* as the title of a play written by Odille Orme, the mother of Regina, to expose those who have wronged her. Much like *Hamlet*'s mousetrap play, the stage drama *Infelice* tells the true story of an event that has been masked by a fabrication, but this account, since it clears up the mystery of the heroine's identity, is withheld until the novel's final pages.

A similar situation confronted Captain Geddes, according to his version of his introduction to Lillie Orleman: "She said she was unhappy, never expected to be happy again, and that what made her unhappy was a secret that concerned only herself and her family." When asked about this statement, Lillie denied having a secret but said that if she had said that she was unhappy, it was a matter concerning only herself. The two statements are strikingly similar: Lillie's denial simplified Geddes's statement without contradicting it. Moreover, her statement was internally inconsistent since she denied that she had a secret, but invoked secrecy by describing her unhappiness as "a matter concerning only herself."

Infelice begins with mystery: out of a stormy night a strange young woman appears at the country parsonage of Dr. Peyton Hargrove. She tells the minister that she is Minnie Merle, whose wedding to Cuthbert Laurance he had performed four years earlier. Without revealing anything further, she obtains proof of her marriage from Hargrove and his promise to act as guardian to her daughter, should it become necessary. The next day he discovers that his study has been broken into during the night and the actual marriage certificate stolen.

Lillie would claim on the stand that what appeared to be her own behavior inculpating her father had been the result of

Geddes's influence over her: "When I was in Captain Geddes's presence I was completely mesmerized and consequently he could make me say and do as he pleased." Although the brand of hypnosis popularized in the nineteenth century by Franz Mesmer was so commonly known that his name became a general noun and verb, Lillie might have gotten the idea of being "mesmerized" from reading *Infelice*. When Regina Orme, the child in question, is brought to Reverend Hargrove, the two enjoy an instant rapport. Commenting on this, Regina's co-guardian, the lawyer Erle Palma, asks Hargrove, "Did you mesmerize her?"[43] Palma lives in New York City and sees Regina infrequently. She finds him stern and remote.

As the plot wends its leisurely and complicated way, shifting between scenes of Regina's mother making her living as an actress in Paris and Regina growing up in America, the novel pauses from time to time to consider the role of women. The young hero of the early part of the text, Hargrove's nephew Douglass Lindsay, argues in favor of the education of women and against the "popular fallacy, that in the same ratio that you thoroughly educate women, you unfit them for the holy duties of daughter, wife, and mother."[44] He asks rhetorically, "Can an acquaintance with literature, art, and science so paralyze a lady's energies, that she is rendered utterly averse to, and incapable of performing those domestic offices, those household duties so preeminently suited to her slender dexterous busy little fingers"?[45]

Such a fear had in fact been promulgated by those doctors who believed that mental activity sapped feminine energy needed for childbearing.[46] And aside from that specific belief, there was a general idea that advanced education unsexed females.[47] Even the highly educated Lieutenant Bigelow recoiled from the idea of educating women to the same degree as men. In a conversation he had with a Miss Bishop, a young woman who regretted not having gone to Vassar, he justified his position that she should instead be congratulated by telling her that women might be damaged by the effect of "strong intellectual effort in the department of science." Rather, they should pursue "the aesthetic studies, poetry and art." Miss Bishop failed to appreciate this argument and reiterated that if she had any daughters, she would send them to Vassar. The exasperated Bigelow concluded that "a woman was not deserving of being taught to think since it was not in her nature to use such a power if she had it."[48]

In the heated debate on the issue in *Infelice,* Douglass's mother announces that notorious bluestockings like Harriet Martineau and Madame Dudevant [George Sand] were impelled by their intellectual pursuits to cast aside the clothing of women and cut their hair short. She maintains that she would prefer to see Regina in her coffin than shorn of her "gloriole of ebon locks."

As the voice of good sense, Reverend Hargrove asserts that there is little danger of Regina's "becoming a blue-stockinged ogre." Such extreme learning "offers little temptation to a young girl." His idea is to educate her only to the point of producing "a cultivated, refined woman, sufficiently conversant with the sciences to comprehend their contemporaneous development, without threatening us with pedantry."[49]

The Reverend's sermon continues by explaining modern-day feminism as a reaction to centuries of repression:

> Amazonian excesses of this epoch are the inevitable consequence of the rigid tyranny of former ages; which sternly banished women to the numbing darkness of an intellectual night, denying them the legitimate and natural right of developing their faculties by untrammelled exercise. . . . This woman's rights and woman's-suffrage abomination is no suddenly concocted social bottle of yeast; it has been fermenting for ages, and having finally blown out the cork, is rapidly leavening the mass of female malcontents.[50]

Douglass objects that his uncle's diatribe confuses a few "ambitious sciolists" with "the noble band of delicate, refined women whose brilliant attainments in the republic of letters, are surpassed only by their beautiful devotion to God, family, and home." Although his long argument winds its way down to a conventional denouement, the description of women's wrongs "fermenting for ages" until they produced an explosion was eloquent enough to make social conservatives uneasy.[51]

Ultimately, the Hargrove home is disbanded upon the death of Reverend Hargrove: Regina must go to her other guardian, Erle Palma, while Douglass becomes a missionary to India.

Meanwhile, Regina's actress mother pursues her long-nourished life scheme of obtaining revenge against the Laurances—the father who destroyed her marriage and the son who has remarried an heiress. (The reader does not learn how these events came about until the end of the novel.) Odille Orme has not taken the customary route of bringing suit for bigamy because such a course would have brought her reputation under attack, and this she preserves for the sake of her daughter. Between her career and her machinations against the Laurances, Odille falls ill and retreats to Naples. She is followed there by General Laurance, who, unaware that he is her father-in-law, has fallen in love with her.

Regina, loyal to the conventions of nineteenth-century women's fiction, has found herself in an unhappy situation at her guardian's house. Palma appears to be a monster of cold ambition; his stepmother, who lives with him, is hostile and cruel to Regina. Madame Palma's own daughter, Olga, is good-natured but fast, a stereotype of the laxly supervised urban girl. When Palma's cousin falls in love with Regina, the rigid and censorious Palma realizes that he loves her, too. Typical of his controlling nature, he informs the girl that when they are alone he will call her Lily.

A villain appears on the scene with the intention of getting money from Regina by claiming to be her father. When Palma discovers Regina's meeting with this man, his accusation that she is seeing a lover provokes a passionate outburst from Regina: "Lover! Oh merciful God! When I need a father, and a father's protecting name;—when I am heart-sick for my mother, and her shielding healing love . . . God grant me a father and a mother, a stainless name."[52] Coming from her different but equally anguished circumstances, Lillie Orleman might have cried out in similar pain.

Not surprisingly, given this need, Regina begins to be attracted to her older, fatherlike guardian, an authority figure with a godlike omniscience and omnipotence. Her youthful love, Douglass, must be removed from the field by death because his desirability as a suitor is compromised by poverty. (In spite of the romantic nature of novels such as Wilson's, a hardheaded Puritan ideology dominates: the favored suitor is invariably rich as well as good.)

In the subplot, after General Laurance discovers that he is actually Odille's hated father-in-law, he dies—possibly of a bad conscience for having separated the young couple and convinced his son that Odille was dead. Other characters are also tidily disposed of: Cuthbert Laurance's second wife and their handicapped child die in a sea disaster, freeing him to return to Odille. When Regina marries Palma, her mother and father are reunited and reconciled, creating the respectable family unit their daughter has always missed.

Infelice thus furnishes a contrasting pair of women protagonists, the active older woman and her passive daughter. Odille Orme brings to her vengeance as much energy, talent, and single-mindedness as any male character might muster. Like a man in her society, she shapes her destiny, while her daughter is passed from one guardian to another without the power to affect her own life. Odille's strength, independence, and ability to act may seem enviable, but the novel hints on more than one occasion that her unwomanly passion for revenge has deformed her character. She is saved at novel's end by becoming a wife once more.

This restoration of the original Laurance marriage is in its way as significant as Regina's marriage. It emphasizes the importance of proper antecedents and the power of the father. As the child of an absent father, Regina never knows domestic security: without the means to resist, she is moved from one surrogate family to another. And as a girl whose father is unknown, she becomes vulnerable to an illiterate ruffian who claims the paternal role. She is horrified when this repulsive man presses his claim, but has no way to refute it—simply an instinctive reaction that they cannot be of the same blood. Her passive endurance is rewarded with marriage to Palma.

Lillie Orleman could have identified with Regina Orme quite naturally. Both girls had spent periods of time in convents. Both had reasons to be unhappy centering on family, and both lacked power to materially affect their situations. Both needed a heroic rescuer.

Reading *Infelice* at a time when her romantic attachment to Geddes was at its peak, Lillie Orleman may have seen in Erle Palma, who called his love Lily, a parallel with her own hoped-for savior. Although Palma appeared forbidding at first because Regina had not learned enough to appreciate him, his great wisdom allowed him to play every male role in his charge's life— God, father, and husband. He had all knowledge in his possession; most important, he recognized that the man who accosted Regina, frightening her more by his assertion of kinship than his demand for money, was a false father.

Lillie could not repudiate her own father as false—such is the difference between fiction and reality—but she might have imagined that Geddes, almost twice her age, could play the role of Palma in her life, extricating her from her unideal family and replacing it with himself.

THE COMMANDER OF FORT STOCKTON

When Major McLaughlen became ill early in 1879, he was replaced as commanding officer of Fort Stockton by Lieutenant Colonel Matthew M. Blunt. Neither of the judgmental Fort Stockton diarists liked Blunt. True to form, Captain Armes dismissed him as "a cowardly sneak and an imbecile," while Lieutenant Bigelow preferred charges against Blunt for having reprimanded him in front of enlisted men. Blunt had taken an extended leave shortly afterward, and the charges appear to have gone astray in departmental headquarters, either intentionally or by chance. Bigelow seems to have accepted lack of closure on what he regarded as Blunt's insult, but he continued to make disparaging remarks about the post's commanding officer in his diary. On one occasion "the Col's weakness made me inclined to take him by the nape of the neck & shake him." Beyond his personal antipathy for the man, Bigelow chafed under the command of an infantry officer who, he felt, knew nothing about the needs of cavalry.[53]

Having to testify in the Geddes trial must have been a distasteful business for Blunt, who was called first by the prosecution and then by the defense. It had been to Blunt that all three parties—Lieutenant Orleman, Captain Geddes, and Lillie Orleman in succession—had first officially told their stories.

As a prosecution witness, Blunt dutifully recalled these events. On March 12, around 5 p.m., Orleman had come to Blunt with his story, which stressed the immediate danger of Geddes's abduction of Lillie that evening. Blunt responded by sending his adjutant, Lieutenant Sweet, to tell Geddes that he could not leave on the stage that night. Geddes came to Blunt around 6 p.m., accompanied by Friedlander. He told his version of events and Blunt asked him no questions. Around 8:30 p.m. Lillie came to Blunt's quarters with her father. In her statement she "confessed an attachment" for Geddes and admitted to having written him two notes.* About the "secret of her life in these notes," Blunt said she told him she meant "the harsh treatment of her father, he refusing her permission to go out with the young officers, and keeping her in great restraint." This first official telling of Lillie's story was the only instance that her father's treatment was characterized in this particular way—as restraining Lillie from seeing young officers. In her court testimony Lillie said that she had begged Geddes not to tell Blunt this secret, yet she herself told him.

For the defense Blunt admitted that Geddes's reputation for "truth and veracity" was good, and—most significant—that he would believe Geddes if he testified under oath. In the army hierarchy, Blunt's opinion would ordinarily have carried great weight since he was the highest-ranking officer at Fort Stockton as well as the post's commanding officer. Moreover, he had been the first to hear the antagonists' competing stories. The best that the prosecution could do with Blunt's testimony was to bring out that Geddes had not served under him for a long period of time—first in 1875 and then in 1879 for only the few months preceding the trial.

The time and sequence of the three visits to Blunt on the evening of March 12 invite speculation. Orleman went alone at five. Three and a half hours after his initial visit, he returned with his daughter. What happened in the interval? Lillie had hoped to leave Fort Stockton with Geddes, but without speaking against her father. By going to Blunt, Orleman had moved events into a

---

*Actually, four notes were entered into evidence.

public sphere where Lillie must support her father or be the agent of his and the family's ruin. Was time needed to persuade Lillie to support Orleman's story? There was certainly time for the Orlemans to agree on the details and for Lillie to rehearse her own account before her meeting with Blunt.

5

THE DEFENSE

Geddes began to testify on August 4, 1879, the fifty-fourth day of the trial. On June 27, he had written to an acquaintance at Fort Stockton to say that "Miss Lillie had tripped three times already on the direct examination, and that he would come out all right."[1] But by the time he was able to tell his story, his confidence must have been shaken by the court's constant denial of defense objections and requests for witnesses.

And by another matter: the openly partisan stance of the powerful departmental commander, General E.O.C. Ord. When faced with the possibility of another trial seven months after the conclusion of his court-martial, Geddes was to write that he couldn't get a fair trial in a department commanded by General Ord.[2] And he was probably right. His repeated efforts to bring Ord's actions before the court, including calling Ord as a witness, were rebuffed. A special plea in bar of judgment made during the trial—in effect, a call for a mistrial—referred to two partisan gestures Ord had made. He had told Friedlander's brother William, a post trader at Fort Clark, "that he should or ought to advise his brother Joseph Friedlander . . . to keep away from the accused as he might injure himself by having anything further to do with him, the accused, or words to that effect." Further, the defense had learned that "during the progress of the present trial," Ord had sent "a written or verbal message to 1st Lt. L. H. Orleman, Tenth Cavalry, expressive of his sympathy and that of his staff for Lieutenant Orleman and his family on account of sickness growing out of the incidents in this case."[3]

Ord had also furnished Geddes's confidential deposition to the retiring board considering Orleman's application to retire on grounds of disability. Here, too, Geddes tried to make this action a trial issue and was frustrated by the obvious solidarity of Ord's subordinates, who testified that no violation of Geddes's rights had occurred.[4]

A man such as General Ord would have been repulsed by the very idea of incest, surely the most taboo subject in American discourse. Psychologically as well as institutionally, it would have been much simpler for Ord to believe that Orleman was a good father like himself rather than a man who would sexually abuse his own daughter, a child who—like Ord's own daughter Bertie—had leaned with confidence against her father, the blue-coated stalwart protector.

But there may have been a more overt and palpable reason for Ord to side so blatantly against Geddes—a reason that had nothing to do with Orleman. It had surely come to Ord's attention before the arrival of Geddes's deposition that the young captain had been having an affair with his commanding officer's wife—a scandalous affair that produced a child and sent the errant wife back to her relatives in disgrace. The cuckold was an old and highly valued officer, Napoleon Bonaparte McLaughlen, a brigadier general of volunteers during the

Civil War and an admired Indian fighter in the Department of Texas. R. G. Carter describes him as "with the exception of Captain Wirt Davis, probably the best pistol and carbine shot in the Army."[5]

Carter relates a dramatic incident in which McLaughlen faced down the renowned Colonel Ranald Mackenzie, who led his troops illegally across the border in 1873 to attack a village of raiding Indians. When McLaughlen discovered the lack of authorization for the raid, he told Mackenzie that had he known, he would not have gone. Mackenzie replied that he would have shot any officer who refused to cross the Rio Grande with him. At this McLaughlen "snapped out sharply, 'That would depend, Sir,' upon who *shot first!*'" Mackenzie did not reply.[6]

The next year, however, McLaughlen commanded a battalion in Mackenzie's famous fight with the Comanches in Palo Duro Canyon. Carter refers to him here as "a gallant officer of long service and much experience."[7]

By early 1879 McLaughlen was clearly feeling the effects of his years of campaigning and, possibly, his personal troubles as well. On January 9, Ord sent him a solicitous telegram admonishing him for risking his health by working too hard:

> When you left here Doctor Taylor told me you were too sick to go to duty, and should take a leave; and now, Dr. Price tells me that you are tasking yourself beyond a proper regard for your health. I assure you I appreciate the resolution which inspired you to stick like a true soldier to your post, but we want your services too much to let you remain, when your own good health requires a change.[8]

Ord was getting McLaughlen away from Fort Stockton and away from the man who had recently cuckolded him.* He assigned McLaughlen to court-martial duty in San Antonio, to be followed

---

*From other sources the affair can be dated to the fall of 1878.

by a lengthy leave, and replaced him at Fort Stockton with Colonel Matthew Blunt.

At the very moment that the Geddes-Orleman affair was reaching a crisis point, a doctor found Major McLaughlen to be seriously ill:

> [He suffered] a serious impairment of the functions of his nervous system, accompanied with occasional attacks of loss of consciousness, loss of voluntary motion, and of sight at times. He has frequently fallen when walking and has a disposition to pitch forward when the eyes are closed. His ultimate recovery is very remote and uncertain. A change of climate and associations are imperative in my opinion.[9]

The last sentence, and particularly the word "associations," lingers: a man who had just discovered his wife's infidelity might well need a change of climate and associations and might also display symptoms that suggest a psychological component.[10]

McLaughlen was rarely well after 1879, and in January of 1882 the general who replaced Ord as commander of the Department of Texas, Christopher C. Augur, supported his request to retire, citing his "long and faithful service in the Army, and his impaired state of health."* At the same time, a medical report indicated "a general breaking up of his whole constitution, the result both of his age, 60 years, and his long and arduous service in the US Army." Attacks of dizziness heralded "impending if not present cerebral disease." In his retirement application McLaughlen cited his desire "to establish a home and provide for the education of his children."[11]

McLaughlen would have a limited time to do this. On October 27, 1884, his wife notified the Army that she had been made

---

*He began service in 1850 and thus had served for thirty-two years.

trustee of his estate, her husband having been declared insane and confined to an asylum. He died at this institution on January 27, 1887. In April of 1892 a lawyer for his wife wrote requesting information about his pension.

Whether or not McLaughlen was its cause, Ord's partisanship was a formidable obstacle to Geddes's defense and must have dashed his spirits. Captain Armes noted in his diary entry for July 11 that he had spent most of the evening with Geddes in his room at the Menger Hotel. He then added, "There seems a determination to force him out of the Army if possible on the false charges they have trumped up against him."[12]

The major theme of Geddes's testimony was his version of his relationship with Lillie, as described in his deposition and Lillie's letters to him. But in addition to presenting himself as a rescuer, Geddes had to rebut the charge that his motive had been Lillie's seduction. After their introduction at the hop—where he said that he made no overtures of any sort to her—he described her as having initiated a conversation when they were standing on their adjacent porches. He was reading a letter from his sister. She asked questions about the sister. She wished that she had had a big brother. When she learned that the sister was "eighteen or twenty, she volunteered that this was just about her own age, but—'I have had the experience of a woman of forty.' " She said that she was unhappy, that she never expected to be happy again, and that the cause of her unhappiness was a secret "that concerned only herself and her family."

Geddes stressed that at this time his friendship was with both Orlemans: "Lieutenant Orleman was frequently in my quarters. We used to play chess together." He denied that he had ever been alone with Lillie in her quarters during the period between the hop and the trip to Fort Davis. When he encountered her several times a day, on the porch they shared, the conversation was general.

Geddes said Orleman had fondled his daughter's breast during the February journey between the two forts, and that she had rebuked him for it with the words "Papa, quit!" In her testimony Lillie had denied this, but said that Geddes had pressed her knees between his under cover of a cape. Geddes claimed that it would have been

> a physical impossibility to do it without placing myself in such a position as would have been noticed by all in the party. . . . I should have had to move my whole body forward to the edge of the seat on which I was sitting, or else let my body drop down in a crouching position in order to cover the distance that intervened between the knees of the parties sitting opposite each other and in the usual position when riding.

Neither side introduced actual measurements of the vehicle's interior to prove or disprove Geddes's assertion.

Joseph Friedlander's testimony gave yet another version of the trip to Fort Davis:

> Lieutenant Orleman reached down and put his hand under his daughter's clothes and took hold of her leg. She, Miss Orleman, looked over at me and looked very much embarrassed and said, "Papa, don't." Lieutenant Orleman then said, "What a big leg you have, Lillie," then told the following smutty story: "There was once a young couple just got married and the first night that they got into bed, he says to her, 'Honey, put your little footsie-tootsies into my lap and let me warm them for you.' About three months afterwards he says to her, 'Keep your dirty old cold feet away.'" While this was being related, Miss Orleman was very much embarrassed as well as myself.

Orleman was never asked if he had told such a story but it's likely he would have denied it. The only point of agreement among the four occupants of the army ambulance was the seating arrangement.

Geddes had not heard the story or seen Orleman grasp his daughter's leg because he had been walking at the time as the ambulance slowly negotiated the road through Limpia Canyon. Taking a stage through the canyon in 1868, San Antonio *Herald* correspondent H. C. Logan noted that "the scenery in viewing the mountains is no longer just beautiful; it is sublimely magnificent."[13] The ambulance arrived in the canyon at sunset, and Geddes remained outside for at least a half hour, easily keeping ahead of it as it negotiated the rough terrain.

Friedlander also testified that Orleman touched his daughter's breasts on the return trip to Fort Stockton: "He would take her in his arms, put his hands around her and fondle or rub her breasts."

Aside from the major areas of contention, there were some minor yet possibly significant discrepancies in the four stories. The Orlemans had said that on the trip to Fort Davis Geddes covered his and Lillie's legs with his officer's cape. Both Geddes and Friedlander testified that the legs of all four passengers were covered by a large buffalo robe. The overcoat worn by Lillie on the return trip was described by Geddes as being merely thrown around her shoulders and entirely unbuttoned, as opposed to her father's account that she had been so encased that it would have been impossible for him to fondle her breasts.

Geddes further testified that he did not call on Lillie Orleman during the time the party spent in Fort Davis: "I saw her, however, nearly every day to merely say good morning or good evening." While there she had been escorted by Lieutenant Landon, and possibly by other officers. Another Fort Davis officer, Lieutenant Scott, testified that he had gone horseback riding with Lillie during her Fort Davis visit. Earlier in the month, when he had accompanied her to the Fort Stockton hop, he had urged her to get to know Geddes. At Fort Davis she told Scott that she had done so, and "had found Major Geddes all that I had said of him. He was a perfect gentleman in every sense of the word." Lieutenant Landon testified that Lillie had complained that Geddes was distant toward her, "albeit a perfect gentleman." Just as Orleman's character witnesses repeatedly described him as a gentleman and an excellent father, so Geddes's witnesses reiterated that he was a "perfect gentleman."

After the Fort Davis trip at the end of February, the next significant date was March 2, when Geddes supposedly heard and witnessed the activity that prompted his accusation. As officer of the day he was required to make periodic checks of post activities for a twenty-four-hour period. That evening he heard voices from the Orlemans' bedroom. He had had suspicions before, "but actually did not credit them, did not think it possible and did not wish to harbor or entertain that such a thing as criminal intercourse was going on between them."

His curiosity piqued by what he had overheard, Geddes began his evening rounds by looking in the Orlemans' bedroom window. He saw Orleman in his nightshirt get on top of Lillie. They appeared to have intercourse. Orleman got off and seemed to be removing a "covering."* He asked Lillie if she wanted a drink and she replied "No." Orleman then crossed the room and poured out a drink which he brought back to Lillie, telling her she would sleep better if she took it, which she did.

The following morning Geddes made this speech to Lillie: "If ever you want a friend under any circumstances whatever and no matter for what, let me know. Don't hesitate to call upon me, and I will do all or anything in my power to protect you and for you." He also exclaimed, "Poor little girl, how I pity you." Later, when they were alone together in her quarters—at her insistence, according to Geddes—she asked him what was wrong. He finally

---

*A condom.

told her, "I don't think your father is treating you right." She pressed him for an explanation, and he added, "'Your father is not treating you as a father should a daughter.'"

At this slightly more explicit utterance, Lillie reportedly "jumped up from her chair, threw up her hands, and said, 'My God, my secret is known,' and would have fallen if I had not caught her. She cried very bitterly, hysterically repeating several times, 'for God's sake don't tell. I knew it would come out at last.'" In Geddes's account, Lillie quickly understood his reference to Lieutenant Orleman not treating her right and acknowledged its truth:

> Miss Orleman then told me with some preliminary remarks that this thing between herself and [her] father had been going on since she was thirteen years of age. . . . She said that he first brought it to her mind by talking to her about such things when she was eight years old, that he accomplished his purpose when she was thirteen.

According to Geddes, between the third of March and the fifth or sixth Lillie constantly accosted him with more stories and details of what she had suffered. She told him that in Austin she had once hidden herself for three days to escape her father's sexual advances. Her father had come into the room where she and her younger sister Daisy were sleeping and wanted to get in bed with Lillie. She protested because of Daisy's presence, whereupon he picked the sleeping child up and carried her out of the room: "She [Lillie] hurriedly slipped on her shoes and what clothing she could and ran off."

At Fort Griffin she had refused to do it. Her father took her out for a ride, stopped, pulled out his gun, and said he would shoot both of them unless she agreed. She told Geddes that her mother knew and people in Austin suspected. When Lillie and her mother threatened to expose Orleman, "he used to say to them that he would give his resignation in, leave the country, and let them and the children get along the best way they could." He would actually write out a resignation. This was always effective in obtaining her submission.

Whenever her father was with her, Geddes quoted Lillie as saying, it seemed impossible for him to let her alone. She said that he never even respected her when she had "her sickness." And she feared that he would begin on her younger sister, ten-year-old Daisy. She also feared that when Geddes confronted him, her father would get his gun and kill himself and her, as he had threatened to do. Geddes told her, "He is not that kind of a man—a man that would act toward his own daughter as he has done towards you has not the courage or manliness enough to shoot anybody."

Eventually, the patient listener related that he became tired of Lillie's stories. One day when she began with "There is something I want to tell you, but it will disgust you so that you will never speak to me again," he cut her off: "I said, 'then do not tell it, Miss Lillie.'"

Above all, Geddes testified, Lillie wanted to be rescued. She repeatedly spoke to him about "taking her away from a life of shame." She "begged me to do so, crying always at the time."

Geddes denied any improprieties in his behavior toward Lillie. Questioned by his attorney, he also denied a number of specific accusations—that, for example, he had threatened to bring a civil suit against her father. He denied having led Lillie to believe he would get a divorce and marry her. He denied having powers of mesmerism. And above all, he denied visiting her in her quarters when her father was at Stables, a time, directly after dinner, when he habitually went riding. His orderly, Private William Phelps, testified that he was instructed to bring the captain's horse to his quarters every day at that time.

Geddes said he had not visited when Lillie was alone, except for one time when she inadvertently locked the door. He went at that time, he said, only because of her repeated invitation. Further, the injunction in one of his letters to her—"please write"—was explained as meaning that if she had anything more to tell him, she should write it (rather than constantly accosting him in person).

This standoffish behavior on Geddes's part seems inconsistent with the noble speech he supposedly made to her on March 3, holding out an unconditional hand of friendship and pledging to do his utmost for her. It was a dilemma for Geddes: admitting to the court that he had intentionally seen her alone would have reinforced the seduction charge, but he also needed to establish his altruism toward Lillie, a young woman trying to extricate herself from a horrible situation. It was difficult to document a laudatory sequence of actions without straying into the negative territory of the seduction plot.

When Geddes finished his testimony, the judge advocate refused the opportunity to cross-examine. The court similarly had no questions.

Geddes was the central witness on his own behalf, but he was supported by others. Captain Armes, who served with Orleman in the Tenth Cavalry, stated that he had seen Orleman on Geddes's porch on March 11—that is, at a time when Orleman denied he was on friendly terms with the captain. In explaining why he remembered the date, Armes worked into his answer one of his typical character assessments:

> I had requested Lt. Orleman to be relieved from a Board of Survey of which he was recorder on the ground that I had publicly denounced him several years before as a low bred individual and that I could not expect fair action upon any examination he would make.

Armes's diary repeated the characterization of Orleman as "low bred." Since the Army regarded Armes as a troublesome officer who had been rightfully dismissed and later reinstated by political influence, his testimony probably did not help the Geddes case. Aside from that, the aristocratic Virginian was always finding his colleagues beneath him and quarrelling with them.

Another defense witness was Geddes's good friend Joseph Friedlander, who had been one of the party on the Fort Davis trip. In one of her frantic notes Lillie had written to Geddes that her father thought Geddes had "told Friedlander," and in fact Geddes *had* confided in his friend.

On the stand Friedlander intimated that the community of Fort Stockton pretty much believed that some sort of illicit relation existed between Lieutenant Orleman and his daughter, but Friedlander was a good friend of Geddes—and a man whose own reputation was persistently assailed by the prosecution. Judge Advocate Clous intimated darkly that Geddes knew damaging information about his friend and was in Friedlander's debt as well.[*] Moreover, a member of the court had objected to Friedlander's not having taken the oath with his hat on since Friedlander was "an Israelite." Clous quoted from a volume entitled *Duties of the Judge Advocate* which asserted that "Jews regard no oath as obligatory unless their head is covered."[†] How strictly observant Friedlander was never entered this discussion.

Clous also hauled into court several witnesses to testify against Friedlander's character. A farmer, Joseph Landa, stated that Friedlander had a bad reputation at Fort Stockton and a low standing in Landa's estimation: "The man has told me lies off and on as long as I knew him and brought me to great losses and represented things

---

[*]Probably this is a reference to an affair Friedlander was alleged to have had with Rachel Beck, an officer's wife.

[†]Benét observes that the court-martial should follow whatever ceremony "most forcibly imposes the obligation of speaking the truth. This can be best effected by swearing witnesses according to the particular mode which they may deem most binding on their consciences" (*A Treatise on Military Law,* 92).

differently what in reality it was [sic]." Cross-examination brought out that there was a long-standing feud between Friedlander and Landa over business matters.

At this point, the trial's fifty-ninth day, tempers must have been frayed. Geddes complained that a member of the court, Assistant Surgeon Brown, had "on several occasions taken it upon himself to snub and reprimand the accused and his counsel *verbally*." Geddes wanted any further reprimands to be put in writing, no doubt with an eye toward establishing irregularities if the verdict should go against him. The court rejected his request.

Unlike the prosecution, which stood or fell on the testimony of Lieutenant Orleman and his daughter, the defense called several witnesses who could corroborate Geddes's accusations and who appeared to be disinterested. Of these witnesses, no one proffered more explicit support of Geddes's story than Michael Houston. If his demeanor in court was as persuasive as the substance of his story was scandalous, he would qualify as the star witness. Houston recounted an experience surprisingly similar to that of Andrew Geddes's lurking outside the Orlemans' window on the evening of March 2. But Houston had had no motive to put himself in the way of revelation: he was simply the stage driver who transported the Orlemans as his only passengers when they left Fort Stockton in April, bound for San Antonio and the coming trial. Houston claimed to have overheard an incriminating conversation during this trip:

> The first that I heard that drew my attention was that Miss Lillie Orleman was crying—next that I heard was Lieutenant Orleman telling that he could have left Fort Stockton liked and respected if he had never took her there, then she says that he could have left that way anyway if he had acted the part of a gentleman. The next I heard her say was that he made her deny the statement she made to the major. He told her he did not. She answered back to him, "Yes sir, you did." Then the next she says was that it was the proudest act

of her life that she had made the statement to the major. Then the next was that that had been going on now for six years.

She says to him, "Papa, you have been raising me as your daughter and using me as a common woman." He says, "I was not the first one that did it." She says, "You were, you were." Next, I heard her say, "Just think of the idea, of your using your own flesh and blood in that manner." Sometime after that he asked her, "How did Lieutenant Bigelow feel—you have felt him all over, I suppose." She answered, "Like any other man, of course." The next thing I heard him say was "would she not wish that her darling Andrew was here tonight."* He says, this is the next I recollect now, he called her a little whore and a puppy. He said that Major Geddes had said that she sat on his lap and [he] finger fucked her. This is the words he said. She said that the major had always treated her like a gentleman. After that he put his head out of the back and asked how far it was to any house.

Houston reported that he heard the sound of scuffling and Lillie's voice saying, "Papa, quit that, stop." After that, he heard nothing but breathing and thought that "criminal intercourse" was going on. Around April 17 when he returned to Fort Stockton he told Michael Francis Corbett, operator of the stage concession and his employer. At that time, he testified, he had never spoken to the accused and knew nothing of matters between the Orlemans and Geddes.

Cross-examined by Judge Advocate Clous, he added, "I heard her say—she was crying at the time—that her mother and her aunt had suspected her. The Lieutenant said it was a lie, that her aunt had not seen her mother for two years."

Clous brought out that in his original statement Houston had reported that when Lieutenant Orleman was committing the act of criminal intercourse with his daughter, "he asked her who did it best: he, Lieutenant Bigelow, or Major Geddes."

*Some of Lillie's letters to Geddes do in fact begin "darling Andrew."

The prosecution suggested that Joseph Friedlander had helped the driver prepare his statement. Houston denied this, or that he had known Friedlander until they had been stage passengers together on the trip to San Antonio for the trial. Discovering their common reason for the stage journey, they had talked about the matter: "He asked me several times if I was positive. I told him I was—I do not remember anything more that I said or he said." Given the length of time necessary to travel by stage from Fort Stockton to San Antonio—five days—the two men had ample time to become acquainted and thoroughly discuss the case.

Clous expressed skepticism that Houston could have overheard a conversation occurring inside the stage. Houston rejoined that the driver's seat was separate from the passengers by a "light canvas," and that the partition was only buttoned down on one side at the time. Clous persisted. Did the driver usually eavesdrop on his passengers? Houston answered indignantly, "I never was and would not have been then if it had not been for the crying attracting my attention." He expressed regret at having become a witness: "I would have come no way, if I had known that I had to stay so long."

Clous returned to Houston's association with Friedlander in order to insinuate corruption. Houston replied, "I am not that kind of a man, to be bribed by Mr. Friedlander or any other man." Perhaps not. But if he had been, the substance of the conversation he testified to hearing would most likely have come to him from Friedlander, who would have heard it from Geddes, who would have had to invent it himself. That Houston, who had no connections with the parties in the case, invented such a convenient story himself strains credulity.

Friedlander was clearly Geddes's confidant, and he might have known that this particular stage driver was, as Clous insinuated, open to persuasion. Nevertheless, it seems improbable that any of the men in this chain of scandalmongering would have made up such details of the story as Lillie's saying that her mother and aunt suspected and Orleman responding that her aunt had not seen her mother for two years.

It was one thing to report—as Geddes did—an episode of incest overheard and partially observed by the occupant of the adjacent quarters. It was quite another to come up with such a full-blown conversation that brought in the name of two other officers as sexual partners of Lillie's. Geddes never suggested, either in his testimony or in his deposition, that Lillie had had relations with a man other than her father. Such a claim would only have muddied the waters and made his motive in rescuing her seem less valid.

According to Houston, Orleman told Lillie that Geddes had admitted "finger fucking" her. That Geddes, or his protective friend Friedlander, would have used such an expression, or asserted that it had come from the mouth of Orleman, is inconceivable. Geddes strenuously denied any sexual or romantic interest in Lillie or any improper behavior. No matter what the context, it would have been counterproductive to place such an idea before the court.

As for the possibility that Houston might have been able to overhear his passengers' conversation, the prosecution made every effort to discredit it. Houston's boss, Michael Francis Corbett (the same Corbett who had had a falling-out with Geddes over the latter's reputation), testified that it would have been impossible for the driver to hear anything from the coach because of the canvas partition. He described the road as being so bumpy that the noise of the voyage would have effectively drowned out any conversation within the stage. Houston stoutly maintained that the overheard conversation had occurred on a smooth stretch of road. Corbett also described Friedlander as a receiver of stolen property and asserted that he would not believe him under oath. He denied "jealousies growing out of commercial rivalry."

Corbett was not asked if Houston had reported the Orlemans' conversation to him when he returned to Fort Stockton.

If there was at least a possibility that Houston was a tainted witness, the prosecution made no such suggestion about the defense's most compelling witness, like Houston a man who had no personal relationship with Geddes and no apparent reason to speak ill of the Orlemans. This was Corporal George A. Hartford of the Eighth Cavalry. He testified that he was stationed at Fort Duncan, Texas, in May 1877, where he saw Lieutenant Orleman and his daughter. He thought, but could not be certain, that it was between the middle and the end of the month. (Orleman later testified to having left the post on May 15.) Corporal Hartford had a detailed and vivid recollection of the scene:

> I was standing near the house that evening. I do not know what one it was, listening to Miss Orleman playing on the piano. While I was standing there, the music stopped, and her father crossed the room, and she walked back with him, Miss Orleman. Lieutenant Orleman sat down in a chair and took Miss Orleman across his knee, sat her down on his knee, and put his arms around her, hugged her a number of times, then run his hand down over her legs outside of her dress, and commenced to lift her up off of his knee and hold her up against his breast. Then he sat her back on his knee again and went feeling her legs. I could not swear that he had his hands under her clothes but it looked like it, and he put his face down against her breast and he appeared to be biting her. He also kissed her. That is about all I recollect now about the matter. He continued this action while I stood there. I think it was about five minutes I stood there. He was still sitting in the same position when I left.

Paschal wanted Hartford to say whether what he saw appeared to be innocent or not, but Clous objected and the motion was sustained. The next series of questions made the answer clear, however.

Q: What induced you to leave at the time you did?
A: Did not care to see any more.
Q: How often did you see him kiss her, and what was his manner toward her when he kissed her?
A: I could not tell exactly the number of times. I did not keep an account of it. Perhaps as many as a dozen times, maybe more. His manner towards her was rather warm.
Q: Explain what you mean by his manner being rather warm.
A: Well, he seemed rather more of a man that was newly married than a father towards his daughter. He had his hand, one arm, around her legs, about the knee. The other under her back or waist and would lift her up bodily off of his knee up against his breast.
Q: How did Miss Orleman act while this conduct was going on?
A: She did not seem to return his embraces. She seemed rather passive in his arms.

Corporal Hartford surely did not know that he was describing a typical response to incest, a state of passivity in which the victim attempts to dissociate herself from what is happening.[14]

In the face of Hartford's powerful story, Clous directed most of his efforts of cross-examination to casting doubt on the date of the alleged incident, attempting to establish that Hartford was speaking about a time when Orleman was away from Fort Duncan. But given an event that happened more than two years earlier, that Hartford might be unable to remember the date precisely hardly discredited his testimony. He met the judge advocate's persistence on the matter by saying, "I am not positive. I think it was [in the last two weeks of May], to the best of my recollection." He *was* positive about what he had seen.

The court asked Hartford if anyone had observed this scene with him. He replied that Private Joseph Smith had, but Smith had been discharged a year ago and was now, possibly, in Brazil. He added to his previous testimony that Miss Orleman appeared to be a grown woman, eighteen or nineteen, a statement that suggests the absence of coaching since the defense would have informed Hartford that Lillie was only sixteen at the time.

Hartford explained his voyeuristic behavior by saying that he had been attracted to the vicinity by the sound of Miss Orleman's playing, and he remained to observe the scene he had described in the hope that she would begin to play again.

The next day Hartford returned to the stand to add that he had suspected criminal intimacy between Orleman and his daughter: "My reasons for thinking so were that I had heard it commonly reported that Lieutenant Orleman slept in the same room with his daughter and frequently in the same bed with her."

If father and daughter had shared the same bed at Fort Duncan, what about at Fort Stockton? The testimony of Private George Sweat, who had taken care of the Orleman bedchamber at Fort Stockton, could have shed some light on this. Sweat was prepared to testify that Lillie's bed frequently showed that it had been occupied by two persons, while the cot [Orleman's bed] was often undisturbed. On one occasion he entered the room after knocking, and "Lieutenant Orleman ran hastily from Lillie's bed to his own, and his daughter lay on her back with her clothing in disorder." Geddes's request to call Sweat as a witness was turned down on the formulaic grounds that Clous invariably invoked—"not material to the ends of justice."

Another such rejected application might also have added a significant piece of information about the father-daughter relationship of the Orlemans. In his own testimony about observing the Orlemans in their bedroom on the night of March 2, Geddes had said that after their intercourse, Orleman had asked Lillie if she wanted a drink of whiskey. She had declined, but Orleman had insisted, telling her she would sleep better. Although nothing was made of this, stage driver Michael Houston included a similar incident in testifying about the Orlemans' trip from Fort Stockton to San Antonio. He remarked that Orleman "had a bottle of whiskey and treated the boys at Pecos Station as well as Houston, and gave his daughter a drink, too." The prosecution did not dispute this testimony.

Another suppressed defense witness, First Lieutenant John W. Pullman of the Eighth U.S. Cavalry, was prepared to testify that in camp near Fort Clark he had observed Orleman giving his daughter "spiritous and intoxicating liquors to such an extent that she complained of the fact to said Lt. Pullman."

In his diary entry of March 25, 1879, John Bigelow had discussed a report of Lillie's drinking that he had heard at Fort Concho:

> I heard something about Miss Orleman which greatly shocked and surprised me . . . that she drank her whiskey straight and that she did it so well as to make Lieut Hodges' head swim. After thinking about it I had to own to myself that I had observed a taste of Miss Orleman's that placed the fact within the scope of possibility, if not probability.[15]

On two of the three occasions when Orleman was allegedly observed giving his daughter strong drink, she was resistant to taking it. Two of the three instances (although not the same two) happened in conjunction with sexual episodes. It would seem that Orleman plied his daughter with liquor in the time-honored manner of reconciling her to sex, or—in the incident reported by Pullman—simply reconciling her to her unhappy situation as the prisoner of her father's desire. Bigelow's observation and the gossip he had heard about her at Fort Concho suggest that her consumption of whiskey was becoming habitual.

The argument over calling Pullman as a witness was especially acrimonious. When the judge advocate gave one of his lengthy speeches to support his denial, Paschal could not forbear. His rejoinder, rather than adducing another point in favor of hearing the witness, conveyed only heat: "If this conduct and treatment of Lieutenant Orleman towards his daughter is considered by the Judge Advocate properly parental and gentlemanlike on the part of a father to a daughter, then the defense does not envy the judge advocate."* Having won the contest, Clous could afford to be lofty:

> The Judge Advocate declines to reply to the argument of the accused as nothing is therein contained to controvert the position he has taken and the law he has quoted. He scorns to pay any attention to the flings of the defense upon him personally or officially.

REBUTTAL

Perhaps the most significant rebuttal witness was one the court did not hear. Lillie Orleman might have been brought back to the witness stand in this part of the trial, but Judge Advocate Clous introduced a doctor's note saying that she was too ill to appear again, "for six weeks, if at all."[16] The doctor added—gratuitously—that her illness had been brought on by the strain of testifying. Geddes responded angrily: "The accused respectfully submits that he believes this certificate is intended for the purpose of creating prejudice against him; otherwise it would not contain an attempt to give uncalled for evidence."

---

*Ironically, neither Clous nor Paschal had or would have children.

Lillie's sickness might well have had something to do with the protracted and painful experience of testifying about the most intimate matters of her life. As well as being embarrassed, she must have been fearful of making a misstep that would call her testimony into question: it was, in fact, weak and at times contradictory, although the court protected her from a sharp cross-examination. There would have been no other woman in the courtroom, and in spite of being allowed to testify with her back to Geddes, she must have been acutely aware of his presence.

Hearing of Lillie's illness, Lieutenant Bigelow immediately imagined that Geddes would be responsible for "sending her with a crushed spirit to the grave." A few days later he called on her father and learned that Lillie had a temperature of 105 degrees. He noted that Lieutenant Orleman "did not appear as depressed in spirit as I expected to find him."[17]

Whether or not they followed the judge advocate in blaming Geddes, members of the court could be expected to regard the breakdown of Lillie's health with sympathy. Clous employed a similar strategy in presenting testimony about Orleman's health, a matter that was directly relevant to the trial. Two doctors testified that at the time of the alleged "scuffling" in the stage driven by Michael Houston, the lieutenant was paralyzed on one side. On March 16, 1879, Orleman had complained of intense headache and lapsed into unconsciousness. He remained unconscious for four hours and was bled. His entire left side was paralyzed and without feeling, but by April 5, Dr. W. C. Henderson testified, Orleman "could hobble around." Assistant Surgeon M. K. Taylor described his arm as "entirely useless, having no voluntary motion except slightly in the fingers and the leg so far paralyzed as to drag it after him when he walked." Could Orleman have engaged in sexual intercourse at this time? The doctor thought it not impossible but improbable. He later ascribed the paralysis to an attack of apoplexy.

When Orleman was recalled, the judge advocate asked him about the state of his "bodily health and vigor up to about the middle of March, 1879." Orleman answered that it was very good except for the persistent disease of his eyes that had kept him away from his duties for a year. He then added to his answer, "My health was excellent." Clous followed this up by asking Orleman if his health had changed, eliciting a defense objection that the accused had not been charged with "altering Orleman's health."

The lengthy speech Clous made to defend his question perfectly illustrates his method. He first "respectfully state[d] that he [was] well aware that the accused [was] not charged with changing the physical condition of the witness." But then he went on to intimate that very thing:

> The Judge Advocate by the question simply desires to elicit the fact whether or not the accusation of the accused had any effect upon the physical condition of the witness. It is evident from the present appearance of the witness and his limping gait that between the middle of March and his appearance here something must have seriously changed his physical condition. There may have been sickness consequent upon the excitement produced by the accusations, the mind may have been overwrought, apoplexy may have been produced. All of which is legitimate to establish, to show the result, if any, the accusations of the accused may have produced on the witness.

The court sustained the objection, but it hardly mattered. Clous had painted a vivid picture entirely outside the scope of the charges but designed to arouse sympathy for Orleman.

Orleman at that time was still awaiting the processing of a request made a year earlier to be retired from active duty for reasons of physical disability.[18] Describing his health up to March of 1879 as "excellent" strains credulity in view of this request

Old Fort Stockton. Officers' Row, where Captain Geddes divided the end house on the left with Lieutenant Orleman and his daughter Lillie [Courtesy of Historic Fort Stockton]

Friedlander's store. The store was just off the post, a brief walk from Officers' Row (left background), where Friedlander often socialized [Courtesy of Historic Fort Stockton]

Department of Texas Headquarters. The lengthy trial of Captain Geddes took place in this building, located on Military Plaza in the center of town. [Courtesy of the Witte Museum, San Antonio]

George Paschal, Geddes's defense attorney. Paschal's kindly eyes may explain some of his popularity as a public figure in later life, but he was only thirty-one at the time of the trial [Courtesy of The Institute of Texan Cultures, The *San Antonio Light* Collection]

John Clous, the Judge Advocate. Clous looks far more respectable in this picture than in the drawings in Captain Armes's autobiography, where he is portrayed as a trumpeter blowing his own horn, a crudely caricatured "Dutchman," just off the boat, and—after his promotion—as a dwarfish brigadier general being introduced to the President [Courtesy of the Civil War Library and Museum]

General E.O.C. Ord, his wife, and their daughter Bertie. Bertie probably got tired of holding her pose for the long period required to take a photograph at the time [Courtesy of the Massachusetts Commander of Military Order of the Loyal Legion and the U.S. Army Military History Institute]

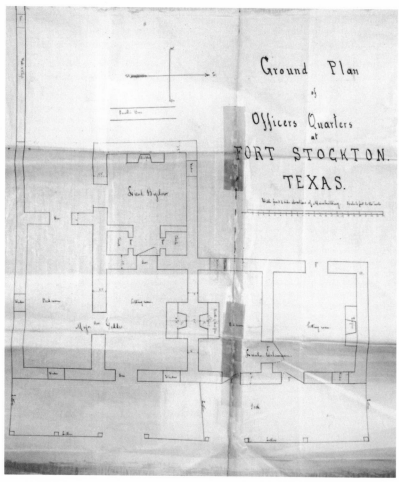

Ground Plan of the Orleman-Geddes quarters prepared by Lieutenant Bigelow for the government's case against Geddes. Bigelow reversed Geddes's bedroom and sitting room: the captain's bedroom was actually next to the Orlemans' bedroom. Bigelow occupied a room at the back of the building [Courtesy of the National Archives]

Lieutenant William Beck, the man allegedly cuckolded by Joseph Friedlander [Courtesy of the U.S. Army Military History Institute]

Major Napoleon Bonaparte Mc-Laughlen, Fort Stockton's commander. McLaughlen, an old soldier with a fine record, wanted his wife's lover to be punished, but without any publicity involving himself [Courtesy of the U.S. Army Military History Institute]

Lieutenant Orleman during his service in the frontier army [Courtesy of Paul Orleman]

The Orleman family in 1894, fifteen years after the trial. Lillie is seated on her father's left; her sister Daisy stands in front of the tree. Orleman holds his first grandson, Louis Henry III [Courtesy of Paul Orleman]

General Ord as commander of the Department of Texas. Sympathy for McLaughlen may have prompted his partisanship [Courtesy of the Massachusetts Commander of Military Order of the Loyal Legion and the U.S. Army Military History Institute]

William Tecumseh Sherman, General of the Army. Sherman's energy, intellect, and determination could be directed toward positive ends, but in the Geddes case these qualities served a darker aspect of his character [Courtesy of the National Archives]

Absalom Baird, Assistant Inspector General. "Chief Inspector Hound" doggedly carried out his mission to dig up everything he could on Captain Geddes. Ironically, his name is that of a Biblical character who committed incest [Courtesy of the U.S. Army Military History Institute]

William Dunn, Judge Advocate General. [Courtesy of the Massachusetts Commander of Military Order of the Loyal Legion and the U.S. Army Military History Institute]

Colonel George L. Andrews, the commanding officer of the Twenty-fifth Infantry and an avowed enemy of Captain Geddes, "evidently so constituted . . . that he would be wretched unless he was in the midst of perfect order" [Courtesy of the U.S. Army Military History Institute]

and of his medical history—an almost unbroken record of health problems requiring leaves of absence. During the Civil War he had a medical leave of absence for diarrhea and debility that lasted fifty-six days. Brought before a commission concerning the over-staying of leaves, he produced documents to account for the entire period and was exonerated.[19]

As an officer in the frontier army, he had taken a number of medical leaves. The earliest was December 10 through 17, 1870, when he was described simply as "sick" at Fort Sill. In April of 1873 he had "tertiary intestinal fever" at Fort Gibson. Then, at the end of both 1873 and 1874, he was treated for piles at Fort Sill. In January of 1874 he had an attack of acute bronchitis there that laid him up for a week. In both May and September of 1875 he had episodes of tertiary intestinal fever at Fort Griffin; in June and August of 1877 he had new bouts of fever at Fort Duncan, fol-lowed in October of that year by "catarrhal conjunctivitis" at Fort Clark. He was granted a leave of absence and was away from his duties for more than a year, returning, this time to Fort Stockton, late in 1878. Another sick leave, this time for apoplexy, began April 14, 1879. He was retired on November 20, 1879.[20]

If Orleman was genuinely ill at the time of the Geddes trial, this would hardly have been unusual: life in a frontier military post tended to be both demanding and unhealthy, and the lieu-tenant had had numerous complaints in the past. How debilitated he actually was, or why, cannot be determined from the courtroom description of his March attack, but there is a peculiar note in the Fort Stockton medical records about it:

Lieut. L. H. Orleman 10th U.S. Cavalry was attacked on 16th March with apoplexy or what was believed to be such. Whether there was any real coma, or only a severe headache with congestion; whether there was any real paralysis or only a paresis or slight loss of power, seem difficult points to be ascertained by me as I did not see the case and the accounts seem conflicting.

As to the etiology in this case; the brain disturbance undoubtedly arose from a quarrel with one of the other officers.[21]

In describing Orleman's March illness, which he had treated, Dr.
W. C. Henderson was forced to make several admissions. First, he
had left Fort Stockton on April 5 and thus could not testify to the
extent of Orleman's recovery by April 13, the day the Orlemans'
stage trip began. Second, he testified that "the post surgeon had
thrown out insinuations that I might be mistaken as to my diagno-
sis." Henderson was a good friend of the Orlemans. He had taken
his meals with them from January 2 until his departure from Fort
Stockton on April 5 and had spent a lot of time in their quarters.

As the trial transcript demonstrates, *appearing* debilitated
enhanced Orleman's case, augmenting his status as a victim to the
extent that General Ord made a partisan intervention to offer him
sympathy, a gesture that would not have been lost on the court.

After the trial, there is no further record of medical problems
until late in Orleman's life. Following his retirement from active
duty, he had a long career as an instructor in various military acad-
emies, and he lived to the then extraordinary age of ninety-four.

Orleman was also asked in the rebuttal phase about stage driver
Michael Houston's allegations. He denied them. He further denied
that he had ever used profane language to his daughter. But there
was a curious addendum to his account, in which he said that during the journey his daughter had slept on the "middle seat." When
M. F. Corbett took the stand to rebut Houston's testimony, he
denied that any of the coaches on the line had a middle seat. Clous
rephrased the question several times in an attempt to save Orleman's story, but Corbett was adamant: there was no possibility that
the Orlemans had travelled in a stagecoach with a middle seat.

On August 18, Lieutenant John Bigelow, Jr., was the trial's
last witness, when Clous recalled him to deny that he had had sexual relations with Lillie Orleman.

On August 19 the court adjourned until the twenty-first. Then, on its sixty-eighth day, Geddes read a brief statement, in which he said that he would make no further defense, but simply point out that "of his thirty-four years, eighteen have been spent as an army officer." Clous declined to make a summation, a typical omission for a court-martial of the period, but hardly typical for a trial of such exceptional length. On the other hand, since the judge advocate deliberated with the court, he had no need to address them here, where his remarks would be part of the record.

The court was cleared and closed for deliberation. How long it deliberated is not indicated in the trial transcript, but the announcement of the verdict occurred on the same day: guilty, exempting only the specification concerning abduction. Geddes was sentenced to be dismissed from the Army and imprisoned for three years. The proceedings, findings, and sentence were approved a week later by General Ord, who, as commander of the Department of Texas, was first reviewing officer. They were then forwarded to army headquarters in Washington, where General Sherman, the Army's highest-ranking officer, signed his approval on November 4.

REVIEW

Not long after the conclusion of the trial, the Army's highest judicial officer, Judge Advocate General William M. Dunn, submitted his review to Secretary of War George W. McCrary, who would in turn forward it to President Rutherford B. Hayes.[1]

The review procedure had been instituted to counterbalance the command influence that could powerfully taint a court-martial verdict. Since the departmental commander decided when a court-martial was warranted and then appointed officers to compose a military court, officers whose own careers were to a large extent dependent upon his good opinion, it has always been an article of faith with critics of the system that a military court is under pressure to return a verdict of guilty.

Through his independence from military hierarchy and from the emotions that a case might generate locally, the Judge Advocate General was in a position to counter this systemic bias toward conviction. In his office in the War Department in Washington he was removed from the politics of working military bases. He was also physically removed: in the Geddes case he was some two thousand miles away from the Department of Texas and the consternation that the court-martial's scandalous subject matter had provoked.

The office had been established in 1862, and General Dunn had become the second Judge Advocate General after an apprenticeship as assistant judge advocate general and a career as a congressman. His picture reveals an earnest countenance; his review of the Geddes trial is a long and thoughtful document.

First of all, General Dunn observed, the charges rested almost entirely on the testimony of Lieutenant Orleman and his daughter, whereas the testimony of Captain Geddes in defense was "supported by that of a considerable number of witnesses."[2] Such an imbalance in the two sides would not necessarily be relevant to guilt or innocence, but Dunn followed up this observation with his own doubts about the Orlemans' testimony. The notes from Lillie to Geddes had struck him as an honest outpouring of feeling, while her later recantation rang false. Dunn pointed to a number of passages in the notes that Lillie had not adequately explained. He concluded that "without a better explanation of the letters in question than that given by Miss Orleman in the replies quoted, they retain unaltered their fatal significance."

The trial materials simply did not persuade Dunn that Geddes would have invented the charge of *incest*

of all others within his reach, and . . . confront[ed] Lieutenant Orleman and his daughter with such a charge, *he knowing the same to be false.* A single instance of harsh reprimand from a father to his daughter, to whom he never before uttered a harsh word, cannot be accepted as a sufficient occasion for a subordinate officer to denounce the offender to his Post Commander.* Nor can a solitary rebuke privately administered by that kind father be rightly designated as a "*secret*" the father was trying to keep, an offense which the community would shun him for if known, and on account of which he talks of taking his life if exposed. An indignant father does not go *crazy* when detected in privately scolding an erring daughter. Nor does that daughter for such a trivial cause iterate and reiterate her appeals to the discoverer to "*swear*" never to divulge it.

Dunn found Orleman's testimony suspiciously similar to that of his daughter: it was "nearly if not exactly similar, word for word, with Miss Orleman's." He had in mind a particular passage:

Orleman: I told my daughter that Captain Geddes had accused me of being too intimate with her and of having had criminal intercourse with her. She answered, "Papa, I do not know what criminal intercourse is." Captain Geddes then spoke up and said, "Miss Lillie, you know your father is not treating you right, is that not so?"

Lillie: [*Quoting her father*] "Lillie, Captain Geddes has just accused me of being too intimate and of having had criminal intercourse with you." I then answered my father that I did not know what criminal intercourse meant. Captain Geddes sat opposite me and said, "Miss Lillie, you know that your father is not treating you right."

Like the members of the court, Dunn was fascinated and preoccupied with the testimony on Lillie Orleman's virginity. Unlike the court, however, the Judge Advocate General was skeptical. Referring only to the actual examination of Lillie, he pronounced

---

*A captain outranks a lieutenant, but Dunn may simply have meant that as a captain Geddes was not a high-ranking officer.

the medical testimony favorable to her innocence, *"so far as it goes."* But he had further thoughts:

> It seems not unreasonable to suggest that the virginal appearance to which Dr. Taylor testified, and which seems to have greatly influenced the Court, may be due to a deliberate care and moderation exhibited by the father of the girl in the gratification of his appetites, or to some unnatural act of coition not involving penetration, with the express purpose of preventing those physical changes which as a rule, it would seem, take place when no precautions are deemed necessary and nature is unchecked. This suggestion, for which some slight foundation may be found in Cap. Geddes' testimony, would seem to reconcile in a large measure the difficulties existing in the case, while it does not diminish in any degree the criminality of the act.

At the end of his review Dunn appended a long note on an article that had come to his attention only after his report was completed. Dr. T. Gaillard Thomas had gathered up some "interesting cases" and published them in the *New York Journal of Medicine*. These cases, which Dunn summarized in detail, raised issues about virginity much like those that had claimed so much of the court's attention:

> Parent Duchatelet in his celebrated work on prostitution, tells of public prostitutes who had for years followed their degrading profession in the streets of Paris, with the hymen so perfect as to leave even the most acute and experienced examiner in doubt as to their chastity.[3]

Prostitutes with perfect hymens! Such extreme cases titillated and baffled the male desire to know and control the sexuality of women—and, much like incest itself, presented a situation that Victorian American society preferred not to confront. The black-and-white nature of Captain Patterson's assertion that a medical examination finding Lillie a virgin would demolish the charge of incest was a more comfortable state of affairs.

Turning to the charge that Geddes had accused Orleman of incest in order to abduct Lillie, Dunn saw the sequence in reverse: "It was necessary to prove him a seducer in order to furnish a motive for his desire to abduct, just as his determination to abduct was the suggested motive for his accusation of incest against her father." But Geddes's notes to Lillie were not "strong enough" to prove the motive of seduction, and he had been acquitted of the charge of attempted abduction.

Just as he rejected the prosecution's portrayal of Geddes as a seducer, Dunn also rejected its portrayal of Orleman as an outraged father:

> It does not appear that Lt. Orleman's conduct was *in any sense* that of a man of honor, who, conscious of the falsity of the infamous charge, is accused in the presence of an innocent daughter of the shameful crime of incest. He listens in silence to the foul accusation; shows his accuser to the door; visits him fifteen minutes afterwards; borrows money of him; repeatedly asks him to his house; renews his request, after the charge of incest has been made, to serve as his daughter's escort to her home; sends down her trunk that there may be no delay, and ends by asking him to pay her fare. Such conduct as this . . . strengthens greatly, in my judgment, the inferences I have been compelled to draw from the falsehoods with which his testimony appears to be studded. A father who finds a libertine pressing his innocent daughter's knees between his own does not deliberately give her insulter every opportunity to repeat his outrage. Yet this is what, according to his own evidence, Lt. Orleman did. . . . The story is not credible; and with this falsehood, if it be a falsehood, at the opening of his tale, his entire testimony tumbles to the ground.

Dunn imagined that if Orleman had actually discovered Geddes pressing his daughter's legs between his own, at the very least he would have insisted on a different seating arrangement on the trip back to Fort Stockton, placing himself, rather than his daughter, opposite the libidinous captain.

Dunn had similar doubts about Lillie's own description of her conduct with Geddes: "I have found it hard indeed to reconcile such conduct as this with the intuitive modesty of a pure and virgin nature." These words indicate that, like most Americans, he shared the Victorian American view of maidenly innocence. He simply did not find that ideal embodied in Lillie Orleman. Lieutenant Bigelow, when faced with a similar contradiction, had continued to believe in Lillie's innocence. As her friend, and a despiser of Geddes, he lacked Dunn's objectivity.

The court had believed the Orlemans too readily, and in Dunn's opinion it had disregarded the testimony of a large number of defense witnesses

> of whom no attempt was made to impeach and among whom were several officers of the accused's own regiment, for that of two parties [the Orlemans], each of whom is interested beyond all others in the conviction of the accused, and whose statements seem to me to be not only incredible in themselves, but in numberless points to be contradicted by irrefragable proof. To me it seems more reasonable to hold that Lt. Orleman is unworthy of belief, and that he has forced his unhappy daughter to sacrifice the truth in his defense.

Dunn believed that there was sufficient proof that the statements made by Geddes in his deposition were neither malicious nor untrue, and that the deposition to General Ord should have been treated as a privileged communication.

On the matter of witnesses, limiting the number of character witnesses for the defense to two must "be acknowledged to have been needlessly harsh and unjust, and highly injurious to the accused." Dunn referred to a favorable letter from C. K. Breneman, a San Antonio lawyer, to the Honorable W. B. Allison, "in which the writer speaks of the character of Capt. Geddes from personal knowledge in the strongest terms." As the trial drew to its close, Geddes had also received a letter of support signed "Gray" (Captain C. A. Gray of the Twenty-fifth Infantry) accompanying a petition dated September 7, 1879:

> We the undersigned Officers of the Twenty-Fifth Regiment of Infantry and citizens of Fort Davis, Texas, certify that we have had an acquaintance of long standing with Captain Andrew Geddes, Twenty-Fifth Infantry, extending in some cases over a period of from seven to twelve years; that we are well acquainted with his character both as an Officer and a gentleman; that we have always looked upon him as a man of undoubted integrity and ability, and an officer whose services did honor to himself and reflected credit on the Twenty-Fifth Infantry.

Among other signatories were two men of local reputation: G. M. Frazer, the County Judge of Pecos County; and Francis Rooney, an early settler and now county commissioner.

Of other witnesses the court had refused to call for Geddes, Dunn singled out for mention the most flagrant instance, that of Private Sweat, who had taken care of Lieutenant Orleman's quarters. Dunn could find no reason for the court's refusal to summon this witness: "The application was in proper form and sworn to by the accused."

The court may have suppressed important witnesses, but Dunn felt he had more than enough evidence to reach the conclusion that the outcome of the Geddes trial was a miscarriage of justice. He wrote that in recommending disapproval of the conviction and sentence he had been "necessarily governed by a variety of considerations outside of the many irreconcilable discrepancies in the testimony offered to sustain the charges":

The first of these is—and to me it seems entitled to much weight—
the relative degree of temptation to perjury [to] which the accuser
and the accused are respectively exposed. On the one hand, while it
may be admitted that Capt. Geddes' temptation to forswear himself
is great, it cannot be said to be so manifestly overpowering as,
almost of necessity, to lead him to see in perjury a venial mode of
saving himself from the consequences of a conviction. The accused is
shown to have applied for certain witnesses to his character for
veracity, who were refused by the court because the judge advocate
admitted that their testimony would be favorable to the accused,
and that they would all testify that his reputation for veracity was
good, and that they would believe him under oath.[4]

Since these officers were all in the Twenty-fifth Infantry, it could
be assumed that they were "acquainted in a greater or less degree
of intimacy with the accused."

Wielding Ockham's razor once again, Dunn could find insufficient reason for Geddes to lie, whereas "to one accused of incest,
who knows the accusation to be true, the temptation to rebut such
a charge even by perjury must needs be so great as with the vast
majority of men to be irresistible."

The Judge Advocate General's exceptionally detailed review of
the Geddes court-martial was forwarded by Secretary of War
George McCrary to President Hayes.

The man who had the power to change the verdict of Andrew
Geddes's court-martial had received the Republican Party's nomi-
nation in 1876, in the aftermath of the Grant Administration's
corruption scandals, because he was considered to be a man
"whose very name is . . . conclusive evidence of the most uncom-
promising determination of the American people to make this a
pure government once more."[5] But he had won the disputed elec-
tion by electoral college politicking. He was, in short, a man of
principle *and* politics. Although, as President, Hayes regarded

ending Reconstruction as his first order of business, what he thought of as his "great work" was reforming the civil service.[6] It was a laudable aim of great consequence to government but less than inspiring, reflective of Hayes himself. As a candidate for the presidency, he had announced that he would run for only one term. As that term drew to an end, his party did not attempt to alter his decision.

Hayes was consistently portrayed in the press as an austere reformer whose wife, a teetotaler, brought Puritanism to the social life of the White House. Still, he had a soft spot for the military. As a young man he had burned to go to war against Mexico but was secretly thwarted by an uncle. Already forty at the beginning of the Civil War, he served with distinction, beginning as a major and finishing the war as a brevet major general. In spite of being wounded five times, once seriously, he looked back on 1861–65 as the best four years of his life. From the battlefield he had expressed his feeling with the simple words, "It is *living*." In 1861, not long into the war, Hayes was already anticipating nostalgia. "These marches and campaigns in the hills of western Virginia," he wrote to his wife, Lucy, "will always be among the pleasantest things I can remember."[7]

This attitude may have been responsible for Hayes's leniency as President in setting aside the deliberations of army courts-martial. During his term he mitigated forty-one out of sixty sentences of officers who had been found guilty of "drunkenness on duty, misuse of public property, selling pay accounts to different individuals, conduct unbecoming an officer and gentleman too gross, vulgar and profane for republication, of cruelty to enlisted men," and other offenses. In the critical words of the *New York Herald,* "Mr. Hayes might justly be called the promoter of intemperance in the Army and the friend and defender of wrongdoers."[8]

The charge described as "too gross, vulgar, and profane for republication" referred to the Geddes trial. On December 3, 1879, President Hayes followed the Judge Advocate General's recommendation to disallow the verdict and sentence: Andrew Geddes would be released from prison and restored to his unit. Read today in conjunction with the trial transcript, Dunn's report is a model of sense and balance. Errors of procedure attributable to prejudice against the defendant were notable in the court-martial, as Dunn rightly pointed out, and on that basis alone, the trial decision merited reversal. About the presence of the obviously prejudiced Patterson on the court, the Judge Advocate General stated that Patterson should have been removed.

But the Judge Advocate General was not without his own prejudices. He seemed to regard character testimony as compelling when it came from fellow officers, the group most likely to close ranks around one of their own. Speculating on the relative probability of a disposition to commit perjury is also questionable. Simply because Orleman had a stronger motive to lie, or had more at stake than Geddes, did not automatically mean that he had lied and Geddes had not. The possible loss of a valued career could well have been sufficient motive for the captain to commit perjury, even though it appears a less compelling motive than being accused of a heinous act. Both men, it might be said, had motive enough to lie.

Dunn is most persuasive in his critique of the trial when he analyzes the evidence itself. The desperate notes that Lillie sent Geddes do have the ring of truth—and they were never adequately explained by the prosecution. On the contrary: the prosecution's effort to account for them was so weak that it enhanced the letters' credibility. Dunn found the Orlemans' statements "incredible in themselves," and beyond that "in numberless points to be contradicted by irrefragable proof." His meticulous, dispassionate review stands as an example of the process at its best.

There were other matters not addressed by Dunn. In finding Andrew Geddes guilty except for the attempt to abduct Lillie Orleman, the court failed to realize that it had entirely pulled the rug out from under the other Orleman charges. It accepted what was patently clear from testimony, that the little world of Fort Stockton had known that Lieutenant Orleman's daughter was taking the stage in the company of Captain Geddes, not as a secret project but as a convenience approved by her father. But if Geddes had no need to abduct Lillie, or to gain her affection—since she had admitted an infatuation with him—he had no motive to charge Orleman with incest. According to Orleman, Geddes had brandished the accusation as a club to coerce the reluctant father into allowing Lillie to leave with him. If there was no need for such coercion, where was Geddes's motive to level such a scandalous charge?

This was only one of the inconsistencies in the Orlemans' story. Lillie's testimony was extremely weak. For the most compelling evidence, her notes to Geddes, she had only implausible explanations, but she was saved by the mores of the times from a blistering cross-examination that might have completely destroyed her credibility. Whenever she was asked an uncomfortable question, a member of the court was sure to object, and the objection would invariably be sustained.[9] Gallantry toward women was part of the code of conduct of an officer and a gentleman, not to be suspended for a judicial procedure. A young woman like Lillie who appeared before a group of male officers in such a vulnerable posture must have brought out the court's protective instincts.

The inexperienced Paschal had more than one moment of frustration as he was repeatedly prevented from questioning Lillie fully. After obtaining her admission that she had *allowed* Geddes to press her knees on the trip to Fort Davis, Paschal tried to elicit her own assessment of what was going on. When he posed the question, she readily agreed with him that the conduct she had accepted was "very ungentlemanly." He tried to follow up on this.

Q: Did you not also realize at the time that this conduct which you have imputed to the accused might compromise you in the mind of all virtuous people, if they knew these things?

A member of the court objected because "Captain Geddes is charged with endeavoring to abduct Miss Orleman and not Miss Orleman with endeavoring to abduct Captain Geddes." The exasperated defense counsel commented, "Hard though it may be, the witness is entitled to no sympathy when the object is the attainment of justice."

Predictably, the member's objection was sustained. Paschal tried to rephrase the question, the member again objected, and the objection was sustained. Paschal exploded: "The accused respectfully asks for an adjournment upon the ground that the rulings of the Court upon questions which the accused relied materially for his defense has so taken him by surprise as to leave him unprepared to go on with the case."

Naturally this request was also denied.

The letters, undated and written in pencil on cheap notepaper, move this story from a confrontation of competing voices to another place. They speak, eloquently, for themselves. After Geddes had told Lillie what he had seen at the Orlemans' bedroom window, she wrote the captain a pleading note:

Please be so kind as to tell my father what you saw and heard a week ago last Sunday and I wish you would please tell him in my presence. But I pray you, dear Major, never let him know what I have told you: never let on to my father, by your words or your actions that I have given you the secret of my life. Please promise me that, dear major. Tell him that you came very near telling Colonel Blunt, but that you did not feel like making it public. You must tell him before you go. He did not know that you were going until this morning. Lt. Quimby told him. He was very angry and said I should not go tonight. Will you please grant me that one request, and that is, to tell my father what you saw and heard that Sunday evening. I want him to know that you know the secret he is trying to keep. But please do not tell on me. He asked me last night if I had said anything to you. I told him no, that you knew as much as I could tell you. What could I have said? I did not want him to know that I had told on him. But you cannot blame me. When you said that you did not think he was treating me right, I could not help telling you all. I felt so unhappy I want you to tell him that, as he has decided not to let me go after you had gotten everything ready so as not to let me go alone. He thinks that it would not be right for me to go and you just tell him that if the people knew what he had done, that they would shun him while they honor and respect you. Please throw this in the fire.

A later note reiterates the themes of the first:

Please tell my father that you will not tell anyone of his secret. He said that he would have to take his life if you were to tell. Please come over and tell him. Please swear to him that you will not tell. He thinks that you have told Joe F. [Friedlander] You must promise me to swear to him that you will not tell. Just think of his family. He says that he is almost crazy. Tell him that you will not ask me if he will let me go. Promise him that, and he will be satisfied. Please say yes.

Lillie's testimony was inconsistent on a critical point, which went unchallenged during the trial but did not escape Dunn, namely, the "secrets" her letters referred to. During her cross-examination she gave this explanation:

Q: Please state what was the secret of your father, concerning which he said he would have to take his life.

A: I meant my father's treatment of me which Capt. Geddes had termed unbecoming an officer and a gentleman.

But on direct examination Lillie had said that her father had always treated her with great kindness, and that her acknowledgment to the accused to the contrary was knowingly false. In other words, there was no secret, nothing about her father's behavior that needed to be concealed or, as the Judge Advocate General asserted, would lead him to take his own life, if exposed, or be shunned by the community. In a time when men were the unchallenged heads of their households and corporal punishment of children was both common and accepted, that Lieutenant Orleman would be driven to commit suicide by the charge that he sometimes spoke harshly to his daughter is preposterous, especially since he grew up in Germany, where he would have been acculturated into an even stronger patriarchal system than that which prevailed in the United States.

The letters indicate that Lillie hoped to use the idea of publicity to secure her freedom: to trade silence about the incestuous relationship for her father's permission to leave with Geddes. This was walking a fine line: the secret must be both promulgated and contained, communicated to Geddes, and from Geddes back to her father, but no further. Were it to be revealed, as both she and her father knew, there could be terrible consequences.

Once Lillie recovered from the shock of a sympathetic young officer's knowing her situation, she was not at all loath to talk about it. Isolated at a frontier fort with her father and "the secret," she must have longed for such a confidant. Her behavior toward Geddes before the revelation—the veiled hints about her unhappy state—and her attempts to discourage her father's sexual abuse by invoking Geddes's name, show that she welcomed the ally she could not have directly approached.

It is tempting to see another of Lillie's actions as symbolic of her real feelings. Lillie accidentally locked the door of the Orlemans' quarters with Geddes inside, her father outside. Locking the door kept Geddes with her and excluded her father.

If Houston, the stagecoach driver, was telling the truth, Orleman made accusations about Lillie's having sexual relations with other men that are typical of the possessive father who fears a rival for his daughter.[10] Paradoxically, making such charges also addresses the incestuous father's need to see the daughter-lover as degraded by this "criminal intercourse," a "whore" who welcomes all comers, including the father, and therefore deserves no respect.[11] For Orleman to accuse his daughter of having had a lover before him would have been another way of denying responsibility and minimizing his own act. His imagining his daughter enjoying the sexual attentions of other men bespeaks an anxiety about his own virility. And his crude language, so unacceptable to Victorian America, would further degrade her.

The trial also focused a great deal of attention on the issue of whether or not Geddes could have seen or heard any evidence of criminal intercourse from the Orlemans' quarters. In addition to ordering a detailed diagram of the premises, the court heard testimony from every witness who might have an informed opinion on the subject.

Lillie in her testimony had recounted her careful preparations on the night in question—drawing the blinds, letting down the curtain, shutting the window—and described in detail the placement of every object in the bedroom. She stated that a normal tone of voice could not be heard through the wall.

Both father and daughter testified that Orleman had entered the bedroom after Lillie had gotten into bed, that he sat on the bed and questioned her with some severity about her relationship with Geddes. In his cross-examination of Lillie, Paschal pursued this:

> Q: When you told the accused on March 3rd that your father had treated you cruelly and meanly, did you tell him in what this cruel and mean treatment consisted?
> A: No sir. I did not. He said he had heard everything that happened that night and I supposed that he had heard our conversation when he said that my father was not treating me right.

The point at issue is what each party understood by certain general terms applied to Orleman. Lillie said that she had thought Geddes's accusations referred to her father's chastising her, and she had agreed that Orleman was "mean and cruel," which Geddes presumably took to be a reference to her father's sexual abuse of her. Lost in this semantic confusion is the contradiction between Lillie's earlier assertion that conversation in the Orlemans' quarters could *not* be heard in Geddes's, and her supposition that the Sunday evening conversation had been overheard. She reiterated this unremarked contradiction in her answer to another question.

> Q: What do you have reference to when you say "what he had seen and heard that Sunday night"?
> A: Captain Geddes had never explained to me what he had heard that night and I naturally believed that he had heard the conversation my father had with me that night.

Once again, Lillie assumed that Geddes *had* heard conversation in the Orleman quarters.

As for Orleman, why would he prefer charges to the commanding officer of Fort Stockton—thus ensuring publicity regardless of the outcome—when Geddes had sworn to keep the matter a secret? If he was not truly a wronged and indignant man, he nevertheless assumed that role by his action. It was the proper role to play, obviously, if there *was* any suspicion about his relations with his daughter. And Lillie's frantic notes to Geddes suggest the motive: Orleman feared that Geddes *had* told others, in particular his close friend Joseph Friedlander. The lieutenant knew the gossipy nature of an army post: by preferring charges he seized the initiative and launched a preemptive strike, one that had in its favor the antipathy of a conservative Victorian-era institution to confront distasteful sexual matters. He must have further realized that he had the advantage of reputation over the womanizing captain and simply needed to play the part that his world had no desire to challenge, that of the honorable paterfamilias.

If Geddes's account of Orleman's repeated pleas to keep silent are true—his emotion, his reference to his family and to his own ruin—Orleman must also have hated Geddes, both for knowing about the abuse of Lillie and for exposing him to the humiliation of having to plead with him. Preferring charges against Geddes gave Orleman the high ground as the victim of scandalous allegations and paid back the captain for discovering Orleman's nasty secret.

Convicting Geddes spared the Army the scandal of finding one of its own guilty of an unspeakable crime and punished a man whose reputation as a philanderer must have told heavily against him in some quarters. Had he confined himself to discreet relations with Mexican servant girls, the rank-conscious Army probably would have shrugged and looked the other way, but to seduce the wife of his post's commander, an officer well known and liked in the Department! That was crossing a line.

Even now, as the military seeks to revise its policy on adultery to bring it more in line with contemporary civilian standards, there is considerable feeling within the armed forces against relaxing the official standard of an officer and a gentleman. Such debates on the morality of officers have occurred periodically. In 1882, the *Army and Navy Journal* defended the ideal against the criticism that many officers failed to live up to it: "It is the pride of the true soldier that a brave man is generous, manly, and unselfish, devoted to works of chivalry, not of devilry."[12]

But Geddes perfectly illustrates a long-standing model of the gentleman, albeit an unacknowledged one: the man who kisses but does not tell. A patriarchal society regarded his married lovers as pathetic victims who had been preyed upon by a depraved seducer, but they may actually have been independent-minded women who had their own reasons for extramarital affairs.

Fannie McLaughlen resembles Kate Chopin's heroine Edna Pontellier in *The Awakening,* a woman bored with a dull routine and ripe for romantic adventure. Fannie came from a monied and socially prominent background in New York. She was married to a man who was growing old and ill, possibly—from the medical evidence—syphilitic. She was marooned in the Texas desert. Into this aridity came a handsome young captain, well versed in the classics of English poetry and equally versed in the art of appealing to women. He changed her completely, from—in the army investigator's censorious telling—"restrained and prudish" to devil-may-care. This liberation came at a price in the stifling venue of a frontier army post, would indeed have been scandalous anywhere in late-nineteenth-century America, and she was packed off to her relatives in disgrace. But Fannie's adultery might have had a positive dimension for her that the Army, an obvious partisan of the wronged husband, would not—could not—entertain.

If rumor and innuendo can be believed, Geddes seems to have found a number of dissatisfied wives on the Texas frontier. Fort Stockton became known for such unsavory doings throughout the Department of Texas—not surprisingly, since the downsized regular army was a small community in which everyone knew everyone else. In a single department, whose units were intermingled at its various forts, everyone must have known of Geddes's reputation.

It hadn't affected his promotion to captain, but the affair with Fannie McLaughlen, followed by the accusation of incest, produced an unwholesome notoriety. During Geddes's trial, Colonel Grierson, commanding officer of the Tenth Cavalry, was preparing a list of officers to appear before a retiring board. Of McLaughlen he wrote:

> This officer has been sick much of the time since joining the regiment, is broken down from long and faithful service, is now absent on sick leave for seven months since March 13, 1879, and it is believed that he will never again be fit for active field service in the cavalry.[13]

The easiest way to bury the scandal of Geddes and Fannie McLaughlen, as well as the incest charge, was to get rid of Geddes.

As competing petitions illustrate, the Twenty-fifth was divided by the Geddes case. According to historian Oliver Knight, in the unwritten code of the army officer corps an officer's personal affairs were "the concern of his regiment alone; it was bad manners for the officers of another regiment to even ask questions."[14] On a small post this line was probably blurred: Lieutenant Bigelow of the Tenth Cavalry had no scruple about intervening to enlighten a possible victim of Geddes's.

The outcome might conceivably have been different if the court had had to choose between an obviously guilty Orleman and a completely innocent Geddes. But the six-hundred-page trial transcript of Andrew Geddes's court-martial is more like the multiple perspectives of *Rashomon* than a choice between clear antinomies. Both sides told some of the truth; both sides lied.

In his review of the trial Judge Advocate General Dunn systematically exposed the Orlemans' lies, but he did not address a problematic area of Geddes's defense, his relationship with Lillie Orleman. She portrayed herself as a romantic dupe of Geddes: the court was invited to see through her testimony the familiar plot of a cad seducing a young and innocent girl. Geddes, of course, characterized his role as that of benevolent and disinterested friend. As a married man, he could hardly do otherwise. I suspect, however, that each of these contrasting versions contains some truth.

In all likelihood, Geddes noticed Lillie at the hop and made advances to her there. She returned his interest: all the reasons that made him a sympathetic, if not irresistible, figure to other women worked on Lillie as well, but emphatically so because she longed to be rescued from the incestuous demands of her father. She and Geddes lived in such proximity that it was no trick for them to see each other often in the natural course of the day. Geddes was touched by her story and wanted to help her, but it must have been difficult for this practiced Romeo to restrict his involvement when she offered him at least some encouragement. If her letters to him convict her father, Geddes's to her convict himself:

> Lillie, I did not think you could be so unkind. Do you regret what happened at the hop? Well, I suppose you are right and that you regret everything that has passed between us. . . . Think of me kindly sometimes. Your unhappy friend.

Geddes had taken great pains to convince the court that exactly nothing had happened between himself and Lillie Orleman at the hop, whereas the note implies that an overture was made and later followed up. Then Lillie pulled back because Geddes was, after all, a married man ("I suppose you are right"). But he had presented himself in the stereotypical and strategic role of the misvalued and unhappy husband, an object of pity. The conclusion of the letter confirms this interpretation.

Another note is simply one line: "Please write. How cross you spoke to me." In court Geddes maintained that he had grown tired of Lillie's constantly accosting him in person with more stories of her incestuous experience with her father. "Please write" was, he said, an attempt to free himself from those repetitive conversations by having her put her complaints in writing instead— an explanation that seems as weak as Lillie's attempt to explain her letters.

Finally, Geddes wrote, "Forgive me, if you will. I would not hurt you for the world. Every tear you shed is like taking a drop of blood from my heart. You seem so unkind at times. . . . Pity, do not condemn. To err is human, to forgive divine. Please forgive. You know what I think of you—" Here Geddes had probably pressed his advances too far and was begging forgiveness. The correspondence is obviously predicated on a mutual attraction: Geddes writes melodramatically that Lillie's tears are like drops of blood drawn from his heart; Lillie's letters typically begin "Darling Andrew." One of hers ends, "Yours truly, if I may call myself."

Geddes may have gone riding every day, as he and other defense witnesses testified, but in spite of his attempt to account for all of the time Lieutenant Orleman was absent at afternoon Stables, his explanation did not preclude rendezvous, possibly brief, between himself and Lillie. They lived in the same building, after all, her door a step away from his. While Orleman was predictably at Stables, a chore that an infantry officer like Geddes escaped, Geddes might have visited Lillie for ten minutes or a quarter of an hour every day between the end of dinner and the time of his ride.

Lillie did not say that Geddes had told her he would get a divorce and marry her. She said that she *thought* he would do so, based, no doubt, on his avowals and behavior toward her. Unlike Mrs. Baily, Mrs. McLaughlen, and the wife of the citizen at Fort Davis, Lillie was a young, unmarried girl. Geddes must have known that, aside from other considerations, it would be fatal to his career actually to seduce the daughter of a fellow officer. Perhaps he was merely enjoying her obvious infatuation, thinking that the flirtation would end of its own accord when he delivered her to her mother in Austin.

Or perhaps, like other compulsive womanizers, he didn't think ahead. The sixty-two-year-old head of the Army, its highest-ranking general, William Tecumseh Sherman, succumbed to a woman who was in her thirties while imagining that he regarded her simply as another of his daughters in need of masculine aid. Geddes might have responded to the importuning Lillie in the same way. After all, a score of women novelists of his era had produced one best-seller after another in which an older guardian suddenly emerged as the heroine's romantic interest. Lillie had recently read one such novel from Geddes's library.

The court had two strong motives for conviction: absolving the Army of being an institution in which the most stringent sexual taboo could be broken and legitimately punishing a vile seducer.

It is only by chance that a case in some ways analagous to that of Andrew Geddes had occurred six years earlier at Fort Stockton and in his own Twenty-fifth Infantry Regiment.* General Christopher C. Augur, then commander of the Department of Texas, set aside the guilty verdict of Sergeant Benjamin Mew, who was accused of attempting to poison his wife and her lover, Corporal Lee. The case rested entirely on the testimony of Corporal Lee and Sergeant Mew's wife, Martha, but Augur observed that the relationship of these two made their statements highly suspect. They were, in other words, interested parties. The language of Augur's decision is cumbersome, but pertinent:

> The motives that influence parties to a trial in their actions, in relation to the subject matter thereof, anything in their evidence causing

---

*But not in Geddes's company. Geddes was stationed at Fort Duncan at the time.

suspicion of their good faith requiring explanation, conversations they had on the matter before the court, wherein their statements may be at variance with their sworn testimony, are all proper subjects of investigation, and relevant to the issue. These remarks are particularly applicable to cases like the present, where the witnesses referred to may be said to rest under the imputation of being strongly and improperly interested in the conviction of the prisoner. As has been said in General Court-Martial Orders from the War Department, *courts-martial had much better err on the side of liberality toward a prisoner, than by endeavoring to solve nice technical refinements in the law of evidence, assume the risk of injuriously denying him a proper latitude for defence.*[15] [my emphasis]

In this, Augur anticipated General Terry's 1876 testimony to Congress that insofar as it was a "despotic" system the military should be especially punctilious in establishing judicial safeguards.

The very thing Augur cautioned against, denying the defense "a proper latitude," occurred repeatedly in the Geddes court-martial. And the Orlemans, who, like Martha Mew and her lover, corroborated each other's stories, were scarcely less disinterested. Although Sergeant Mew may have been, like Geddes, an innocent victim, his trial exposed only a relatively banal adulterous love plot, not a deeply held taboo like incest. Karin Meiselman, a present-day writer on the subject, observes that "overt incest, like murder, is one of those human events that is so unthinkable to most people that there is a tendency to suppose that anyone who would do it *must* be 'crazy.'"[16] I would modify this assertion in one important respect: to most people incest is even *more* unthinkable than murder.

There is another crucial difference between the Mew and Geddes cases. Both the Mews and Lee were black, and the two men were enlisted men. They were not held to the high standard of "an officer and a gentleman." Mrs. Mew, established as an adulterous spouse attempting to get rid of her husband by a false accusation of murder, received no sympathy from the court. But Lillie Orleman, who was an officer's daughter, and a victim regardless of the truth of her story, was constantly protected from reasonable questioning by the same court that explored her virginity in such detail.

After the trip to Fort Davis, Friedlander told Geddes that he believed the Orlemans guilty of criminal intimacy: "No pure-minded honorable father would put his hand under his daughter's clothes in my presence." Friedlander testified that after Geddes had left Fort Stockton, Orleman sought him out and reproached him for having taken sides against him, saying, "I have always been a good friend of your brother's at Fort Clark and done everything that I could to help him and have also been a friend of yours here." He then showed Friedlander an affidavit his daughter had made, which Friedlander rejected as false. As he recounted their conversation for the court, Friedlander told Orleman, "'You know what I saw.' He said, 'What was that'? I said, 'I saw you put your hand under your daughter's clothes, take hold of her leg, she asking you to desist.' He said, 'That was nothing.'"

Such a response might be construed to mean that Orleman thought that his grasping his daughter's leg was insufficient grounds for Friedlander to take Geddes's part or to imagine that a criminal intimacy existed. Yet it sounds uncomfortably dismissive as well, another veiled assertion of his paternal right to touch his daughter's flesh without interference or censure.

If it happened, Geddes's alleged pressing of Lillie's knees was done under cover of his voluminous officer's cape or a lap robe and thus was intended to be unobserved. The actions and speech Friedlander attributed to Orleman were just the opposite—so obvious that the other occupants of the ambulance could not have failed to notice. If Friedlander's account is accurate, Orleman's actions could have been unconsciously motivated by a desire to warn off the other man. Taking hold of his daughter's leg was a flourishing of proprietorship in the face of a man who might have sexual designs on her.* Orleman's crude comment, "What a big leg you have, Lillie," can be compared to the husband's remark about his wife's feet in the story Orleman told: in both cases, possession cancels the need for flattery.

In spite of the enlightened views he had frequently expressed about fair trials, General Ord was not predisposed to rein in a judge advocate who was injuriously denying a defendant a proper latitude for defense when that same defendant had made a scandalous charge against one officer—and had had an affair with his commanding officer's wife to boot. It would take the Judge Advocate General to act in the interest of justice rather than politics or passion.

---

*Although Friedlander and Orleman were almost the same age, since Friedlander was a bachelor, Orleman might have considered him to be a possible rival.

Three

FINALE

AFTERMATH

The Judge Advocate General's argument was logical and dispassionate, but the Army immediately resisted it, thereby guaranteeing that Geddes would not be able to resume normal life with his regiment. He did return to duty, but his company was immediately exiled from Fort Stockton to the remote camp of Peña Colorado ("painted rock"), an uninhabited area fifty miles south of the post.[1] Whatever the possible reasons for assigning an army unit to this area, departmental correspondence demonstrates that Company F of the Twenty-fifth Infantry was chosen in order to remove Geddes from Fort Stockton.[2] Instead of being rotated back to the post, as would ordinarily have occurred, the company was kept in wilderness isolation at Peña Colorado until it was transferred to the Department of Dakota.

While Geddes was virtually imprisoned in the West Texas desert, General William Tecumseh Sherman was feverishly plotting to expel him from the Army by some other means—by any other means, it appeared.

As General of the Army, Sherman could have accepted the reversal of the court-martial and labeled the dossier "case closed." Instead, he mounted a determined effort to rid the Army of Geddes. In the spring of 1880 he dispatched Absalom Baird, the assistant inspector general, to undertake a wide-ranging investigation of Geddes's character, with the object of dredging up damaging information that could result in new charges. In this quest Sherman seemed willing to accept any scurrilous innuendo or gossip at face value. More than willing—avid.

Sherman committed himself to whatever was necessary to end the military career of an officer who had a distinguished field record and much support within his regiment. As Sherman would write to General Alfred Terry after the report was complete, "I see no escape from a trial by a General Court Martial, unless Captain Geddes resigns as I think he should do."[3]

The simplest explanation for Sherman's zeal to rid the Army of Andrew Geddes is his long friendship with General E.O.C. Ord. They had been friends ever since their cadet days at West Point, and Sherman was intensely loyal to Ord. At the time of the Geddes case Sherman was trying to persuade President Hayes not to forcibly retire Ord, one of a group of generals the President had targeted. Sherman had sloughed off the criticism of Ord by Philip Sheridan, the Army's second-ranking general, who had complained in 1877, "I have lost confidence in his [Ord's] motives and his management of his department is a confusion which is demoralizing to his subordinates." In 1879 Sheridan again complained, this time of Ord's "eccentricity of character and the devious methods he employs to accomplish his ends."[4] Sherman, who would lose the battle to keep Ord from being retired, would have been predisposed at any time to accept the judgment of his "life-long friend" on a court-martial.[5]

Yet friendship is ultimately not a compelling argument to explain Sherman's extraordinary vendetta against Geddes. Ord's

AFTERMATH

fate would not be decided or even affected by the disposition of the Geddes matter. What emerges from the record is the intensity of Sherman's conviction that Geddes was a monster.

Like Dunn, Sherman was removed from the immediate vicinity of the case and might have been expected to view it without emotion. But incest and seduction were emotional issues, even when they occurred elsewhere. As the reviewing judge, Dunn had been able to set aside powerful cultural attitudes in his assessment of the judicial record. Sherman was not similarly immune.

Concerning women, particularly young and vulnerable women, Sherman was a gallant who envisioned himself in the ideal male role of defender of the weaker sex. When the young widow of George Armstrong Custer addressed a moving plea to him for help in removing a statue of her husband from West Point, Sherman enthusiastically embraced her less-than-reasonable cause.* He instantly replied, "I sympathize with every pulsation of your wounded heart," then told her how to make the strongest case in another letter that she would address to him and that he would send with his endorsement to the Secretary of War.[6] For Sherman, Libbie Custer represented suffering womanhood in need of his masculine power to aid and comfort. She was also young and beautiful.

Sherman was a man of his time in seeing women as delicate creatures who required the protection of men. Had Lillie Orleman appealed to him in person, he would undoubtedly have been sympathetic to her youth and vulnerability. But his partisanship in the case may have had its source in a more veiled aspect of his being, one that he could not so readily articulate as simple charity to a young female unfortunate.

*Mrs. Custer had never personally seen the statue of her husband but hated it because she had not been consulted about it.

The devoted father of daughters as well as sons, Sherman was strongly attracted to young women. At the very time that he set in motion the post-trial effort to oust Geddes, he was, at the age of sixty, on the threshold of a long involvement with the widow of his Civil War aide, Major Lewis Audenreid, a woman in her thirties. In the years directly preceding the Geddes court-martial he had had a similar intimate and secret relationship with the beautiful young sculptress Vinnie Ream.[7]

Had he chosen to scrutinize his own conduct, Sherman might have seen himself in uncomfortable proximity to both protagonists in the San Antonio court-martial. Lieutenant Orleman had been accused of illicitly transforming a fatherly role into that of sexual partner. This was, in fact, an issue that would preoccupy Sherman in his coming liaison with Mary Audenreid. Early in the relationship he struggled to impose a respectable order on his feelings:

> As the wife of my aide you were of my family, and I really feel to you as I do to Elly or Rachel [his daughters], to caress and love you as a child rather than as a woman. If I were twenty years younger, I would not even trust myself with you, in the close intimacy in which you hold me.[8]

The rationalizing is transparent. Later, his writing to her "I realize that I must play the part of father, not that of lover" articulates a struggle whose expression on paper is an attempt at mastery, not a statement of accomplishment, as if one were to write "I realize that I must give up smoking" without acting on the intention. As Peter Gay observes in his history of the nineteenth-century middle class, "The love for the father . . . was a highly visible occupation of many women's lives in the nineteenth century."[9] Sherman could imagine Mary to be another daughter, whose obvious feelings for him, as his for her, could be comfortably subsumed under the rubric of respectable affection.

Nevertheless, although Sherman was troubled by the difficulty of reconciling his erotic impulses with his fatherly role toward Mary, his feelings for her and other young women were not incestuous. They were directed outside the family circle rather than toward his own daughters. They were, in fact, reminiscent of those of the older male guardians who married their wards in such popular novels of the period as *Infelice*.

Still, an unfriendly critic might well view Sherman's relations with Mary Audenreid and Vinnie Ream as similar to Orleman's exploitation of his daughter for his own sexual satisfaction. And while the vigorous and powerful head of the Army seemed far removed from the mere lieutenant whose physical disability would soon result in his retirement, the two men shared certain characteristics. Both had large families: in Orleman's case, larger than he could easily support; in Sherman's case, larger than he wanted. Whatever Mrs. Orleman's feelings for her husband, the two were effectively separated for long periods of time, and Lillie had taken her mother's place at her father's side. In the late 1870s Sherman had undergone a similar experience: his wife and children had removed from Washington to St. Louis except for one daughter, who continued to live with her father. The separation endured for several years, and the Sherman marriage remained stormy.

As a strong-willed patriarch who felt underappreciated by his wife, Sherman basked in the admiration and gratitude of younger women. As he once told the sympathetic Mary Audenreid, his wife, an ardent Irish Catholic, regarded "an Irish drayman who gets drunk six times a week and belabors his wife and children—yet who has kept the true faith and goes to Church on Sunday—as a higher type of mankind than a patriot soldier at the head of a victorious army." While the need for ego gratification is palpable in Sherman's many complaints about his wife, he saw his behavior toward younger women as beneficent, even when he was warning them off other men. In 1886, Mary Audenreid would start to see General Absalom Baird, who was by then the Inspector General of the Army. Sherman informed Mary that Baird, four years younger than Sherman, was too old for her.[10] She never did marry again.

Except for the development of intimacy, Sherman's relationship with Vinnie Ream began much like the correspondence with Mrs. Custer. (Had the young and attractive widow of George Armstrong Custer lived in Washington, Sherman would certainly have seen her in person rather than writing her sympathetic letters.) Sherman was on the committee to award the commission for a statue of Admiral David Farragut. Ream had submitted a proposal. At first, Sherman simply gave her advice on securing the commission, but by the time she won the competition he had become a regular visitor to her atelier. Their correspondence, redolent of intimacy and oblique sexual references, was broken off in 1878 when Ream married, but was later resumed intermittently until Sherman's death.[11]

If the age difference between Sherman and the women he loved, and his attempt to view them through the lens of paternal feeling, linked him to Orleman, he was, like Geddes, a married man who had affairs. The puzzling intensity with which Sherman pursued Geddes may have concealed his fear of being exposed as an adulterer. He prided himself on the discretion of his liaisons, instructing both Ream and Audenreid to destroy his letters, as he did theirs. (Both women saved his letters, however.) While Sherman envisioned himself as a protector of women, he described Geddes as a despoiler "of *the fair fame of ladies* [who] ought to resign his commission rather than subject them to the publicity and scandal of a trial" (my emphasis). In his brief letter of June 17, 1880, to General Terry, whose department was inheriting Geddes from Texas, Sherman uses this significant phrase twice. Because "the case involved *the fair fame of ladies* entitled to our protection," he informs Terry, "I ordered a thorough examination by Inspector General Baird whose report is herewith" (my emphasis).[12]*

The repetition of this curiously archaic and romantic phrase, "the fair fame of ladies" suggests how important this justification was for Sherman. According to one historian of the frontier army, "an officer would go to any length to protect a lady's name, even if silence should damn him."[13] Glossing over the common denominator of adultery, Sherman saw himself as circumspectly protecting "the fair fame of ladies" while Geddes destroyed it through his reckless behavior, bringing down "publicity and scandal" on the delicate reputations of women. Like society as a whole, Sherman found it more palatable to believe that Orleman was a good father and Geddes an evil seducer—and a slanderer, to boot.

Ironically, to achieve his goal of removing Geddes from the army, Sherman himself was willing to sacrifice the fair fame of whatever ladies could get the job done.

The point of departure for Absalom Baird's investigation was an affidavit that had been made in June 1879, while the Geddes trial was in progress.† Lieutenant Owen J. Sweet, Twenty-fifth Infantry, had solicited the affidavit on his own initiative in order "to shed light on the moral character of Captain Geddes." When Colonel Blunt forwarded this document to Judge Advocate Clous, he commented—tellingly—that Sweet "was about the only officer then at Stockton who could be relied upon for any assistance the prosecution might need."[14] Not only did the other officers of Geddes's own regiment remain loyal to him, the officers of *Orleman's regiment* also refused to aid the prosecution.

---

*Baird was actually an assistant inspector general at the time.

†See Appendix B for the text of the Baird Report.

Lieutenant Bigelow's diary entries reveal his estimation of Sweet as "mean and deceitful," as well as a gossip—a type Bigelow detested. Early in May 1879, Sweet had visited Bigelow's quarters for the purpose of discussing current scandals, but when Sweet began, Bigelow pointedly demanded that they speak of something else. After relating the episode in his diary, Bigelow went on to give his impression of Sweet:

> He likes to go among officers, I imagine, and draw them out on personal matters and then go home and have a good talk over them with Mrs. Sweet, reporting everything that he has heard. He delights in the Orleman and Geddes affair, pretends to be very much shocked and amazed at the occurrence of such scandal, but it furnishes just the kind of excitement that he and Mrs. Sweet thrive on.[15]

Evidently, the prying Sweet and his stout wife were well suited to each other.

Sweet was either an enemy of Geddes or simply an interfering gossip who delighted in exposing the sins of others. It had been his wife who had filled Lillie Orleman's ears with accounts of Geddes's amours among the officers' wives at Fort Stockton. No doubt Sweet knew where to find a witness to Geddes's affair with Fannie McLaughlen. Reading the affidavit Sweet had solicited, which was forwarded to him as the prosecutor of the case against Geddes, Judge Advocate Clous commented piously, "It is hard to conceive the social ethics of some of the people who were at Fort Stockton and figure in the recent disgraceful scandals."[16]

As another witness to Geddes's scandalous behavior, the laundress Mary Stewart provided an account of parallel and collusive affairs engaged in by Geddes with Mrs. McLaughlen and Friedlander with Mrs. Beck. As Clous wrote to Sherman after the 1879 verdict was overturned, Mary Stewart's character "does not seem to be bad," but unfortunately for the general's plan, the laundress had a significant liability. Clous continued with his evaluation:

> It is said that she is living with and is married to a colored soldier for a number of years, and that her behavior was good. Under all the circumstances, it is doubtful whether a clear case could be made upon Mary Stewart's accusations alone . . . the prejudices against a white woman living with a Negro, would weigh heavily against her.[17]

J. C. Nott and George R. Gliddon, in their widely read book on race, believed that the characteristics of offspring differed according to both the sex and the race of each parent. That is, intelligence was inherited from the mother, race more strongly inherited from the father. But this theory came up against a problem if the mother was white and the father black since whiteness was assumed to improve blackness. However, the authors claimed to have no firsthand knowledge of such a case since the pairing of white women and black men was so rare.[18]

It was not surprising that in spite of their extensive research in the South, Nott and Gliddon had found no such couple. Even consensual sex between a black man and a white woman could result in the man's being lynched. Aside from the reality of physical danger at worst and social ostracism at best, for a white person to marry someone of another race in Texas in 1879 was against the law. There was a strong gender bias in society's attitude toward this transgression, a racial extension of the double standard that controlled the sexuality of white women while allowing freedom to white men. The Texas law endured until 1967, when the Supreme Court declared such statutes unconstitutional.[19]

For Sherman, once the Geddes court-martial had been reversed, Mary Stewart's account was the logical place to begin the effort to unearth more evidence against Geddes, thus laying the groundwork for a new trial. He gave Baird a wide mandate. Special Orders

No. 25, issued on March 13, 1880, dispatched Baird from Chicago to Fort Stockton "and such other points as he may find necessary for the purpose of making the investigation ordered by the General of the Army."[20] By the time Sherman wrote to General Terry in June of 1880, he had received Baird's report on Geddes, which frankly branded the captain a libertine.

That Baird's report is studded with condemnatory interjections is hardly surprising, given his explicit charge to discover information useful to Geddes's reprosecution. The particulars he gathered fall under the general rubric Baird sets forth close to the beginning: according to reports Geddes appeared to be "a man totally destitute of any sense of right and wrong, or of moral propriety as regards casual intercourse between men and women in the society into which his commission as an officer of the army has admitted him."[21]

In a community the size of Fort Stockton such goings-on could scarcely have been kept secret. Indeed, Baird added that "the name of Fort Stockton became a bye word [sic], a shame and a reproach throughout the Department of Texas."[22] Yet for all the presumed facts Baird included in his report, the hopes of a new prosecution were pinned on a single problematic document—the affidavit of Mary Stewart, a laundress. Like Sherman and Clous, Baird saw Stewart's testimony through the lens of race and class prejudice.

Baird's evaluation was accompanied by a communication from Assistant Adjutant General R. E. Drum to General Ord, who had wanted to know if—on the strength of the Stewart affidavit—he could remove Rachel Beck from Fort Stockton. Drum indicated that the military requirement of discipline, rather than guilt or innocence, should decide the matter:

> The commanding officer is not bound to inquire into the question of adultery in such a case as this; the question with him is how will her presence effect [sic] the discipline and good order of his post. An

innocent person, who is imprudent and defies public opinion of the garrison so far as to cause scandal, may be dismissed from the Post. On ships of war, women untouched by scandal are not admitted as subversive of discipline. . . . If Mrs. Beck's presence would impair discipline in the Army, or would scandalize or degrade the service, her removal would not only be proper, but should be required.[23]

There were complications, however. "Improper women" could be removed, but this term was intended to describe prostitutes: "It is not supposed that Mrs. Beck could be classed with [such women]." Moreover, Mary Stewart had simply given her opinion that Mrs. Beck was guilty of adultery. And "besides," Drum felt compelled to reiterate, "she is a white woman married to a negro, and is laundress to a company of the 10th Cavalry. . . . Her statements are denied by Lieutenant Beck, by Friedlander, and would probably be denied by Mrs. Beck."[24] All interested parties regretfully concurred with this assessment of the affidavit: Stewart's class and social transgression made her testimony worthless for their purposes.

Lieutenant Beck appears to have been an extremely trusting or naïve husband. Although Mary Stewart said that Friedlander had given her money to buy her silence about the affair, Colonel Blunt told Clous that "it was the common talk at Stockton that Mrs. Beck received valuable presents from Friedlander, mentioning as some of the articles a silk dress all made up and a diamond ring."[25] In response to the allegations of impropriety, Beck had told Blunt that his wife was "imprudent and defied public opinion." The furthest he would go still left room for a benign interpretation of his wife's activities: "It may be that during my wife's illness," he wrote to Clous, "the cure of her by a person who since proved to be a bad woman [Mrs. McLaughlen] was the ostensible reason used by that person to meet her associate [Captain Geddes]."[26]

The compressed narrative of Beck's remark dovetails with Lillie Orleman's trial testimony that an officer's wife had seen Mrs. McLaughlen and Geddes running from the back of the hospital together, and with correspondence between Alice Grierson and her family referring to Rachel Beck's illness and Fannie McLaughlen's care of her. To her son Charlie, Alice wrote on October 18, 1878: "For more than a week, Mrs. Beck had been very sick, and Mrs. McLaughlen had been helping take care of her."[27] That Beck was desperate to preserve his own picture of reality seems confirmed by Clous's reference to his "many wild assertions."

If Lieutenant Bigelow's description can be believed, the Beck household was chaotic at best. When he first came to Fort Stockton in 1878, Bigelow took his meals with the Beck family but soon made other arrangements.* He had a host of complaints beyond the overpriced and inadequate food and Mrs. Beck's "ugly temper." The Beck children were annoying, "ill bred; beside which their teeth are not clean and they talk horrible English, which their parents do not correct."[28] The unattended children suggest that the parents had other concerns. Beck's was drinking—his behavior under the influence led to a court-martial—and his wife's was her affair with Friedlander.

In any case, quite aside from the impression Mary Stewart might make as a witness, an affair between Mrs. Beck and Joseph Friedlander was irrelevant to Sherman's goal of retrying Geddes, and Major McLaughlen's aversion to publicizing his cuckoldry would have made prosecution on this ground difficult.

Friedlander had not been idle during the efforts to brand him the adulterous lover of Mrs. Beck. Before either General Ord or

---

*To make extra money, individual officers, with or without family, would undertake to provide meals for those officers who wanted such an arrangement. "Mess" is the army term for taking meals.

Colonel Blunt could investigate the Stewart affidavit, he secured
an affidavit in his favor from one Quanelo, a man in his employ
who, Stewart had indicated, knew of the affair. According to
Friedlander's business rival, M. F. Corbett, Quanelo was a person
whose opinion could be bought. In his own affidavit for the 1879
court-martial Friedlander had complained that he was the object
of an army vendetta because he had refused to be "bulldozed" by
the prosecution in the Geddes court-martial.

In a report dated February 10, 1880, in which Clous addressed
the credibility of both Stewart and Friedlander, he dismissed
Friedlander's accusation that the Army was out to get him because
it had been made on June 6, 1879, before Friedlander had been
called as a witness in the trial. This time sequence would not necessarily invalidate such a charge. It must have been clear well
before the trial how he would testify, since Friedlander had been
summoned as a witness for the defense.

Still smarting from the reversal of the court-martial, which he
maintained—incorrectly—had nothing to do with the facts of the
case, Clous claimed that Friedlander's affidavit was false:

> A person who, under oath, states that he heard through a solid wall
> of two feet, persons softly walking over the floor in their stocking
> feet, and that floor is shown to have been thickly carpeted, has too
> elastic a conscience to be accredited with any truthfulness in a crime
> where his own misdeeds are in issue.[29]

Friedlander was an interested party in the matter of Mrs. Beck,
but the prosecutor's reference to Friedlander's trial testimony
about hearing noise from Orleman's quarters shows how easily
facts became obscured by biased interpretation in the Geddes
court-martial. Orleman had testified that the floor was covered by
a "heavy layer of hay and a carpet stretched over it." The thickness
of the carpet had not been specified, and a "heavy layer of hay"

may well have crackled when walked over, producing the sounds Friedlander (and others) had testified to hearing. Moreover, the canvas ceiling could have negated the effectiveness of the two-foot partition wall—if indeed the wall was that thick.

In writing of the court-martial, Baird blamed Geddes for subjecting Lillie Orleman to "all the cruel torture which unscrupulous lawyers employ to shield guilty clients from just punishment."[30] Like Clous, Baird disregarded the many substantive matters Dunn's review had raised. He stated that the verdict had been overturned "on the ground of certain rulings of the Court thought to be erroneous, and in no way effecting [sic] the facts in issue"—in other words, because of a technicality.[31] This simply was not true.

The libertine behavior attributed to Geddes was certainly an offense to morality, but Baird, like his taskmaster Sherman, was less than objective in his conclusions. In the course of events leading up to the court-martial Geddes had not attacked "the fair fame of ladies" with the scandal of public exposure. Like most men who have affairs with married women, publicity was the last thing he wanted. He had intended his deposition about the Orlemans to be a privileged communication to the departmental commander, and he had submitted it only when Orleman preferred charges against him.

Baird reveals his determination to believe in the Orlemans' innocence when he justifies their sleeping arrangements. He writes, arrestingly, "that this fact of a father sleeping in the same chamber with his daughter already on the verge of womanhood should excite remark is not strange, but it is natural that the father would be the last one to perceive the changes from childhood to maturity in his own child."[32]

In transmitting the Baird report to Judge Advocate General Dunn on June 15, Sherman made his own position emphatically clear:

I suppose I have no right to call on you officially to aid me in the discharge of my duties, yet I have no doubt you will privately. I send you herewith, all the papers in the case of Captain Geddes, 25th Infantry, against whom charges were made which would have opened up terrible scandals, and before ordering a Court-Martial, the whole matter to be inquired into by Inspector General Baird, to whose report and appendix I ask your attention. By these papers Captain Geddes is not a proper person to be an officer of the Army, indeed [he] must be a sort of a monster, ruining women who have been honorable wives, virgin children, overwhelming a father by the monstrous charge of debauching his own child, and by perjury and ingenuous complications making it highly undesirable to try him by a General Court Martial.[33]

Sherman's characterization suggests that he had not read Dunn's meticulous analysis of the trial, or at the least, that he had brushed aside its conclusion that Geddes was more believable than Orleman. For Sherman, Geddes had ruined "virgin children"—although the only person to qualify for that category would have been Lillie Orleman—and brought a "monstrous charge."

Baird's goal had been to obtain further information that could lead to new charges against Geddes, but while the large fund of anecdotes that he had brought back from Texas might have been true, it seemed unlikely to stand the test of judicial scrutiny. As Clous had observed, invoking a legal authority, "it is very rare, indeed, that the parties are surprised in the direct fact of adultery."[34]

Although the Baird report made for spicy reading, Dunn's opinion, speedily rendered the day after he received the packet of documents from Sherman, confirmed that the material was not well suited to its intended purpose, that of convicting Geddes in another court-martial. On June 16, 1880, he wrote to Sherman that he could not advise reprosecution:

As to the charges of illicit conduct with Mrs. McLaughlin [sic] and the girl named Nevares [Josephine]—the latter does not appear to be sustained by explicit testimony; and, as to the former, the evidence is so far conflicting that it might very likely raise a reasonable doubt with the court in favor of the accused. In view of the great scandal to the service which a trial upon these charges would induce, and the doubtful result and profit of such a trial, I should hesitate to advise—*upon the evidence thus far submitted*—a resort to a court martial. At the same time the reputation, influence and example of Capt. Geddes (as they appear from the within statements), are such as clearly to make it desirable that his resignation should be induced if practicable.[35]

Dunn, who had been impressed by the testimony of officers loyal to Geddes, now made an institutional decision that the appearance of scandal was strong enough in this case to override the question of guilt. Or he may have realized that Sherman could not be dissuaded from his commitment to rid the Army of Geddes, and the preferred way to achieve this end was to have Geddes resign.

In spite of Dunn's strong opinion that another trial would be ill-advised, Sherman forged on. He wrote to General Terry the next day that he "saw no escape from a trial by a General Court Martial unless Captain Geddes resigns."[36] Dunn's caution about "the great scandal to the service" seems to have made no impression on Sherman, nor did the potential for another round of scandals that Dunn did not mention: the shattering of "the fair fame of ladies" who might have engaged in an adulterous relationship, even though they were characterized in Sherman's account as "honorable wives" who had been "ruined" by Geddes rather than as sinners in their own right. But if Sherman's paternalism deprived the guilty women of volition, it did accurately reflect their status. This was a contest between men in which women, in keeping with their societal powerlessness, were to be used as necessary in realizing male objectives, regardless of the detriment to the women's own interests.

•   •   •

Captain Geddes's resignation could not be "induced." When he was first informed that Baird was investigating him at Fort Stockton, he wrote to the assistant inspector general that he had "great pride in and love of my profession." He added that he considered his trial to have been unfair "from beginning to end—which also seems to have been the opinion of the revising and reviewing authority."[37] Sherman's idea had been to confront Geddes with what Baird had learned, supported by two letters of Mrs. McLaughlen's—a blatant attempt to force his resignation. Geddes's reply showed that he could play hardball, too:

> I am pained greatly by the fact that, if I am brought to trial thereon, the name of a lady will be thrown broad-cast about the country in the most public and scandalous manner. The lady in question is connected socially with some of the first people of New York and elsewhere, and when I think of the newspaper notoriety which will certainly ensue, I am filled with feelings of the greatest repugnance at the mere contemplation of such an unfortunate result. The lady in question has always borne an untarnished reputation, and that it should now be blasted by the mere testimony of a monstrosity of the basest description—viz., a white woman who has been living with a Negro for ten years—is to be regretted of all good people.[38]

Like everyone else who read the Stewart affidavit, Geddes knew that the laundress's crossing the color line would discredit her testimony. He told Baird that she had been indicted by a grand jury for miscegenation and was awaiting trial: "It will always be easy to prove her a perjurer." Mary Stewart, who had lived with a black man for ten years in a community that was both socially and legally racist, must have come to regret her intervention in the Fort Stockton scandal.

Whatever the reliability of Mary Stewart as a witness, there seems little doubt that some part of the accusations against Mrs. McLaughlen were true. Baird's report said that McLaughlen had not denied the affair, nor was it denied in Geddes's letter. McLaughlen professed himself satisfied if his wife behaved herself in New York. In keeping with the mores of the times, the McLaughlens did not divorce.

Geddes, after twitting Baird with the weakness of the Stewart affidavit, concluded his letter with simple dignity: "It would be hard to give up a career and profession followed since my boyhood, a captain at sixteen and Lieut. Col. commanding a regiment at nineteen. I had four brothers in General Sherman's army."[39] In other words, Geddes was unwilling to resign. And he did not suspect at the time, or possibly ever, that his most formidable enemy was the head of the Army—General Sherman himself.

The impasse would be resolved from an unexpected quarter. At the end of July Geddes and his company had made the transfer from Texas to Dakota, the last of the regiment to be sent. On September 11 a telegram from General Terry, commanding general of the Department of Dakota, announced to Sherman that new court-martial charges had been filed against Geddes, and that he would suspend action on the "old matter" and try Geddes on the new charges: "We may thus save all scandal."[40]

Again, Sherman's reply to this news reveals the depth of his determination to see Geddes cashiered. He telegraphed Terry, "That is well—order the trial of Captain Geddes on the new charges. The old can await unless the Statute of Limitations compels an immediate trial."[41] If the new charges did not succeed in removing Geddes, Sherman would insist on pursuing the old—no matter how much the "fair fame of ladies" or the reputation of the Army itself suffered.

FINAL ACT

D
r. Benjamin Pope, a meditative army surgeon at Fort
Stockton in the 1870s, found in his experience that soldiers could be sharply divided into two classes: "First,
those who are chronic transgressors of the law, and second, those
who are never in that category."[1] This may have been true in general—or true of enlisted men—but it fails to capture the nuances
of Andrew Geddes's encounters with military law. Even given the
high rate of courts-martial in the frontier army period, three trials
within eight years would place him in Pope's category of "chronic
transgressors." Yet Geddes doesn't fit the typical profile of the
repeat offender, the man whose vice—usually alcohol—is a recurring source of grief. All of Geddes's trials were exceptional in one
way or another.

Geddes went on trial for the third time at Fort Randall,
Dakota Territory, on the most common charge in the frontier
army: drunkenness on duty. The date was October 1, 1880,
exactly a month after the incident in question. Charges had been

preferred by Colonel George L. Andrews, the commander of the Twenty-fifth Infantry Regiment and the author of an official statement sent to General Ord earlier that year saying that he did not consider Captain Geddes to be a proper person to have command of a company.[2]

The particulars of the case were not in dispute: the issue was one of interpretation. Geddes had consumed a number of drinks during the afternoon of September 1. That evening at dress parade he became unsteady and then left the field. As he mounted the step to the porch of Company G quarters, he "seemed on the verge of falling."[3]

Captain Charles Bentzini testified that he had seen Geddes during the afternoon at the post trader's: "Before I left the signs of inebriation became apparent on the accused by a flushed face and what I can only express by saying his tongue was beginning to be heavy." At evening parade, "his body was oscillating to and fro and he showed the most positive signs of drunkenness." A group of witnesses for the prosecution corroborated that Geddes had been drunk on duty, and that he had had to turn over command to Lieutenant McMartin during dress parade and make a precipitous departure. Lieutenant McMartin himself testified that Geddes was "under the influence of liquor . . . to such a degree that it became necessary for him to leave the Parade." One witness described Geddes as "reeling and staggering." Another characterized him as "unsteady as he stood in front of his Company." A third baldly asserted that Geddes was drunk.

The defense responded that Geddes had been sick rather than intoxicated. Geddes himself testified that he had been sober. During parade he felt "dizzy with an extreme desire to get to a privy." After leaving the field and using the band privy, he felt much better, but for the next few days he had diarrhea. A series of defense witnesses testified that he had been sober at dress parade and had not "staggered." First Lieutenant Wallace Tear had seen Geddes walking to and from parade and affirmed that on both occasions he appeared sober. He also confirmed Geddes's frequent visits to the privy and had overheard him saying that he had "the trots."

The line between drunkenness and illness was not necessarily clear-cut. Just as illness could cause unsteadiness of the sort attributed to Geddes, so a drunken man might feign illness as a cover. In deciding between the two conditions a number of factors—such as the reliability of witnesses on both sides and the past conduct of the accused—might be brought to bear in a particular case.

Even if one did not know the behind-the-scenes machinations of the Army's top brass to get Geddes out of the service, several matters in this trial would raise suspicion. Much of the testimony for the prosecution just as easily supported the defense as the prosecution or was significantly undercut by cross-examination. For instance, the prosecutor called the post trader and the bartender to establish Geddes's afternoon drinking. Both confirmed that he had been drinking but testified to his sobriety as well. Major Joseph Bush had been working with Geddes that afternoon at the trader's. He said that Geddes "showed he had been drinking liquor . . . [but] I considered him able to do his duty. We compared the books together." Bush might as readily have appeared for the defense.

First Sergeant Wilson Buckney testified that on the parade ground Geddes was "a little unsteady" and told Lieutenant McMartin to take charge of the company because he was sick. This was during the latter part of the parade, and, according to Buckney, Geddes had performed his duties in the ordinary manner up to that time. Sergeant Buckney hadn't seen him stagger or reel and said that if this had happened, he would have seen it.

Corporal Richard Craige, of Geddes's own Company F, was sitting on the porch of Company G quarters with a Private Truett when he saw Geddes leave the parade and seem on the verge of falling when he negotiated the porch step. "It occurred to me that he had been suddenly taken sick," he testified. He noticed no "signs of liquor" about Geddes. Cross-examination provided an explanation for Geddes's stumble: the step was unusually high and the condition of the floor at the place where he stepped was bad, "the end of one of the boards being broken."

Perhaps the most damaging prosecution witness to the prosecution's own case was the post surgeon, who testified that he had treated Geddes for diarrhea. He refused to say that this condition could be a "natural outcome of excessive drinking," although he admitted that whiskey was a laxative. He indicated that he had seen Geddes on September 1 and found him to be "perfectly sober." More than that, he maintained that Geddes had not exhibited any "symptoms of intoxication" during the entire period relevant to the charge.

On cross-examination the doctor was asked if in his experience he had ever known of cases where men had "reeled, staggered, and even fallen in ranks from other causes than drunkenness." He replied "Certainly," and went on to name a number of possible causes for such behavior, among them, vertigo, epilepsy, apoplexy, and sunstroke. Even Second Lieutenant McMartin, who insisted that Geddes "was under the influence of liquor . . . to such a degree that it became necessary for him to leave the Parade," supported Geddes's account of having diarrhea. He had seen Geddes making repeated trips to the privy. William Ridell, a carpenter who had observed the September 1 dress parade, seemed like a particularly weak prosecution reed. When asked if Geddes appeared sober, he answered, "I could hardly tell, as I only remember to have met him once before."

Second Lieutenant Robert Loughborough was queried about possible prejudice against Geddes. He told the court that he had no personal prejudice against the accused but had expressed prejudice against him "on occasions." The court requested clarification and was told, "I mean I expressed myself prejudiced against the conduct of the accused for which he was tried in San Antonio. I should have said I was prejudiced against his conduct but not against himself personally." Other testimony substantiated that Loughborough had confessed prejudice against Geddes.

Loughborough should be regarded as only the tip of the iceberg. After the San Antonio trial, the Twenty-fifth Infantry had become factionalized, with groups of committed pro- and anti-Geddes officers. Given such a scandalous case within a small social group, it was inevitable that the majority of officers would have an opinion and choose a side. When the entire military hierarchy, including the regimental commander and the head of the Department of Texas, had taken a public position against Geddes, it is hardly surprising that junior officers would be inclined in that direction. Geddes, who knew nothing of Colonel Andrews's protest to Ord that Geddes was unfit for command, must nevertheless have known the regimental commander's feelings about him. The defense tried without success to get a witness to admit that Andrews was out to get Geddes.[4]

In a replay of the flagrant procedural violation that had caused Judge Advocate General Dunn to overturn the San Antonio trial, the Fort Randall prosecutor disallowed a number of defense witnesses. While every possible prosecution witness was heard, including the useless carpenter, two privates who were prepared to support the testimony of noncommissioned officers that Geddes had been sober were excused from testifying. The defense offered thirteen character witnesses, including Geddes's commanding officer at Fort Meade, but the court declined to call any of them on the ground that they were not material witnesses. Yet since the testimony of the material witnesses was divided, some character testimony would have been pertinent.

Worst of all, Geddes was forced to defend himself because his counsel, Olliver Shannon, was unavoidably absent for three days during the trial and the court had refused to grant the customary postponement.

The determination to cashier him emanating from the highest quarters of the Army gave Geddes's attempts to defend himself a pathetic dignity. He submitted the commendation he had received from Lieutenant Colonel W. R. Shafter in 1875 for the famous pursuit of Comanches that Geddes had led, along with other exhibits testifying to his excellence in performing his duty. In his written statement to the court Geddes retraced his military career, beginning with his enlistment in the Civil War at the age of fifteen and his distinguished war service. Then he stated, "The accused is too old a soldier to go upon the parade ground if he were staggering drunk; but would rather remain in his quarters and take the consequences of being absent from parade." Finally, he asked, "In all candor, if intoxication was the cause of this unsteady motion at parade, would it not have been seen by some of these parties at some of these points *before* or *afterwards*"? The charges against him, he asserted, "were trumped up."

Geddes was speedily found guilty of drunkenness at dress parade and sentenced to dismissal from the Army. This time his sentence was approved all the way up and signed by President Hayes exactly a year after the President had disallowed the San Antonio conviction.

Why did Judge Advocate General Dunn not call attention to the same procedural violations that he had pointed out in the earlier trial? Because of what he had learned in the interim about the captain's personal life, he had been converted to Sherman's view that the Army must rid itself of Geddes. He had not been convinced of Geddes's guilt in the San Antonio trial. Nor had he been willing to recommend reprosecution on the dubious collection of hearsay and gossip that Baird had brought back from Texas. But he must have felt that there was enough truth in the stories to brand Geddes an undesirable: Geddes had been too close to scandal on too many occasions for an honorable man to overlook.

Whether it played a part in his decision or not, Dunn now knew how determined Sherman was to dismiss Geddes. Had Dunn once again disagreed with his superior in rank by recommending that the captain's court-martial be reversed, Sherman would have proceeded to the far more inflammatory matter of a new trial in Texas. At this point—right or wrong—the choice was between the Army and Geddes. Dunn had thought Geddes should resign, and when he didn't, signing off on the Fort Randall court-martial in the best interest of the Army must have seemed to be the lesser evil.

If Geddes was bitterly disappointed at the outcome of his 1880 trial, his counsel, Olliver Shannon, was simply astonished. "My experience before courts-martial, varied as it has been," he wrote to his client, "prepared me very little for the extraordinary finding in your case. . . . The testimony of the prosecution carried a preponderance in your favor." Concerning the denial of postponement during his absence, Shannon commented that "such adjournments are common, and their refusal, when unavoidable absence of counsel is the reason, are very rare. I don't think the books or cases reported furnish such a case."[5]

Like many a dismissed officer, Andrew Geddes tried to obtain reinstatement through congressional action, an avenue that had worked repeatedly for the well-connected George Armes, but was usually not fruitful. In 1882, House Bill 3205 was introduced into the 47th Congress, first session, to reinstate Geddes, but it was not recommended by the Committee on Military Affairs. Geddes might have suspected but had no way of knowing what he was up against: the machinations of his enemies remained secret. In a letter to the Adjutant General, he wrote of the Baird Report:

> Were these reports *true,* I would forever hide my face from the sight of man. I ask you to please furnish me with a copy of Col. Baird's report; and earnestly hope, in simple justice, that my request may be granted. In self-defense I consider that I should know with what I am charged.[6]

This basic constitutional right was denied. A few days later, Geddes was informed by letter that the Baird Report was regarded as a privileged communication, and, accordingly, he would not be provided with a copy of it. The day before this letter was sent, someone in the Adjutant General's office had pencilled a note on it: "The writer [Geddes] is so bad a man that it don't seem worth while to have anything to do with him."[7]

In conjunction with Geddes's reinstatement effort a group of seven officers at Fort Randall, including Colonel Andrews, wrote to the President on January 30, 1882, to say the following:

> Owing to his scandalously immoral conduct, only a small part of which is recorded in the proceedings before the General Court Martial published in General Court Martial Orders, No. 66, War Department Adjutant General's Office, 1879, no officer in the Army could permit the ladies of his family to, in any way, recognize Andrew Geddes, and a majority of the officers would hold no other but necessary official relations with him.[8]

Of the seven officers of the Twenty-fifth Infantry who signed this letter, Colonel Andrews had brought the Dakota court-martial charges against Geddes, and Captain Bentzini had testified against him at the trial.

Geddes would never again be an active army officer. He went to work for the Department of Agriculture in Washington, where he rose to the position of chief clerk, the Department's highest ranking bureaucrat.[9] In this sedentary job, much of his time was spent in routine or low-level correspondence. To the editor of a publication called *American Agriculturist,* he wrote, "Replying to that portion of your letter of June 23rd relating to the utilization of celery refuse, I would say that the Department of Agriculture has never investigated this subject."[10]

A number of letters Geddes penned addressed a perennial concern of government agencies, the desire of political figures to obtain jobs for friends or constituents. Geddes wrote to assure Chicago congressman Hugh Belknap that he was giving proper attention to Belknap's "very earnest letter in behalf of Miss Johanna Quilty": "I at once made inquiry and find that a large number of microscopists in Chicago have been furloughed on account of slack in the work there."[11] The letter goes on to reassure the congressman that every consideration will be given his applicant when hiring resumes. Most letters indicate that the Department of Agriculture already had its full complement and might in fact be discharging rather than hiring.[*] Nevertheless, the petitioner's candidate would be kept in mind if a vacancy occurred, and so forth. Although he wrote many such letters, Geddes always individualized the predictable message and couched it in sympathetic language.

By 1891, this life was taking its toll. At the age of forty-seven, Geddes suffered from severe rheumatism, an enlarged heart, and "disease of the eyes." He was six foot one, but at 197 pounds probably heavier than he had been as a young officer.[12]

By 1899, when he was fifty-three, Geddes made still another attempt to remove the stain of dismissal from his record. For this

---

[*]Since hiring decisions were made by the Secretary of Agriculture, no doubt when an applicant received a job, the good news went out over the Secretary's name.

effort he submitted a long letter to the Committee on Military Affairs. It began with the by now familiar reprise of his military career, then continued with an account of the events that resulted in dismissal:

> My dismissal was the result of charges, trumped up, without any foundation in fact, maliciously concocted, and the outcome of as despicable, unjust, relentless, and bitter a persecution as ever disgraced the annals of our Army or any other. As was said at the time, it was better to sacrifice me than give publicity to an army scandal by trying and punishing the very party who had been guilty of incest with his own daughter. I was victimized; the other (God save the mark!) honorably retired. It was an infinite, dastardly outrage.
>
> The officer who preferred the charges against me, on which I was dismissed, threatened, after the President had disapproved the proceedings, findings, and sentence in the former case, that he would follow me until he "did me up." His charges were false and born of malice. The trial [the Dakota court-martial of 1880] was a mockery, the result a travesty upon justice, and an indelible wrong. I was misled and curtailed in my defense. There were several witnesses whose testimony was material and pertinent; but a prominent member of the court asked if the evidence of these witnesses would be in the same line as that already in—to effect that I was not under influence of liquor, as charged—and when the accused answered yes, he said it would only be a waste of the time of the court, and that he was satisfied. I concluded that he was satisfied of my innocence and that the other members were so, too; therefore did not call these material witnesses. This evidence would have established the proof of my innocence beyond any question; it would have given an overwhelming preponderance in my behalf. I consider and submit that this was a great wrong. . . .
>
> This court was bent on conviction. Congressman Perkins's paper at the time gave as an item that members of the court in Sioux City, en route to Yankton, expressed the opinion that it would probably go bad with Geddes on account of a former trial in Texas. This alone disqualified them to sit on the trial. . . .

During these last eighteen years I have suffered under this great wrong and injustice. Not an hour or day all those years that this outrage and disgrace have not been present; not a night that I have not in prayer appealed to Him that this burning stigma might be wiped from my name. It has covered me as with a pall of blackest night. In attempts to secure honorable position it has, Banquo like, risen to thrust me back and hold me down. It broke an aged, beloved, and Christian father's heart. It has deeply hurt and pained dearly loved sisters, brothers, and friends, but thank God, never alienated their affection and respect, for they have ever believed in my innocence, truth, and manliness. Were I gifted with the language of a Milton or Macaulay I could not express the deep oh, the bitter humiliation and mortification of those eighteen long, saddened, heavy-laden years. Death has taken father, mother, brothers, sisters, a son, and two lovely little daughters. I believe that an all-merciful God has sustained me with the consciousness of my innocence and truth.

I was proud of my profession. My family for generations were soldiers. From 16 to 35 I had given my every thought to love of our flag and its service. Therefore it is that I appeal to the Congress and to the President to right as far as possible this great wrong; to take away from an honored name this blot; to at least, now that I am marching the downgrade of life to the inevitable "taps," by this act of clemency, kindness, and justice make that forced march as light and easy as possible, enabling me at last to leave to wife and children a name cleared of dishonor and stain. . . .

With depth of feeling inexpressible, I appeal to you to remove this life sentence.[13]

At the time of the Texas court-martial Geddes was living apart from his wife, Florence Towers Geddes, and had no children. It seems impossible that Mrs. Geddes knew nothing of her husband's philandering, or that, since they lived apart, they were a happy couple. In fact, Geddes had acknowledged his marital unhappiness in the 1879 trial, and Lillie's testimony indicated that it was common knowledge at Fort Stockton: "I had been told that he did not love his wife and had been made to marry her." Yet he and Mrs. Geddes apparently began to live together after his dismissal and relocation in Washington and had, in addition to the three children who died, a son and two daughters. Geddes fathered another daughter after his wife's death.

The Senate Committee on Military Affairs followed its counterpart in the House in favorably reporting out a bill to authorize the President to place Geddes on the retired list with the rank of captain. Its report pronounced that "a great injustice has been done Captain Geddes in the action of the court-martial and that a full investigation of the facts will demonstrate to impartial men that his restoration to the Army, with the rank held at the time of his dismissal, is an act of simple justice."[14]

In support of this action Geddes's old commanding officer, now Brigadier General William R. Shafter, once more wrote of that long-ago time:

> While under my command Colonel Geddes's conduct was always exemplary. . . . Colonel Geddes's war service is well known. He was one of the youngest officers of his grade in the Army, and as a mere boy, served as a commissioned officer with distinction.[15]

The passage of this bill in 1901 changed Geddes's dishonorable discharge to retirement. The only real justice would have been the continuation of his military career without prejudice, but clearing his name was at least a partial reparation. He died in Washington in 1921 and is buried next to his wife in Arlington National Cemetery.

After his retirement from active duty in 1879, Louis Orleman immediately left the state of Texas and took up a position as military instructor at Peekskill Military Academy in Peekskill, New

York, where he remained, rising to the position of commandant in 1890. In that year, according to a surviving catalogue, the school had 130 students. It was inspected by an officer on the Inspector General's staff who gave Orleman an enthusiastic evaluation:

> The military professorship is in charge of First Lieutenant Louis H. Orleman, U.S. Army (retired), who is a officer of fine ability, and zealous and conscientious in the discharge of the duties confided to him. He gives entire satisfaction to the authorities, and, so far as I can see, they have every reason to congratulate themselves on the possession of so industrious an officer.[16]

One of Orleman's younger daughters graduated from the Academy in 1897, the only female student in the class. She went on to Cornell.[17]

Orleman's health began to deteriorate early in the twentieth century. In 1901 he asked to be relieved of his Peekskill duties because of "facial paralysis, neuralgia of the head, and heart trouble."[18] In 1906 he requested permission from the Army to leave the United States for health reasons. Five years later, his daughter Daisy wrote to the Adjutant General that her father's mental condition was "disturbed." He had been talking about resigning, but Daisy wanted the Adjutant General to understand that this was "the result of his condition" rather than a genuine intention.[19] By 1916 his son Carl, by then acting as his guardian, referred to Orleman as "mentally incapacitated."[20] He was to live another twenty years in that condition.

When Orleman died at Atlantic City on December 27, 1936, at the age of ninety-four, he was described in a newspaper account as leaving four daughters, two of whom—Daisy and Violet—were physicians.[21]

Lillie, who had settled in Peekskill, was also named as a survivor. She remained single until late in life and evidently had lived with her family until the late 1920s, when she married a widower eight years her junior. By 1935 the Peekskill directory listed her as a widow.[22]

Lillie's life between her role in the Geddes trial and her late marriage generated no publicity. Given the drinking that was observed in Texas, she might have been a quiet alcoholic all those years, but this is mere speculation. Did her father's abuse continue? Were possible suitors repelled by what they knew or conjectured about her situation? Geddes had testified that Lillie had told her father that she would never marry without first telling her prospective husband what her father had done to her, whereupon Orleman had replied, "You little fool! Nobody will know it—nobody can tell it." Whatever her later life, in 1879 Lillie was the victim of a code that was officially devoted to protecting women but was willing to sacrifice them for male satisfactions. Even if her father had been innocent of "criminal intimacy" with Lillie, he might have placed her good above his own desire to defeat Geddes with public vindication. Having already been exonerated of wrongdoing by the retiring board, he might have eschewed charges against Geddes that would subject his daughter to the painful experience of testifying before the all-male court—not to mention those repeated gynecological examinations.

In his determination to triumph over his adversary, Orleman acted as Wade Hampton did when he circulated explicit charges against James Henry Hammond, the uncle who had abused Hampton's daughters. Hammond's biographer writes that "out of either allegiance to the former governor or more general feelings of delicacy, most legislators had declined to examine the materials Hampton had made available." While Hammond rode out the storm, Hampton's daughters were ruined: "Their father had won a victory of sorts . . . but the father triumphed at his children's

expense: Harriet, Catherine, Ann, and Caroline were far more vulnerable than their uncle."[23]

If Lillie paid the price of victimization, the sister she had
wanted to shield was a success. According to her entry in the *Dictionary of American Biography,* Daisy Orleman Robinson became a
prominent dermatologist and surgeon as well as a wife. Among a
number of achievements, she was decorated by the French government for her work in France during World War I.

Geddes's defense attorney in Texas, George Paschal, went on to
become a leading citizen of San Antonio and to have a successful
public career there. He was elected district attorney in 1885, the
same year in which his was the first signature on a telegram signed
by members of the San Antonio bar recommending that John
Clous be promoted to major.* An obituary notice described
Paschal as "the best prosecuting attorney the district had ever
had . . . [he] made a statewide reputation as a fearless and fearful
prosecutor and state's advocate, his very name being a terror to all
evil-doers, and his record of convictions being one of the largest in
the annals of courts of law."[24]

By the time of his death in 1894 at the age of forty-six, Paschal
had established a reputation for two qualities, legal brilliance and
courage: "[He] had no fear to do what he thought was right."
Eventually he served as a popular mayor who inaugurated "a great
many improvements and many radical reforms." A victim of
Bright's disease, a kidney ailment, he died unexpectedly in office.
Paschal was attended in his final illness by Dr. George Cupples,

*The telegram was sent to Texas senators S. B. Maxey and Richard Coke.

one of the San Antonio doctors who had testified on virginity for the defense at the Geddes trial.[25]

General E.O.C. Ord found himself abruptly retired by President Hayes on December 6, 1880—much against his will and that of the people of Texas, where his vigorous pursuit of border raiders had made him popular. It was now a different era, and even his old friend Sherman was no longer interested in defending Ord against the criticisms of the Army's second general, Philip Sheridan. When Sheridan wrote "that it is my belief that we cannot have any quiet or peace on the Rio Grande, as long as Ord is in command of Texas," Sherman promptly agreed with him: "I am more than convinced that a cool and less spasmodic man in Texas would do more to compose matters on that border than the mere increase of the cavalry."[26]

Ord's beautiful daughter Bertie, who married the Mexican general Gerónimo Treviño in 1880, died in 1883, the same year as her father.

When George Armes appeared at Geddes's trial as a witness for the defense, he noted that his testimony seemed to offend Judge Advocate Clous: "I am satisfied," he told his diary, "he will watch his chance to get me the first opportunity that occurs."[27] This was not long in coming. Three months later, Clous arrived at Fort Stockton in connection with a prospective court-martial of Armes. "Clous is going among my men," Armes wrote, "manufacturing all the evidence he possibly can to win the case. He has sufficient control of those negro soldiers to make them swear to anything that he may fix up."[28]

A week later Armes was accusing Clous of "an underhanded and villainous act," an attempt to obtain evidence by subterfuge. A month later he wrote that many had predicted his acquittal, "but knowing Clous as I do and his underhanded way of managing cases and picking his courts, I feel that I have been found guilty. . . . Clous is a man I cannot expect justice and fair dealings from, and having full control of the court, he handles the members as if they were his puppets."[29]

Since Armes had as much genius for getting out of trouble as for getting into it, he continued to survive encounters with military law and to meet his enemy in new judicial proceedings. On July 31, 1880, he wrote in his diary about the beginning of still another trial, "I objected to Clous on the ground that he was not a gentleman, or a man who could be relied upon under any circumstances."[30]

Eventually, even luck and political pull were not enough to keep Armes in good standing. After "twenty-three arrests, eight trials," and a sanity hearing, he was forcibly retired.[31] Once his stormy army career was over, Armes settled in the Washington area and made a fortune in real estate. His dislike of John Clous endured beyond his separation from the military. When he heard that Clous might be promoted, he wrote to the Secretary of War:

> Believing you do not wish to reward dishonest persons, who happen to be shielded by a uniform, is one of my reasons for calling your attention to a character who is a disgrace to the service, and at the same time manages to escape the punishment he justly deserves.[32]

His fellow diarist, John Bigelow, Jr., continued an army career of solid accomplishment. He finally saw action in 1898 in the Cuban campaign, where he was wounded and awarded the Silver Star for gallantry. After his retirement in 1904 he taught French, studied strategy, and wrote books. His *Principles of Strategy* was reprinted as late as 1968.[33]

Victorio, the Apache who had bedevilled Mexico and the Southwest for so long, was finally killed in Mexico on October 29, 1880. The fight on January 29, 1881, against the remnants of his band was the last Indian battle fought on Texas soil.

Fort Stockton, having outlived its purpose, was abandoned in 1886. The town remains, now a community of 8,524.* Like so many frontier communities, it never achieved the large-scale development and population dreamed of in the heyday of expansion. Today Fort Stockton has modest tourist attractions, among them a larger-than-life statue of a roadrunner and "Historic Fort Stockton"—a few original buildings, some that have been reconstructed, and the old fort cemetery. The *Texas State Travel Guide* notes that the birth and death dates on the gravestones here show that few people lived beyond the age of forty, an "indication of hardships among those who opened and settled this harsh country."[34]

And Clous. Three years after the Geddes case he served as the judge advocate in a court-martial that would live on in history, the trial of the first black graduate of West Point and first black army officer, Lieutenant Henry Ossian Flipper. While Flipper had been acting commissary of subsistence at Fort Davis, a sum of government money in his charge disappeared, and he was tried for embezzlement

---

*According to the 1990 census.

and conduct unbecoming (because of misleading statements he made about the money). Flipper believed that a cabal of prejudiced white officers had taken the money, a hypothesis that seems plausible but could not be proved. Although no one thought he had actually embezzled the missing funds, Flipper was found guilty of prevaricating about the incident and was cashiered—a harsh penalty since there were instances of admitted white embezzlers in the Army who had received lesser punishment. The case lived on as an example of racism in the American military until its final disposition in 1999.*[35]

Clous's rise was steady, if not spectacular. From 1886 to 1890, he served as assistant judge advocate general, the next in line to head the Judge Advocate General's office. Then he was an instructor at West Point from 1890 to 1895. At the very end of his career, when he had reached mandatory retirement age, he was appointed Judge Advocate General for a few days so that he could retire from that position. He died in 1908 at the age of seventy-one.[36]

For a man as methodically ambitious and as "zealous" as John Clous, not attaining the highest position in his field until it meant nothing more than a few days served to inflate his pension must have been a cruel disappointment.

In Clous's voluminous army file there is nothing for the year 1879.

---

*Flipper died in 1940. In 1976 the Army overturned his dishonorable discharge. In 1999 he was completely exonerated by presidential action.

EPILOGUE:
INCEST AND JUSTICE

A Scots gentleman named Bell Macdonald who subscribed to papers from all over the British Isles between 1839 and 1862 amassed a nine-million-word collection of clippings related to police and trial accounts. In addition to violent crime, these newspaper stories enshrine "a compendium of vice, including seduction, rape, adultery, transvestitism, illegal abortion, prostitution, bigamy, sadism, and indecent exposure."[1] Everything but incest. Yet at the same time, the practice flourished in nineteenth-century pornography: "The violation of man's sacred taboo, especially on the part of virile father and pubescent daughter, offers dependable pairings sure to keep the reader's interest at a high pitch."[2] But not until the 1970s, almost a century after the Geddes court-martial, did incest begin to appear in public with increasing frequency: on the criminal court docket, in scholarly investigation, and in a spate of books and articles, both popular and learned. Most state statutes against incest received their current formulation in the 1970s.[3]

Until then, incest was generally brought up and dismissed as the supreme taboo of humanity. In Peter Gay's words, "civilization . . . is among other things a moat against incest."[4] But however prohibited in practice, incest has mystified and provoked the attention of numerous fields of inquiry from anthropology to psychoanalysis. It has been theoretically explained in countless ways, although the prominent sociobiologist Edward O. Wilson wrote in 1983 that "to a large degree the taboo has defeated all such attempts to understand it."[5]

Historically, in the European tradition incest was a matter for ecclesiastical courts, a sin rather than a crime. This attitude on the part of the state conformed both to the conception of patriarchy that had evolved in Western societies and to the Biblical tradition in which the father's power over the child is absolute. Modern law has inexorably reduced this power: in our society today a man who intended to sacrifice his child because God told him to do so would be treated for mental illness rather than lauded for religious devotion. And slowly but surely, remedies have come into being for groups formerly denied redress by law—among them, women and children.

Where the Bible speaks explicitly on the subject of sexual relations, Leviticus 18, it addresses men throughout as those who control sexual relations. Only once is a woman mentioned as an agent, although here, too, the admonition is delivered to men as those who are responsible for the sexual behavior of women: "Neither shall any woman stand before a beast to lie down thereto."[6] The chapter first issues a general prohibition against a man's approach "to any that is near of kin to him," and then goes on to proscribe a large number of relationships, many of which—like those by marriage—are not blood kin, but which in terms of family harmony it seems sensible to rule sexually out of bounds:

> Thou shalt not uncover the nakedness of thy daughter in law: she *is* thy son's wife; thou shalt not uncover her nakedness.
>
> Thou shalt not uncover the nakedness of thy brother's wife: it *is* thy brother's nakedness.[7]

To ensure communal harmony, "thy neighbor's wife" is also forbidden, as is a male partner or an animal. Strikingly absent from the long and intricate list of forbidden sexual partners is a man's daughter.

Dr. Judith Herman conjectures that this omission speaks to the assumption that female sexuality is a male possession. A man is forbidden to have sex with his daughter-in-law because she belongs to his son and with his brother's wife because she belongs to his brother. But the unmarried daughter "belongs to the father alone. Though the incest taboo forbids him to make sexual use of his daughter, no particular man's rights are offended, should the father choose to disregard this rule." No man, she concludes, "is in a position to challenge a father's power over his daughters."[8]

Incest has always tended to be deeply buried within the family, more hidden than other sexual relationships and other familial matters of ecclesiastical concern such as marrying outside the faith. How seriously or how often a young woman's surrogate father, the church, was willing to step in and challenge a father's power over her is far from clear, but the notorious case of Beatrice Cenci at the end of the sixteenth century would not have offered much hope to incest victims of an earlier age. Count Francesco Cenci was archetypal in his evil, a Roman noble with a long record of acts of violence and two imprisonments—one for blasphemy, the other for sodomy.[9] Yet when his abused daughter conspired with other members of her family to kill him, the Pope was more concerned about the challenge to paternal authority than the crime that provoked the murder. The twenty-two-year-old Beatrice was tortured to extract a confession, tried, and condemned to death. She was beheaded.[10]

Sigmund Freud, who not long after the Geddes case called the attention of Western culture to the relationship between sexual behavior and psychology, originally believed his female patients who accused their fathers of incest. He later abandoned the idea to the extent that in 1916 he made an emphatic blanket assertion about girls who identified their fathers as seducers: "There can be no doubt either of the imaginary nature of the accusation or of the motive that has led to it."[11]

The state's record has not been notably better. A standard legal reference book, John Henry Wigmore's *Evidence in Trials at Common Law,* advances the premise that women and girls are likely to lie in making sexual accusations.[12] First published in 1904, *Evidence* has had at least eighteen editions and is still used today in spite of its extreme bias. Female complainants, Wigmore writes, should automatically undergo psychiatric evaluation, a process that he makes clear will treat them with hostility:

> Modern psychiatrists have amply studied the behavior of errant young girls and women coming before the courts in all sorts of cases. Their psychic complexes are multifarious, distorted partly by inherent defects, partly by diseased derangements or abnormal instincts, partly by bad social environment, partly by temporary physiological or emotional conditions. *One form taken by these complexes is that of contriving false charges of sexual offenses against men.*[13] [my emphasis]

As Dr. Herman observes, in support of his position Wigmore was willing to do some lying himself:

> Where . . . published case reports suggested the possibility of real sexual abuse, Wigmore, like Freud, falsified or omitted the evidence. For example, in his discussion of incest, Wigmore cited case

reports of two girls, ages seven and nine, who accused their fathers of sexual assault. In both cases, the original clinical reports documented the fact that the children had vaginal infections. . . . This and other corroborating evidence was systematically omitted in Wigmore's presentation, and the cases were discussed as examples of pathological lying in children.[14]

Herman concludes, somberly, that Wigmore's supposedly fact-based views "remained unchallenged for decades in the legal literature, and still retain great prestige and influence in the courtroom."[15]

Assistant Inspector General Absalom Baird, charged by the General of the Army with investigating Captain Geddes after his first conviction was overturned, was akin to Wigmore in seeing such matters through a veil of prejudice that all but ruled out the possibility of incest. Like most people of his time and much later, he would have been shocked and horrified to learn that very young children can be victims of parental sexual abuse or that, as one researcher wrote in 1990, "among women, incest is so common as to be epidemic."[16] This was not knowledge that society was eager to embrace since it placed corruption in the bosom of the primary social unit, the family, and identified the agent of this corruption as the father.

Everything conspires to deny credibility to an accusation of incest. Since it is a family crime, it exists within the private sphere where witnesses are rare. Family members who know have strong motives to conceal this quintessentially guilty knowledge: both their own implication and the scandal that would descend on guilty and innocent alike continue to be powerful inducements to silence, as well as the likely dissolution of the family that would follow such exposure and its attendant economic upheaval.

In the discussion of a bill to protect children from parental cruelty, one English legislator acknowledged that the evils addressed were "enormous and indisputable," but, he went on to say, "they are of so private, internal, and domestic a character as to be beyond the reach of legislation."[17] As late as 1971, Robert Roberts wrote of the slum neighborhood in which he grew up that everyone knew what houses harbored incestuous relationships, "but I don't recall a single prosecution: strict public silence saved the miscreants from the rigours of the law."[18]

Incest was and remains such a deep-seated and universal taboo that the majority of Andrew Geddes's countrymen preferred to believe—*regardless of evidence*—that it simply did not occur, or if it did occur, it occurred elsewhere, perhaps among uncivilized peoples on the other side of the globe or the ignored underclass of urban ghettos, those beings that so many native-born Americans found so different from themselves. Throughout the nineteenth century researchers were documenting "the prevalence of incest among the poor," but neither the topic nor the word ever appeared in the press.[19]

Such things happened, it was beginning to be said, only among the urban underclass, where an entire family might occupy only one room. Orleman and his daughter sharing a bedroom might have seemed strange to middle-class Americans of 1879, but it would not have suggested a comparison with the crowded conditions of city tenements. The class difference was too overwhelming: Orleman was an army officer, and his daughter was convent educated, a girl who read literature and played the piano.

Society seemed to collude with the guilty in agreeing that the public was better off not knowing: the word *pollution* had been used by more than one critic to characterize Harriet Beecher Stowe's accusation of Lord Byron. In the late nineteenth century, a well-bred person would never entertain ideas about incest since, given the unlikelihood of its actually taking place, any such thought would indicate a morbid imagination.[20]

While there is no one type of incestuous father, the clinical studies that have been ongoing since the 1950s have suggested some characteristics that could readily apply to Henry Louis Orleman. A career military officer, born in Germany, he might well have been an authoritarian patriarch: the father who rules his family with an iron hand is a staple of incest literature.[21] Such fathers rarely have to coerce their daughters physically because the daughters are cowed and anxious to begin with. They fear the father's desertion of the family and its consequences, for which they would feel responsible if they opposed their father's wishes or published his advances.

One researcher who studied six military men who were incestuous fathers even concluded that incest was a strategy on the victim's part to preserve a family threatened by dissolution.[22] Lillie had confided in Geddes, he said, that her father had made various threats—among them, violence to himself and to her and desertion of the family. Lillie was also the oldest daughter, a typical attribute of incest victims.[23] Another consequence she feared—rightly, as modern investigators have also confirmed—was her father's turning to his next youngest daughter for sexual gratification.[24]

Researchers have noted, incidentally, that incestuous families have a "surprisingly large number of children."[25] Orleman, as Lillie confessed, had difficulty supporting his family of eight children, but as the family provider, he nevertheless might have demanded more attention and care than the mother of such a large brood could give him. A sense of being neglected by their wives is common among incestuous fathers. Mothers in these families appear to be "overburdened, and unable to protect their daughters or exert a restraining influence on their husbands."[26] This might be an accurate description of Mrs. Orleman since Lillie told Geddes that her mother knew, but that whenever she and her mother threatened to expose her father, he threatened in turn to abandon the family. Mrs. Orleman was also a native of Germany; thus she, too, had been acculturated into a strong form of patriarchy.

Orleman had physically isolated Lillie from her mother and younger siblings by taking her with him to various army postings while the family remained elsewhere. This in itself would have been frowned upon by late-nineteenth-century advice books for mothers, which stressed the need for maternal supervision during adolescence.[27] Medical authorities of the time also emphasized the formative importance of this period in a girl's life.[28]

In all outward respects, as a number of witnesses testified, the Orleman family was perfectly conventional. In our own time, when far more bureaucratic entities exist to channel societal scrutiny than existed in nineteenth-century Texas, an incestuous family still seems like any other family from the outside: for the most part the family is unknown to "mental health services, social agencies, or the police."[29] The father who terrorizes within the family circle may seem "sympathetic, even admirable" to outsiders.[30] Captain Noel Lustig's study of the six military men who committed incest describes them as "strongly motivated to maintain a facade of role competence as the family patriarch in the eyes of society."[31] They succeeded in this goal. Of one subject, who was brought to trial for allegedly raping his eight-year-old daughter, Lustig writes that "during the trial his associates rose to his defense and character witnesses were uniformly and emphatically flattering despite the character of his alleged crime."[32] This held true for Orleman. His army file was full of letters that professed him to be "a gentleman in every respect, and a very efficient and capable officer."[33]

Baird's report refers to Orleman as "a man of little force or energy of character and lacking in bodily strength," a description obtained from people Baird interviewed rather than firsthand.[34]

Just as Clous had suggested in the trial that a partially paralyzed man could not have been responsible for the "scuffling" Michael Houston said he heard, so Baird's characterization was meant to establish that Orleman did not have the physical or mental qualities to commit incest. Present-day research suggests just the opposite, that passivity and a feeling of inadequacy are often found in incestuous fathers.[35] Such men may be weak in their relations with the outside world while maintaining patriarchal dominance within the family. Orleman had reasons to feel inadequate in the late 1870s: he had a large family that drained his resources and no hope of earning more because of the scarcity of opportunities for promotion in the frontier army; with the diminishing of the Indian threat, the possibility of military glory receded, and in the immediate past Orleman had been plagued by a persistent ailment that had reduced his vision and incapacitated him for a year. He was on the verge of retiring from active duty for reasons of health.

Lillie had told Geddes that her father's sexual demands were constant, even during her "sickness": "She told me that whenever he was with her it seemed impossible for him to let her alone." On the strength of this particular, Orleman may have belonged to that subgroup of incestuous fathers who are hypersexual.[36] As a man of only thirty-eight in 1879, he was still likely to have had a vigorous sexual appetite, but he was separated from his wife for long periods of time.

Lillie's desperate attempts to end the incestuous relationship with her father are also in keeping with what clinicians have discovered. In Herman's study *no* such relationship was ended by the father.[37]

One aspect of Orleman's treatment of his daughter seems at first glance unusual. Whereas daughters involved in incestuous relationships in our society are often made to feel special by their fathers and are wooed with presents and privileges, Orleman apparently employed little ceremony with Lillie. In the conversation allegedly overheard by Michael Houston, when Lillie upbraided her father for using her like a woman of the street rather than a daughter, Orleman appeared unmoved. Geddes reported that Lillie had told him that her father had often compared sleeping with her to sleeping with a side of bacon, "her father saying to her that he would as soon sleep with a side of bacon with a hole in it as with her." This coarse remark is of a piece with his commenting on the size of her leg in front of Friedlander and with the rest of the overheard conversation in which Orleman used crude language to assail Lillie about other men.

Such behavior could have been more of the same patriarchal attitude of female commodification that made it possible for Orleman to commit incest in the first place. It might also have reflected a particular hostility toward women. Some clinical studies have found that incestuous fathers come from a background of childhood maternal abandonment or neglect with a consequent negative reaction that in adult life settles first upon the wife and then upon the daughter.[38]

Had Andrew Geddes followed the Stowe-Byron scandal of 1869–70, he might have concluded, ominously for his own case, that the Anglo-American world regarded publicity about incest as worse than the crime itself. The most extreme view of that case expressed disbelief that incest had been committed at all and condemned both Lady Byron and Harriet Beecher Stowe for their parts in disseminating such a monstrous charge.

Although countless books and articles have now been written about it, and all states have statutes against it, at the beginning of a new millennium incest still remains relatively unpunished, not because penalties do not exist but because victims often refuse to testify, or the crime is uncovered long after it has been committed. In 1879, Lieutenant Orleman was vindicated by the military judicial system and remained a member of the Army in good standing. His accuser's career and reputation were irrevocably ruined.

Officers were by definition gentlemen, a concept that yoked together a buried class marker and an overt ideal of behavior. The gentleman supposedly followed the code of behavior of the "gently born," but beneath the accretion of class lay a principle of gender. A man behaved in a certain way, summed up by the popular nineteenth-century adjective *manly*. When Judge Advocate Clous accused stage driver Michael Houston of receiving money for his testimony, Houston responded in language that invoked this principle: "I am not that kind of a man, to be bribed by Mr. Friedlander or any other man." At the other end of the scale, when Lillie told Geddes that she feared her father would kill her and himself, Geddes replied, "He is not that kind of a man—a man that would act towards his own daughter as he has done towards you has not the courage or manliness enough to shoot anybody."

The trial of Andrew Geddes centered on the question of who was guilty of ungentlemanly acts: was Geddes a would-be seducer and abductor of a fellow officer's daughter or was that officer an incestuous father? The court answered the question one way; history, I believe, must render another judgment. It must also cast a colder eye on the concept of the officer and gentleman than the military writer who identified it with all the virtues—generosity, unselfishness, works of chivalry. As officers and gentlemen, one man sexually abused his daughter, another seduced other men's wives, and many others closed their minds to evidence and reason. General Sherman, the Army's most powerful officer and gentleman, threw aside the scrupulous review of his institution's highest judge in order to pursue Geddes relentlessly. Sherman's example belies his ringing defense of the Constitution, which serves as this book's epigraph, and reminds us that any governing document or code of justice is only as good as the human beings who administer it.

What is most disturbing about this miscarriage of justice is the apparent sincerity of those who upheld Orleman and condemned Geddes. It was a simple case for them: a man who could be labelled a "vile seducer" brought a terrible charge against another officer, merely—it seemed—to gratify his own immoral appetites. Geddes's past, and the gynecological examination of Lillie Orleman, convicted Geddes, but had the captain lived an exemplary life the result would have been the same. A stronger motive led the court to accept uncritically the flimsy story of the father and daughter: the desire to preserve their idea of fatherhood as beneficent and incest as both unspeakable and unimaginable.

APPENDIXES

NOTES

BIBLIOGRAPHY

INDEX

APPENDIX A

Ranks of Commissioned Officers in the United States Army,

from Highest to Lowest

Major General
Brigadier General
Colonel
Lieutenant Colonel
Major
Captain
First Lieutenant
Second Lieutenant

APPENDIX B

The Baird Report

Headqrs. Mil. Div. of the Mo.
Inspector General's Office
Chicago, May 1880.
To the Adjutant General of the Division

Sir:

I have the honor to return herewith the papers referred to me from your office on March 12th. relative to charges preferred against Captain & Brevet Major Andrew Geddes, 25th Infantry, by the Colonel of his regiment, Colonel George S. Andrews—"for conduct unbecoming an officer and a gentleman": and "perjury to the prejudice of good order and military discipline." In this connection, I was ordered to visit Fort Stockton and other points in Texas, in order to ascertain for the information of the General of the Army whether the charges could probably be proved if the case should be brought to trial.

In returning them, I have to report that I went first to San Antonio, Texas, in order to learn something of the case which appeared to have grown out of a previous trial of Capt. Geddes, but of which trial I had no official or other information beyond that contained in the papers given to me. From that point I proceeded to Fort Stockton and ultimately to Fort Davis, and I returned by the same route.

I obtained important information at the Department Headquarters, and I had interviews with officers having knowledge of the facts involved both at Fort Stockton and Fort Davis. I caused Captain Geddes to be summoned to Fort Stockton to meet me, and I there gave him copies of the charges, and invited him to submit any statement in reply that he might choose to make. My letter to him and his letters in reply are enclosed, and I invite attention to them.

I examined no witnesses for the reasons, first,—that my instructions gave me no authority to administer an oath, and second,—that any testimony I might take would be of no value on a trial of the case; besides which, it might be regarded as objectionable by one side of [sic] the other to tamper with witnesses by an examination of them in advance of a trial.

The information obtained came mostly from officers having a general knowledge of circumstances—such as is generally made the ground for preferment of charges and a trial. It is my belief that every specification and each charge against Captain Geddes is true, and that they can be proved to be so to the satisfaction of any impartial Court without great effort in collecting the evidence.

And in consideration of the enormity of the crime involved in the subject matter of the original accusations made against Lieutenant Orleman by Captain Geddes—that of incest by a father with his daughter—I do not think that a trial can be avoided, or that public sentiment, so far as the best people of the Army are concerned, will be satisfied until the truth or falsity of the accusation is pronounced upon by an official tribunal, and the criminal punished with all the severity due to his crime. The matter of cost in such a case should not I think be considered.

In order that the General may the more readily decide whether the case should be brought to trial or not, there are a few incidents in the past history of some of the persons involved, which are not matters of proof, but only such as go to give to an individual a reputation in the community in which he lives—that it seems well that he should know. Captain Geddes, as appears from the Army Register, was born in Canada, but entered the Volunteer service of the United States in 1861 from the State of Iowa, as Captain of the 8th. Iowa Vols. He was afterwards appointed a lieutenant in the 4th U.S. Infy. and later transferred to the 25th Infy., still as Lieutenant. He served in the Western Armies, and received a brevet of Major for services about Vicksburg. He says that he was but 15 years of age when first made an officer, and that he has held a commission ever since. General Ord, his present Department Commander, and other officer[s] who know him, esteem highly his activity, enterprise, and efficiency as a soldier. Genl. Ord regards him as more valuable for field duty than almost any other officer of his grade, and has no prejudice against him. But Capt. Geddes appears to be according to reports a man totally destitute of any sense of right and wrong, or of moral propriety as regards casual intercourse between men and women in the society into which his commission as an officer of the army has admitted him.

It is said that his name appeared disreputably in the public prints in connection with that of Mrs. Baily, wife of Surgeon Baily of the Army, whose trial a few years ago brought great scandal on the service.

It is also said that about eight years ago he married, under threats of personal violence from her male relatives, a young woman of Mississippi or Alabama whom he had seduced. She is now his wife but is not with him at his post.

It is furthermore openly asserted that at the post of Fort Davis he formed an intimacy with the wife of a citizen in some civil employment of the Government living close upon the confines of the post, which intimacy led to such scandalous comment in the garrison and in the neighborhood that coming to the knowledge of the woman's husband, he directed a loaded shot-gun at Capt. Geddes' head and discharged it, and the life of the latter was saved only by the intervention of a bystander who threw up the muzzle of the gun.

So far as I can learn, it was at Fort Clark, Texas, that his intimacy with Mrs. McLaughlen, the wife of the Lieutenant Colonel of the 10th Cavalry, stationed at the same post began. She is described as a woman of culture belonging to a family of high social standing in the City of New York, but no longer in the bloom of youth, formerly rather restrained and prudish in her intercourse with gentlemen, but Capt. Geddes soon succeeded in bringing both her name and his own into notoriety by the scandalous comments which their behaviour towards each other excited in the garrison.

These relations between them were afterwards continued at Fort Stockton, where their most intimate associates were other persons both male and female of tarnished reputation, and the conduct of this set was such as to draw a social line across the garrison, separating from them all who cherished a regard for purity of life and a fair reputation.

This line of social separation extended itself through other neighboring posts, to the great injury of the service, and the name of Fort Stockton became a bye word, a shame and a reproach throughout the Department of Texas.

In the end Col. McLaughlen was compelled to take his wife back and deliver her over to her relatives in New York, where she soon gave birth to a child of which he is not the father while every circumstance seems to fix the paternity upon Capt. Geddes.

It was during this period of the intercourse between Mrs. McLaughlen and Capt. Geddes at Fort Stockton that his attention seems to have been drawn toward the young Mexican girl, Josephine Nevares, a servant in the family of the post trader and his wife highly reputable.

From a statement made by this girl, it would appear that Mrs. McLaughlen assisted in procuring her for Capt. Geddes, which probably it was not very difficult to do, although there is every reason to believe that she was perfectly pure until he debauched her.

The last person so far as I have learned towards whom the lustful propensities of Capt. Geddes directed him was Miss Lilly Orleman, the daughter of Lt. L. H. Orleman, an officer of the 10th Cavalry stationed with him at Fort Stockton, the two officers occupying adjoining sets of quarters in the same adobe building.

According to the Army Register, Lieut. Orleman is a native of Germany who entered the service of the United States as a private of New York Volunteers in 1862 and served until 1865, having in the meantime become a Captain.

Soon after his discharge, he was appointed lieutenant of the 10th Cavalry, in which regiment he continued to serve until retired in November of last year.

He is described as a man of little force or energy of character and lacking in bodily strength.

Having a wife and several children whom he could not well care for in the quarters to which his rank entitled him at his post, he located his family at Austin, Texas, but took with him this one daughter, a girl between 17 and 18 years of age at the date of the present trouble. Having but one sleeping apartment they occupied it in common—the position of the bed of each is shown on a diagram given in evidence on the first trial. That this fact of a father sleeping in the same chamber with his daughter already on the verge of womanhood should excite remark is not strange, but it is natural that the father would be the last one to perceive the change from childhood to maturity in his own child, and so far as I can learn the only persons who did comment on this particular matter are persons talked about as loose in their own lives and their own conduct.

Upon the presumed want of force of character in Lieut. Orleman, and confidence in his own power, Capt. Geddes appears to have calculated in his approaches toward the daughter.

I invite the attention of the General to two statements from Miss Orleman, copies of which are forwarded.

It is evident from these that the girl had passed completely under the influence of Capt. Geddes and was mentally in his power. All that was wanting was a favorable opportunity in order to accomplish her ruin.

APPENDIX B

Lieut. Orleman, in spite of his presumed stupidity, was sharp enough to think that the intimacy of a married man with his young daughter was not proper, and the opportunity sought for by Capt. Geddes was prevented.

Geddes then applied to the Department Commander for a leave of absence on the ground of severe illness in his family living East of the Mississippi, and obtained it while the girl got her father's consent to return to her mother, the two having arranged to leave the post on the same stage. When Lieut. Orleman discovered this, he prohibited his daughter from going, and thus frustrated Capt. Geddes went boldly to Lieut. Orleman and charged him with having long lived in a state of incest with his daughter and threatened that if he Geddes was not permitted to rescue the girl and take her to her mother, he would make an exposure.

There was no threat of exposure, but an implied promise to suppress everything, provided Lieut. Orleman would deliver his daughter over to Geddes in order that he might take her from the post and rescue her from the unhallowed relations in which she was compelled to live.

Contrary to expectation Lieut. Orleman, stunned and stupefied by the frightful accusation, went at once to the commanding officer, told him of it, and demanded an investigation. An inquiry was ordered, but the commanding officer for reasons of his own permitted Geddes to depart on his leave. He arrived at San Antonio and at once engaged the service of a lawyer, although there was no accusation against him, and he delayed there so long as to attract the attention of the Department Commander, who had granted his leave in consideration of severe illness requiring his presence with his family East of the Mississippi.

He explained to General Ord that he was awaiting intelligence from Fort Stockton, but soon after left for his home.

Report of the inquiry at Fort Stockton began to arrive, and at the same time the lawyer of Capt. Geddes so pressed himself upon General Ord that the General was forced to say that any communication Capt. Geddes might wish to make must be official and in writing.

Following this came the sworn statement of Capt. Geddes, specifying the circumstances of the criminal acts charged against Lieut. Orleman.

Orleman in turn appeared before a retiring board at San Antonio for examination as to retirement, his breaking down in health being unquestionably hastened by the charges of crime against him made by Capt. Geddes.

General Ord, unwilling to overlook these accusations against Orleman and not disputing the possibility of their truth, determined that he should not be placed on the retired list while they were hanging over him. He accordingly sent the affidavit of Capt. Geddes and the other reports to the Board and directed them to be considered.

After a full investigation, the Board recommended that Capt. Geddes should be tried for false swearing in the matter, and the President of the Retiring Board, Colonel Andrews, who is also the Colonel of Capt. Geddes' regiment, preferred the charges.

A long and tedious trial before an impartial Court ensued, and the young girl, Miss Orleman, was subjected during a long examination to all the cruel torture which unscrupulous lawyers employ to shield guilty clients from just punishment.

The result was that Captain Geddes was found guilty on each of the three charges on which he was tried, and was sentenced to be cashiered and to be imprisoned in a penitentiary for a period of three years.

Such was the judgement of the second body of officers who inquired into the facts of this case, fully sustaining the opinion of the Retiring Board.

Captain Geddes' lawyer made no defense before the Court, to which, had he done so, the Judge Advocate might have replied. The Court had granted him access to the record during the progress of the trial, so that he might be fully aware of what he had to answer without the trouble of keeping a record himself. This privilege he failed to avail himself of until after the case was closed, the sentence fixed, and the proceedings, certified to by the President and Judge Advocate, were forwarded to the Department Commander. Then an application to see the record was made and General Ord refused to grant it. The lawyer followed it to Washington and there according to his statement in the Office of the Judge Advocate General the record was placed in his hands and he was given facilities to reply to it.

This reply, a printed document of 81 pages full of falsehoods, and accompanied by several ex parte statements from officers as to the good character of Capt. Geddes, in which all allusion to his moral habits is avoided, went before what is called "the revising authority" along with the record, and according to Capt. Geddes had its weight with the "revising authority" when preparing an opinion for the guidance of the revising authority on final action.

G.C.M. Order No. 66, series of 1879, shows that the findings and sentence were disapproved on the ground of certain rulings of the Court thought to be erroneous, and in no way effecting [sic] the facts in issue. There was barely an expression of doubt by the "revising authority" as to the findings being fully sustained by the evidence.

Thus this grave case, in which one of two officers must have been guilty of infamous crime, was disposed of, and the one pronounced guilty by two sets of officers in succession, was restored to duty without censure, and the other officer after the investigation was ended was thought worthy to be placed on the retired list.

Public sentiment in the military circles to which Capt. Geddes returned, and indeed in the Army generally, was not satisfied, so that the Department Commander found it advisable to isolate Captain Geddes' Company in order to remove him from contact with others who were unwilling to be associated with him. Of this Capt. Geddes complains as a grievance.

The outcome of this trial was not satisfactory to the officers in the Department of Texas, since it restored to association with them a man pronounced worthy of a criminal's cell, and the charges now under consideration are the result.

The important charge is that of perjury in having sworn falsely in his own defense in the previous trial, and the fundamental facts are the same that were investigated on the previous trial.

With regard to this charge, a lawful oath was regularly administered to him, and he testified knowingly and willingly in a matter material to the issue then being tried. The only question to be determined is whether his testimony was true or false. If true, then Lieut. Orleman should be put out of the Army and turned over to the civil authorities for punishment. If false, Capt. Geddes deserves the severest punishment.

On one side there will be the oath and testimony of Capt. Geddes. In denial of this, the evidence of Lieut. Orleman and Miss Orleman. Then the plan of the building will be exhibited to show the improbability if not absolute impossibility of Capt. Geddes having heard the conversation between Lieut. Orleman and his daughter which he claims to have heard, or seen what he claims to have seen. If he saw what he relates, he must have made an eavesdropper of himself, going far out of his way to put himself at the window of Lieut. Orleman's bedroom; and even then few believe in the possibility of his obtaining the view he claims to have had. These will be the questions for the Court to decide upon.

Beyond this there will be the testimony of two distinguished Surgeons of the Army, whose reputation either as men of medical experience or as gentlemen of integrity is not surpassed, asserting that, at the time of Captain Geddes' trial, Miss Orleman carried on her person the most undoubted evidence of her virginity, and that she has never had connection with any man.

The theory of the defense on the trial was that Lieut. Orleman and his daughter had commenced this vile intercourse when she was but 13 years of age, and that it had been kept up during 5 years until she was 18, and while the one act of intercourse which Capt. Geddes says he witnessed might have left no marks which experts could detect, it is not possible that doctors could be deceived had these relations been continued for a length of time.

This will be the matter to be decided on so far as the charge of perjury is concerned.

The accusation of adultery with Mrs. McLaughlen I advised should be charged as conduct to the prejudice of military discipline, and not as conduct unbecoming an officer and a gentleman, for the latter charge is often regarded as covering only some few crimes of a very degrading character, and not as embracing all the acts which an officer should not commit, and a gentleman would not. Col. Andrews failed to see that a majority of the officers of a Court might change the finding and thus weaken the force of the case, and he declined to modify the charge.

As Col. McLaughlen was and is the person most injured in this affair, it seemed to me that the General might wish to know his wishes in regard to having it referred to a Court Martial for trial. With this in view, I went to Fort Davis to confer with Col. McLaughlen. I found that he had not sought redress for his wrongs before the Civil Tribunals, and that in consideration of the feelings of his wife's relatives, he declined to become prosecutor before a Military Court, so long as she should remain quietly with her people and deported herself properly; but he was most anxious that Capt. Geddes should be brought to trial by some one else, and was desirous of telling all that he knew regarding the case.

His testimony will show conclusively that the child to which Mrs. McLaughlen gave birth after reaching New York was not his, and he will testify to many circumstances convincing him that Capt. Geddes is its father. He will likewise testify that his wife, Mrs. McLaughlen, did not dispute or deny that Geddes was the parent when he charged it upon her that such was the case.

Numerous witnesses can be found to testify to this improper and suspicious intimacy between Capt. Geddes and Mrs. McLaughlen. One of these, a white woman, Mrs. Stewart, laundress in Capt. Bentyoni's [sic] company and married to a colored sergeant of the company.

Capt. Geddes, anticipating that this woman would be a witness against him, asked me to examine certain citizen friends of his—one of them the local judge—as to her character and want of credibility on the ground that she was living in adultery with a negro. This I learned to be untrue, as the woman had been married twice to this man, once by a Protestant preacher and once by a Catholic priest with the consent of the Captain of the company. Since my return from Texas, Captain Geddes informs me in a letter that she has been indicted in the Texas Courts for miscegenation, which if true, has been done without doubt at his instance to break down her testimony as a witness against him and Mrs. McLaughlen.

The additional charge of conduct unbecoming an officer and gentleman in having seduced the Mexican Josephine Nevares, I likewise recommended should be charged as to the prejudice of discipline, as the criminal intercourse of an officer with any female belonging to a household in the garrison—even the servant of the trader—must be destructive of discipline and order. The accusation that he made use of violence in the specification does not seem to me to comport well with the term seduce; and as the girl is now married to a soldier, I would recommend that this charge be dropped, leaving the girl to find her redress in Civil Courts, unless it be thought desirable to try it in order more clearly to display the character of Capt. Geddes as a libertine.

> Most respectfully
> Your obedient servant,
> (signed)
> Brevet Major General, Asst. Inspr. Genl.

APPENDIX C

Documents Relating to the Reinstatement of Andrew Geddes

1. Petition of Officers of the Twenty-fifth U.S. Infantry Against the Reinstatement of Andrew Geddes

Fort Randall D.T.
January 30, 1882

To

The President of the United States
Washington, D.C.
(Through Channels)

Sir

Having been informed through the public press that Andrew Geddes has attempted to be re-instated in his commission in the Army, we, the undersigned, respectfully ask that before any action in his favor be taken the following facts be considered.

Andrew Geddes during his career in the Army was dismissed from the service by sentence of General Courts Martial in 1872, again in 1879, and in 1880. (See G.C.A.G.O., A.G.O. No. 28 of 1872, No. 66 of 1879, and No. 64 of 1880)

To again restore him to the service would be an encouragement to the vicious, and a great injustice to the honorable gentlemen who have to serve with him, and to the soldiers who have to serve under him.

Owing to his scandalously unusual conduct, only a small part of which is recorded in the proceedings before the General Court Martial published in 1879 no officer in the Army could permit the ladies of his family to in any way recognize Andrew Geddes, and a majority of the officers would hold no other but necessary official relations with him.

That such conditions cannot be otherwise but to the disadvantage of the service cannot be denied.

That the sentences of Courts Martial are just and proper, when resulting in the removal from the service of the offender, the sequels of the restoration to it, by legislative and executive action, of Sam. K. Thompson, 25th Infantry, T. J. Spencer and Geo. A. Armes, 10th Cavalry, E. R. Clark, 10th Infantry, and others abundantly establish, as all of these persons have again been dismissed, though some of them still hold their commissions through the intervention of executive clemency.

As the person seeking restoration makes use of everything seemingly in his favor, we take these means of respectfully inviting attention to the other side of the case.

Charles Bentzoni, Capt 25th Infantry

Geo. L. Andrews, Col. 25th Infy, Comdg Regiment

C. L. Hodges, 1Lt 25 Inf.

Henry P. Ritzius 1Lt 25 Infy

Gaines Lawson Capt 25th Infantry

H. B. Quimby, Capt 25th Infantry

D. B. Wilson, 1Lt & Adjt 25th Inf

2. Geddes's Appeal to the Congressional Committee on Military Affairs for Reinstatement

UNITED STATES DEPARTMENT OF AGRICULTURE

OFFICE OF THE CHIEF CLERK, *Washington, D.C., February, 1899.*

The Honorable COMMITTEE ON MILITARY AFFAIRS.

GENTLEMEN: I have the honor to submit the following:

I was dismissed, to date December 31, 1880, after a service of nearly nineteen years, at which time I held the rank of captain, Twenty-fifth United States Infantry, and brevet major, United States Army. During all those years I performed many and varied duties, and in all truth can say that I never failed in any respect to discharge them faithfully, zealously, capably, and to the entire satisfaction of my superiors.

I enlisted at the age of 16 in Company K, First Iowa Volunteer Infantry, in April, 1861, and served until the muster out of that regiment, the latter part of August, 1861. Was present at the battle of Wilsons Creek, Mo., and very close by General Lyon when he fell, mortally wounded, and with a few others hauled off guns of Totten's Battery (horses having been shot) at the close of that hard-fought and heroic battle. October 1, 1861, I was unanimously elected captain of Company D, Eighty Iowa Volunteer Infantry—probably the youngest officer of that rank in the United States service.

Served in that capacity for more than three years, when I was unanimously elected lieutenant-colonel of my regiment by the officers—the youngest officer of that rank in the United States service. Although there was a vacancy I could not muster in as colonel, the regiment being reduced by active and long service below the minimum required by law. Commanded regiment and took it home to Davenport, Iowa, for final pay and muster out May 6, 1866, after a service of five years. Was at Shiloh, Jackson, Vicksburg, Memphis, Spanish Fort, and many other minor engagements, and always at the front. Was several times mentioned in orders for gallantry; was a prisoner of war for more than six months and suffered unspeakable cruelty at Tuscaloosa, Ala., under Wirz, and at Macon and Madison, Ga., and in "Libby." At Madison, for attempting to escape, was threatened with death, taken to a murderer's dungeon, kept there for two weeks, and taken out in a starved and half-dead condition.

While yet in my teens was chief of ordnance of District of West Tennessee on General Washburn's staff, aide-de-camp to Gen. E. A. Carr, and several times assistant adjutant-general of division. In the regular service twice saved large commands of troops at risk of my own life, and did other perilous service.

Had five brothers in Iowa regiments, all of good and even distinguished service. In July, 1867, appointed first lieutenant in the Regular Army, and did active and serious service receiving high recommendation from commanding officers. (See Gen. William R. Shafter's letters herewith, marked "A;" Colonel Young's, Third United States Cavalry, and others, marked, respectively, "B," "C.")

My dismissal was the result of charges trumped up, without any foundation in fact, maliciously concocted, and the outcome of as despicable, unjust, relentless, and bitter a persecution as ever disgraced the annals of our Army or any other. As was said at the time, it was better to sacrifice me than give publicity to an army scandal by trying and punishing the very party who had been guilty of incest with his own daughter. I was victimized; the other (God save the mark!) honorably retired. It was an infinite, dastardly outrage.

The officer who preferred the charges against me, on which I was dismissed, threatened, after the President had disapproved the proceedings, findings, and sentence in the former case, that he would follow me until he "did me up." His charges were false and born of malice. The trial was a mockery, the result a travesty upon justice, and an indelible wrong. I was misled and curtailed in my defense. There were several witnesses whose testimony was material and pertinent; but a prominent member of the court asked if the evidence of these witnesses would be in the same line as that already in—to the effect that I was not under influence of liquor, as charged—and when the accused answered yes, he said it would only be a waste of the time of the court, and that he was satisfied. I concluded that he was satisfied of my innocence and that the other members were so, too; therefore did not call these material witnesses. This evidence would have established the proof of my innocence beyond any question; it would have given an overwhelming preponderance in my behalf. I consider and submit that this was a great wrong. After sentence was promulgated I secured the affidavits of these witnesses, which are herewith submitted, marked "K"—eleven depositions.

This court was bent on conviction. Congressman Perkins's paper at the time gave as an item that members of the court in Sioux City, en route to Yankton, expressed the opinion that it would probably go hard with Geddes on account of a former trial in Texas. This alone disqualified them to sit on the trial. I was refused a reasonable time to secure counsel. (See Judge Shannon's letter, marked "F.")

Particular attention is called to the orders publishing the findings and sentence. Two specifications charge me with drunkenness, not only on the same day and date, but within fifteen minutes of each other; the fact being that I passed from one duty to the other in the time mentioned, barely having time to change my uniform. I was found "guilty" of the latter and "not guilty" of the former charge. The absurdity of the thing is apparent.

During these last eighteen years I have suffered under this great wrong and injustice. Not an hour or day all those years that this outrage and disgrace have not been present; not a night that I have not in prayer appealed to Him that this burning stigma might be wiped from my name. It has covered me as with a pall of blackest night. In attempts to secure honorable position it has, Banquo like, risen to thrust me back and hold me down. It broke an aged, beloved, and Christian father's heart. It has deeply hurt and pained dearly loved sisters, brothers, and friends, but, thank God, never alienated their affection and respect, for they have ever believed in my innocence, truth, and manliness. Were I gifted with the language of a Milton or Macaulay I could not express the depth of the bitter humiliation and mortification of those eighteen long, saddened, heavy-laden years. Death has taken father, mother, brothers, sisters, a son, and two lovely little daughters. I believe that an all-merciful God has sustained me with the consciousness of my innocence and truth.

I was proud of my profession. My family for generations were soldiers. From 16 to 35 I had given my every thought to love of our flag and its service. Therefore it is that I appeal to the Congress and to the President to right as far as possible this great wrong; to take away from an honored name this blot; to at least, now that I am marching the down-grade of life to the inevitable "taps," by this act of clemency, kindness, and justice make the forced march as light and easy as possible, enabling me at last to leave to wife and children a name cleared of dishonor and stain.

Had I remained in service my rank would be that of major or lieutenant-colonel, with a fair probability, considering my age, of becoming a colonel before retiring age of 64.

I also call your attention to Special Orders, No. 1, Headquarters Union Veteran Legion of the United States, herewith marked "Exhibit G."

With depth of feeling inexpressible, I appeal to you to remove this life sentence.

Very respectfully,

ANDREW GEDDES,
Chief Clerk Department of Agriculture.

3. General William Shafter's Recommendation of Geddes for Reinstatement

HEADQUARTERS DEPARTMENT OF CALIFORNIA,
San Francisco, Cal., December 24, 1897.
SIR: I understand that an effort will be made by the friends of Col. Andrew Geddes, now chief clerk, Department of Agriculture, and late captain, Twenty-fifth Infantry, for reinstatement to his former rank in the Army.

Colonel Geddes served under me and under my observation for several years in Texas, both in garrison and in the field. In the field he was one of my most trusted officers, energetic and fearless, and always ready for any duty, no matter how hazardous. On one occasion, in 1875, while scouting under my orders, he swam the Pecos when it was much swollen and then rode 60 miles to Fort Stockton to obtain imperatively needed supplies. On the same expedition, with a detachment of two companies, he followed an Indian trail from the center of the Staked Plains, near the head of Brazos River, for nearly 500 miles, and captured and killed the entire party he was pursuing when within a few miles of the Mexican border, toward which they were fleeing.

While under my command Colonel Geddes's conduct was always exemplary, and I do not hesitate to recommend him to your favorable consideration in the matter which he is about to bring up.

He claims to have been treated with great injustice, and I believe will be able to show that he has been.

He is personally well known to the Major-General Commanding the Army, under whom he served as adjutant of his regiment.

Colonel Geddes's war service is well known. He was one of the youngest officers of his grade in the Army, and, as a mere boy, served as a commissioned officer with distinction.

I am, very respectfully,

WM. R. SHAFTER,
Brigadier-General, U.S.A., Commanding Department.
THE SECRETARY OF WAR, *Washington, D.C.*

NOTES

The following abbreviations have been used in the notes:

ACP   Appointment, Commission, and Promotion
AGO   Adjutant General's Office
JAG   Judge Advocate General
NARA   National Archives and Records Administration
OR   *The War of the Rebellion: A Compilation of the Official Records of the Union and Confederate Armies*
RG   Record Group
USMA   United States Military Academy

Chapter I

1. QQ1387, JAG, General Courts Martial 1812–1938 RG 153, NARA. Geddes's statement occupies pp. 9–14. The original affidavit he submitted to General Ord is in Appendix C. Further quotations from the trial will not be identified with note numbers; all came from this transcript. Spellings of some words have been modernized.

2. William T. Generous, Jr., *Swords and Scales: The Development of the Uniform Code of Military Justice* (Port Washington, N.Y.: Kennikat Press, 1973): 8.

3. Luther C. West, *They Call It Justice* (New York: Viking Press, 1977): 17. The court for the Geddes trial was composed of seven officers. Many courts-martial had six or even five.

4. Generous, *Swords and Scales*: 8.

5. Stephen Vincent Benét, *A Treatise on Military Law and the Practice of Courts-Martial,* 6th ed. rev. (New York: D. Van Nostrand, 1868): 71.

6. West, *They Call It Justice*: 5.

7. Generous, *Swords and Scales*: 10.

8. Jack D. Foner, *The United States Soldier Between Two Wars* (New York: Humanities Press, 1970): 36.

9. *Annual Report of the Secretary of the Army for the Year 1879,* vol. 1 (Washington, D.C.: Government Printing Office, 1879): iii, 191.

10. Marcos Kinevan, *Frontier Cavalryman: Lieutenant John Bigelow with the Buffalo Soldiers in Texas* (El Paso: Texas Western Press, 1998): 78.

11. Sherman to W. S. Hancock, December 9, 1879, Sherman Papers, containers 90–91 (reel 45), no. 202. Manuscript Division, Library of Congress.

12. *A Sketch of the History and Duties of the Judge Advocate General's Department, United States Army, Washington, D.C., March 1, 1878 as prepared at the request of the Commission (of 1876) on the Reform and Reorganization of the Army, with additions* (Washington, D.C.: T. McGill, 1878): 11.

13. Garrard Glenn, *The Army and the Law* (New York: Columbia University Press, 1943): 44.

14. Secretary of War, *Annual Report, House Executive Documents,* 44th cong., 1st sess., 1 (Washington, D.C.: Government Printing Office, 1876): 123.

15. *Report of the Secretary of War, House Executive Documents,* 47th cong., 2d sess., 11 (Washington: Government Printing Office, 1883): 115–16.

16. S. J. Wright, *San Antonio de Béxar: Historical, Traditional, Legendary* (Austin: Morgan Printing Co., n.d.): 93.

17. PP2691, Court-Martial of Andrew Geddes, August 19, 1872, JAG, RG 153, NARA. Holt's report was dated September 11, 1872.

18. PP2691: Andrew Geddes to William W. Belknap, September 8, 1872.

19. Harriet Beecher Stowe, "The True Story of Lady's Byron's Life," *The Atlantic Monthly: A Magazine of Literature, Science, Art, and Politics* 24 (1869): 295–313.

20. Harriet Beecher Stowe, *Lady Byron Vindicated: A History of the Byron Controversy from Its Beginning in 1816 to the Present Time* [1870] (New York: Haskell House, 1970).

21. Alice Crozier, *The Novels of Harriet Beecher Stowe* (New York: Oxford University Press, 1969): 195.

22. Forrest Wilson, *Crusader in Crinoline: The Life of Harriet Beecher Stowe* (Philadelphia: J. B. Lippincott, 1941): 428.

23. "The True Story of Lady Byron's Life," reprinted in *Lady Byron Vindicated*: 450.

24. J. Paget, "Lord Byron and His Calumniators," *Blackwood's Edinburgh Magazine* 107 (January 1870): 138; cited in Elizabeth Ammons, ed., *Critical Essays on Harriet Beecher Stowe* (Boston: G. K. Hall, 1980): 183.

25. Justin McCarthy, "Mrs. Stowe's Last Romance," *The Independent* (August 26, 1869): 1. Cited in Ammons, *Critical Essays on Harriet Beecher Stowe*: 171.

26. "Mrs. Stowe on Lord Byron," clipping without date or place of publication preserved in Harriet Beecher Stowe's Scrapbook on the controversy, Harriet Beecher Stowe Library, Hartford, Ct.

27. *The World,* October 6, 1869, Stowe Scrapbook.

28. *Spectator,* no date; "The Byron Revelations," August 26, 1869, Stowe Scrapbook.

29. "The Byron Mystery," *Saturday Review* (September 4, 1869): 311.

30. Ammons, *Critical Essays on Harriet Beecher Stowe*: 180; cited in Joan D. Hedrick, *Harriet Beecher Stowe: A Life* (New York: Oxford University Press, 1994): 365.

31. Stowe Scrapbook.

32. James Russell Lowell to Edmund Quincy, September 15, 1869, in *New Letters of James Russell Lowell,* ed. M. A. DeWolfe Howe (New York: Harper and Brothers, 1932): 146.

33. George Curtis, "From the Editor's Easy Chair at *Harper's*: In Defense of *Lady Byron Vindicated,*" *Harper's New Monthly Magazine* 39 (1869): 767.

34. Elizabeth Cady Stanton, "The Moral of the Byron Case," *Independent* (September 9, 1869): 1; reprinted in Ammons, *Critical Essays on Harriet Beecher Stowe*: 174, 175.

35. Stanton, "The Moral of the Byron Case," in Ammons, *Critical Essays*: 175, 176.

36. Stowe, *Lady Byron Vindicated*: 162–63, 428, 343.

37. Stowe, *Lady Byron Vindicated*: 74.

38. Benita Eisler, *Byron: Child of Passion, Fool of Fame* (New York: Alfred A. Knopf, 1998): 487.

39. John S. Chapman, *Byron and the Honourable Augusta Leigh* (New Haven: Yale University Press, 1975): 215, confirms the absence of any "record that Augusta was with her husband [George Leigh] during the period of conception."

40. Phyllis Grosskurth, *Byron: The Flawed Angel* (Boston: Houghton Mifflin, 1997): 230; Byron to Lady Melbourne, April 25, 1814, in

"Wedlock's the Devil": Byron's Letters and Journals 1814–1815, ed. Leslie A. Marchand, vol. 4 (Cambridge, Mass.: Harvard University Press, 1975): 104, 99n.

41. Malcolm Elwin, *Lord Byron's Wife* (New York: Harcourt, Brace, and World, 1963): 254; Margot Strickland, *The Byron Women* (New York: St. Martin's Press, 1974): 166, 172.

42. "Mrs. Stowe's 'Vindication of Lady Byron,'" Stowe Scrapbook.

Chapter 2

1. Theodore A. Dodge, "The Battle of Chancellorsville," *Southern Historical Society Papers* 14 (1886): 277, 284, 287.

2. Dodge, "The Battle of Chancellorsville": 282; Augustus Choate Hamlin, *The Battle of Chancellorsville* (Bangor: n.p., 1896): 32.

3. Schurz to Stanton, May 18, 1863; Report of Major General Carl Schurz, May 12, 1863, cited in Hamlin, *The Battle of Chancellorsville*: 170, 168.

4. Captain Joseph B. Greenhut, OR I: vol. 31, pt. 1 (Washington: Government Printing Office, 1890): 143.

5. OR, vol. 31, pt. 1: 209.

6. Cited in Hamlin, *The Battle of Chancellorsville*: 157.

7. 0159 CB 1866*—consolidated Civil War file of L. H. Orleman, Letters Received by the Commission Branch of AGO 1863–1870, roll 286, RG 94, NARA.

8. E. H. Brininstool, "The Rescue of Forsyth's Scouts," *Collections of the Kansas State Historical Society 1926–1928,* ed. William Elsey Connelley, vol. 17: 848; Edward L. Glass, *The History of the Tenth Cavalry 1866–1921* (n.p., 1921): 16.

9. "A Terrible Experience: Pen Pictures of a Prairie Pilgrimage," by Lt. Orleman of the Tenth Cavalry, St. Louis *Daily Democrat,* January 12, 1875.

10. Orleman to Adjutant General, Department of Texas, October 28, 1877, and July 15, 1878, 0159 CB 1866*.

11. Unless otherwise indicated, information comes from the consolidated ACP file of Andrew Geddes, No. 6373, AGO, RG 94, NARA.

12. OR, I: vol. 39, pt. 1 (1892) *Reports*: 479.

13. OR, I: vol. 49, pt. 1 (1897): 268.

14. N. B. Baker to Edwin M. Stanton, April 4, 1867.

15. William Loughridge, 4th Congressional District, Iowa, to Edwin M. Stanton, March 13, 1867.

16. PP2691, JAG RG 153, NARA. All references to this court-martial are taken from the trial transcript.

17. The review, signed Bureau of Military Justice, September 11, 1872, is eleven handwritten legal-size pages, unnumbered.

18. Daniel E. Rankin to Wm. W. Belknap, September 9, 1872, ACP File of Andrew Geddes.

19. C. L. Carpenter to Wm. W. Belknap, September 5, 1872, court-martial PP2691, RG 153, NARA.

20. Andrew Geddes to William W. Belknap, September 8, 1872, in PP2691.

21. James Evetts Haley, *Fort Concho and the Texas Frontier* (San Angelo, Tex.: San Angelo Standard-Times, 1952): 235, 236.

22. Lieutenant Hans J. Gasman, entry of October 31, 1875, cited in Haley, *Fort Concho and the Texas Frontier*: 236.

23. Haley, *Fort Concho and the Texas Frontier*: 237.

24. Haley, *Fort Concho and the Texas Frontier*: 237–38.

25. In many records the name of Dr. Baily is misspelled "Bailey." I have silently corrected this in the text wherever it occurs. Baird Report (see Appendix B of this book, p. 231).

26. Court-Martial of Elisha Baily, PP1207, JAG RG 153, NARA. All citations are taken from the trial transcript, whose pages are unnumbered.

27. Testimony of James B. Burbank for the defense, twenty-second day: PP1207.

28. Exhibit FF: PP1207.

29. "Court-martial of Surgeon Elisha J. Bailey," August 13, 1870, *The Army and Navy Journal* 7 (1870): 817.

30. Deposition of Private Robert Jones, QQ1387, Box 1926.

31. Deposition of John Burton, QQ1387, Box 1926.

32. Baird Report (see Appendix B of this book, p. 232). John Bigelow, Jr., Journal, January–November 1878, John Bigelow Collection, Union College.

33. Entry of September 4, 1877, John Bigelow, Jr., Diaries, USMA Archive.

34. Entries for August 18 and August 25, John Bigelow, Jr., Journal, January–November 1878, John Bigelow Collection, Union College.

35. Entry of July 16, 1879, John Bigelow, Jr., Diaries, USMA Archive.

36. See James Morton Callahan, *American Foreign Policy in Mexican Relations* (New York: Macmillan, 1932): 278–340, for a detailed treatment of the French threat; see also George W. Grayson, *The United States and Mexico: Patterns of Influence* (New York: Praeger, 1984): 13–17; and Jasper Ridley, *Maximilian and Juárez* (New York: Ticknor & Fields, 1992).

37. House Miscellaneous Docs., 45th Cong., 2d sess., no. 64: 26; cited in Robert M. Utley, *Frontier Regulars: The United States Army and the Indian 1866–1891* (New York: Macmillan, 1974): 350.

38. Ord to E.O.C. Ord. Jr., n.d., Edward Otho Cresap Ord, 1818–1883, Correspondence and Papers, Box 9, Bancroft Library, University of California at Berkeley.

39. Letter of Ord to Pacificus Ord, May 17, 1843, Preston Collection of Ord Papers; cited in Bernarr Cresap, *Appomattox Warrior: The Story of General E.O.C. Ord* (New York: A. S. Barnes, 1981): 16.

40. Gideon Welles, *Diary of Gideon Welles, Secretary of the Navy under Lincoln and Johnson,* ed. John T. Morse, 3 vols. (Boston: Houghton Mifflin, 1911) 3: 245.

41. Ord to Pacificus Ord, February 27, 1845, Alexander Collection of Ord Papers, cited in Cresap, *Appomattox Warrior*: 20.

42. *Daily Herald,* April 18, 1856; cited in Cresap, *Appomattox Warrior*: 43.

43. Cresap, *Appomattox Warrior*: 77.

44. Ord to President Abraham Lincoln, February 19, 1864, Letters Received, Army Headquarters, 1821–1903, RG 108, NARA.

45. Grant to Charles A. Dana, August 5, 1863, Charles A. Dana Papers, Manuscript Division, Library of Congress.

46. Ord to Sherman, August 14, 1863, W. T. Sherman Papers, Box 12, Manuscript Division, Library of Congress.

47. John M. Carroll, ed., *The Black Military Experience in the American West* (New York: Liveright, 1971): 261; Cresap, *Appomattox Warrier*: 307.

48. Robert E. Denney, *The Civil War Years: A Day-by-Day Chronicle of the Life of a Nation* (New York: Sterling, 1992): 441.

49. Ord to Levi Maish, Edward S. Bragg, and Harry White (draft), February 14, 1878, Correspondence and Papers, Box 1, Outgoing Letters, 1852–1881, Bancroft Library, University of California at Berkeley.

50. Peter Gay, *The Education of the Senses,* vol. 1 of *The Bourgeois Experience: Victoria to Freud* (New York: Oxford University Press, 1984): 103.

Chapter 3

1. Glenda Riley, *Women and Indians on the Frontier 1825–1915* (Albuquerque: University of New Mexico Press, 1984): 156.
2. Cited in J. W. Wilbarger, *Indian Depredations in Texas* [1889] (Austin, Tex.: Pemberton Press, 1967): 554.
3. Cited in Wilbarger, *Indian Depredations in Texas*: 554, 560.
4. Carl Coke Rister, *Border Captives: The Traffic in Prisoners by Southern Plains Indians, 1835–1875* (Norman: University of Oklahoma Press, 1940): 107.
5. Herman Lehmann, *Nine Years Among the Indians, 1870–1879* [1927], ed. J. Marvin Hunter (Albuquerque: University of New Mexico Press, 1993): 216–17.
6. Frederick Law Olmsted, *A Journey Through Texas: Or, A Saddle-Trip on the Southwestern Frontier* (Austin: University of Texas Press, 1978): 296.
7. Brevet Major Earl Van Dorn, cited in Robert Wooster, *Soldiers, Sutlers, and Settlers: Garrison Life on the Texas Frontier* (College Station: Texas A&M Press, 1987): 149.
8. Governor Richard Coke, *Journal*: 37, 14 Legislature, 2 sess., January 1875; cited in Carl Coke Rister, *The Southwestern Frontier 1865–1881* (New York: Arthur H. Clark, 1928): 149–50.
9. Cited in R. G. Carter, *On the Border with Mackenzie, or Winning West Texas from the Comanches* (Washington, D.C.: Eynon, 1935): 299.
10. *The Army and Navy Journal* 10 (April 26, 1873): 586–87.
11. Report of the Secretary of War, *Executive Documents,* House of Representatives, vol. 1, 2d sess. 46th Cong. 1879–80 (Washington, D.C.: Government Printing Office, 1880): 90.
12. S. E. Whitman, *The Troopers: An Informal History of the Plains Cavalry, 1865–1890* (New York: Hastings House, 1962): 17. The comparison of hell and Texas has also been attributed to various other people, but it sounds like the kind of thing the plain-speaking Sherman would say.
13. Larry McMurtry, *In a Narrow Grave: Essays on Texas* (New York: Simon & Schuster, 1968): xxiii.
14. Cited in William H. Leckie and Shirley A. Leckie, *Unlikely Warriors: General Benjamin H. Grierson and His Family* (Norman: University of Oklahoma Press, 1984): 220. The Leckies title this chapter "Banished to West Texas."

15. Lydia Spencer Lane, *I Married a Soldier, or Old Days in the Old Army* [1893] (Albuquerque: Horn & Wallace, 1964): 22, 25, 42.

16. *Report on the Hygiene of the United States Army,* Circular No. 8, War Department, Surgeon General's Office, Washington, D.C., May 1, 1875: 195–96.

17. Zenas R. Bliss, "Reminiscences," vol. 5: 187–90, Eugene C. Barker Texas History Center, University of Texas, Austin; cited in Clayton W. Williams, *Texas' Last Frontier: Fort Stockton and the Trans-Pecos 1861–1895,* ed. Ernest Wallace (College Station: Texas A&M University Press, 1982): 158.

18. Medical History of Post—Fort Stockton—May 1869–October 1871, vol. 63: 10; July 1874–June 1886, vol. 362: 12; Entry 547, AGO, RG 94, NARA.

19. "Medical History of Post": 28–29.

20. DeB. Randolph Keim, *Sheridan's Troopers on the Borders: A Winter Campaign on the Plains* (London: George Routledge and Sons, 1885): 59; Chaplain George G. Mullins to AGO, October 1, 1875, ACP record, RG 94, NARA.

21. B. F. Pope, Medical History of Post, December 1874: 6; James Evetts Haley, *Fort Concho and the Texas Frontier* (San Angelo, Tex.: San Angelo Standard-Times, 1952): 14.

22. George A. Forsyth, *The Story of the Soldier* (New York: Appleton, 1900): 109; Shirley A. Leckie, ed., *The Colonel's Lady on the Western Frontier: The Correspondence of Alice Kirk Grierson* (Lincoln: University of Nebraska Press, 1989): 231 n.; Fairfax Downey, *Indian-Fighting Army* (New York: Charles Scribner's Sons, 1941): 110.

23. Robert J. Casey, *The Texas Border and Some Borderliners* (Indianapolis: Bobbs-Merrill, 1950): 124; James Cook, *Fifty Years on the Old Frontier* (New Haven, Conn.: Yale University Press, 1925): 12; E.O.C. Ord to F. A. Binney, July 19, 1878, Edward Otho Cresap Ord, 1818–1883, Correspondence and Papers, Box 1: Outgoing Letters, 1852–1881, Bancroft Library, University of California at Berkeley.

24. Williams, *Texas' Last Frontier*: 262, 260; Report of the Secretary of War, 1879–80, 1: 20–21.

25. Francis Paul Prucha, *A Guide to the Military Posts of the United States, 1789–1895* (Madison: The State Historical Society of Wisconsin, 1964): 109. The fort was named after Commodore Robert Field Stockton, a hero of the Mexican War.

26. Report of Sergeant J. D. Bingham to the Assistant Adjutant General, March 16, 1869, "Fort Stockton," Box 1083, Office of the Quartermaster General Consolidated Correspondence File 1794–1915, RG 92, NARA.

27. [Peter Cleary, post surgeon], Medical History of Post, 1870–71: 12.

28. *The Army and Navy Journal,* 9 (July 20, 1872): 785; and 20 (January 13, 1883): 526.

29. Captain John G. Bourke, cited in Edward L. Glass, *The History of the Tenth Cavalry 1866–1921* (n.p., 1921): 21; Olmsted, *A Journey Through Texas:* 299.

30. Sanitary Report of February 1875, Records of Fort Stockton (M1189), NARA.

31. Medical Records of Fort Stockton, October 1878: 97–98.

32. Patricia Y. Stallard, *Glittering Misery: Dependents of the Indian Fighting Army* (San Rafael, Calif.: Presidio Press, 1978): 13; Sanitary Report, May 31, 1878, Records of Fort Stockton, National Archives, M1189, roll 3.

33. Bigelow, cited in Erwin N. Thompson, "The Negro Soldier and His Officers," *The Black Military Experience in the American West,* ed. John M. Carroll (New York: Liveright, 1971): 259; Arlen L. Fowler, *The Black Infantry in the West, 1869–1891* (Norman: University of Oklahoma Press, 1996): 47.

34. Jack D. Foner, *Blacks and the Military in American History: A New Perspective* (New York: Praeger, 1974): 55.

35. *Christian Recorder,* March 5, 1864; cited in James M. McPherson, *The Negro's Civil War: How American Negroes Felt and Acted During the War for the Union* (Urbana: University of Illinois Press, 1982): 198–99; *New York World,* December 13, 1864; McPherson, *The Negro's Civil War:* 203.

36. Sherman to Ord, December 26, 1865; cited in William S. McFeely, *Grant: A Biography* (New York: W. W. Norton, 1981): 259.

37. William H. Leckie, *The Buffalo Soldiers: A Narrative of the Negro Cavalry in the West* (Norman: University of Oklahoma Press, 1967): 26.

38. Cited in Haley, *Fort Concho:* 263–64. Historians of the frontier army agree that black soldiers performed well and exhibited less negative behavior in proportion to their numbers than their white counterparts. Marcos Kinevan, in *Frontier Cavalryman: Lieutenant John Bigelow with the Buffalo Soldiers in Texas* (El Paso, Tex.: Texas Western Press, 1998): 158, writes: "Desertions of blacks . . . were dwarfed by those of

whites," and gives the statistics to prove it. While noting that their general lack of basic education created some problems, Robert M. Utley observes that the black soldiers "excelled in discipline, morale, patience and good humor in adversity, physical endurance, and sobriety. Above all, they performed well on campaign and in combat. Even their severest critics testified to their exceptional record of field service." (Robert M. Utley, *Frontier Regulars: The United States Army and the Indian 1866–1891* [New York: Macmillan, 1973]: 26.)

39. Letters Received, Inspector General's Office, File No. T 21, RG 159, NARA.

40. J. C. Nott and George R. Gliddon, *Types of Mankind* (Philadelphia: Lippincott, 1868): 260; January 24, 1878, John Bigelow, Jr., Journal January–November 1878, John Bigelow Collection, Union College.

41. The report is not signed, but the post surgeon, whose responsibility such reports were, was Peter Cleary; Nott and Gliddon, *Types of Mankind*: 278.

42. Whitman, *The Troopers*: 34. George Armstrong Custer was one officer who preferred being a lieutenant colonel in a white regiment to becoming the colonel of a black regiment.

43. Thompson, "The Negro Soldier and His Officers": 262.

44. Report to the Assistant Adjutant General, Department of Texas, November 21, 1872, RG 393, Pt. 1, NARA.

45. N. H. Pierce, *The Free State of Menard: A History of the County* (Menard, Tex.: Menard News Press, 1946): 137.

46. Report of the Secretary of War, 45 Cong., 2d sess. (Washington, D.C.: Government Printing Office, 1877), 1: 80–81.

47. Roberts, cited in Garna L. Christian, *Black Soldiers in Jim Crow Texas, 1899–1917* (College Station: Texas A&M University Press, 1995): 42; Frank N. Schubert, "Black Soldiers on the White Frontier: Some Factors Influencing Race Relations," *Phylon* 32 (1971): 415.

48. Report to Adjutant General, San Antonio, November 13, 1899, AGO file 292843, RG 94, NARA.

49. Foner, *Blacks and the Military in American History*: 64; Leckie, *Buffalo Soldiers*: 98.

50. Dr. Pope, Medical Records of Fort Stockton, vol. 362: 18.

51. Pope, Medical Records of Fort Stockton, vol. 362: 19; Cleary, "Medical History of Post, 1870–71": 7.

52. "Cases Tried by a General Court Martial," PP3542, JAG, RG 153, NARA. The charge of mutiny was reduced to "unauthorized conduct," which mitigated the severity of the punishment.
53. "Cleary, Peter J. A.," Personal Papers of Medical Officers and Physicians, Box 114, AGO, RG 94, NARA.
54. "Cleary, Peter J. A.," Personal Papers.

Chapter 4

1. Charles S. Merchant, Brevet Brigadier General, recommendation for promotion, March 30, 1866, ACP of John Clous, no. 247, RG 94, NARA.
2. Letter of November 16, 1867, to Major General L. Thomas, Adjutant General, Clous ACP File.
3. Correspondence in Clous ACP file.
4. William H. Leckie describes Armes as "an able but contentious and controversial officer. His long military career was dotted with arrests and quarrels with his superiors. He was dismissed from the service in June, 1870, but the dismissal was later amended to provide an honorable discharge. He returned to the Tenth Cavalry in May, 1878, and was retired in 1883." (Leckie, *The Buffalo Soldiers: A Narrative of the Negro Cavalry in the West* [Norman: University of Oklahoma Press, 1967]: 22–23n.)
5. George A. Armes, *Ups and Downs of an Army Officer* (Washington, D.C.: privately printed, 1900): 2–3, 297.
6. Stephen Vincent Benét, *A Treatise on Military Law and the Practice of Courts-Martial,* 6th ed. (New York: D. Van Nostrand, 1868): 78.
7. Mrs. Hart's husband, Captain Daniel Hart, died at Fort Stockton in March of 1878. Geddes, his replacement, arrived in May of that year. Since the Harts had been about to celebrate their twenty-fifth wedding anniversary when the captain died, Mrs. Hart, like Mrs. McLaughlen, was a woman of a certain age.
8. Clayton W. Williams, *Texas' Last Frontier: Fort Stockton and the Trans-Pecos 1861–1895,* ed. Ernest Wallace (College Station: Texas A&M University Press, 1982): 224.
9. Robert Safford to John Bigelow, March 9, 1879, Bigelow Diaries, USMA Archive.

NOTES TO PAGES 84–96

10. Cesare Lombroso, introduction to Gina Lombroso Ferrero, *Criminal Man* (New York: G. P. Putnam's Sons, 1911): xv.

11. Cesare Lombroso, *Crime, Its Causes and Remedies,* trans. Henry P. Horton (Boston: Little, Brown, 1918): 35.

12. Nancy A. Harrowitz, *Antisemitism, Misogyny, and the Logic of Cultural Difference: Cesare Lombroso and Matilde Serao* (Lincoln: University of Nebraska Press, 1994): 142n., notes that "Lombroso's theories had the most influence in the United States. The Lombrosian school was quickly and frequently translated into English." Discussing Lombroso's physical description of the criminal, Jacques Barzun, *Race: A Study in Superstition,* 2d ed. (New York: Harper & Row, 1965): 130, states that "facts are powerless against it."

13. Stephen Schafer, *Theories in Criminology: Past and Present Philosophies of the Crime Problem* (New York: Random House, 1969): 191–92; James Q. Wilson and Richard J. Herrnstein, *Crime and Human Nature* (New York: Simon and Schuster, 1985): 100–102.

14. Reflecting the nineteenth-century popularity of phrenology, its entry in the eleventh edition of the *Encyclopædia Britannica* (New York: Encyclopædia Britannica Company, 1911) 21: 534–41, was seven pages. In the fifteenth edition this entry had shrunk to five sentences.

15. Robert Grierson to Alice Grierson, in *The Colonel's Lady on the Western Frontier: The Correspondence of Alice Kirk Grierson,* ed. Shirley A. Leckie (Lincoln: University of Nebraska Press, 1989): 56.

16. William H. Leckie, *The Buffalo Soldiers: A Narrative of the Negro Cavalry in the West* (Norman: University of Oklahoma Press, 1967): 36, calls Carpenter "one of the finest officers on the frontier."

17. Homer W. Wheeler, *Buffalo Days: Forty Years in the Old West,* 2d ed. rev. (Indianapolis: Bobbs-Merrill, 1925): 250–52.

18. Entries for May 15, and May 27, 1879, Bigelow Diaries, USMA Archive.

19. This comment was Bigelow's reaction to first hearing about the Geddes-Orleman scandal. Entries for May 15, July 15, and March 25, 1879, Bigelow Diaries.

20. Entry of July 3, 1879, Bigelow Diaries.

21. Entry of May 20, 1879 [sic], Bigelow Diaries. In the second week of June, Bigelow began forgetfully dating his entries "May."

22. Entries of July 22, and June 11, 1879, Bigelow Diaries.

23. Numerous commentators on nineteenth-century American life refer to a widespread emphasis on purity. Mary P. Ryan, *Womanhood in America: From Colonial Times to the Present* (New York: New Viewpoints, 1975): 160, is representative in claiming that middle-class women of the time were "inundated with the value of female purity."

24. Nina Baym, *Woman's Fiction: A Guide to Novels By and About Women in America, 1820–70,* 2d ed. (Urbana: University of Illinois Press, 1993): 314.

25. Robert T. Francoeur, *A Descriptive Dictionary and Atlas of Sexology* (Westport, Conn.: Greenwood Press, 1991): 702, offers this definition: "An intact hymen, a tight vagina and bleeding during defloration are commonly said to be signs of virginity although none of these signs guarantees that the female has not had vaginal intercourse. Likewise, their absence is not proof that she has had coitus." A popular manual, Ruth K. Westheimer, *Dr. Ruth's Encyclopedia of Sex* (New York: Continuum, 1994): 279, is more emphatic: "While an intact hymen has historically been used to verify a woman's virginity . . . this is a totally false notion."

26. I am indebted for this explanation, and for information on changes in the female breast, to Thomas Lowry, M.D., formerly a clinical associate of Dr. William Masters at the Reproductive Biology Research Foundation in St. Louis.

27. Judith Lewis Herman, with Lisa Hirschman, *Father-Daughter Incest* (Cambridge, Mass.: Harvard University Press, 1981): 11.

28. Sigmund Freud, "The Taboo of Virginity" (1918), in *The Standard Edition of the Completed Psychological Works of Sigmund Freud,* trans. James Strachey (London: Hogarth Press, 1957), vol. 11: 193.

29. Virginia Woolf, *Three Guineas* (New York: Harcourt, Brace, 1938), 167n.

30. Hammond Diary, January 31, 1844, Library of Congress; cited in Drew Gilpin Faust, *James Henry Hammond and the Old South: A Design for Mastery* (Baton Rouge: Louisiana State University Press, 1982): 242.

31. Drew Gilpin Faust, *James Henry Hammond and the Old South*: 242, 290.

32. Philip Sheridan to William T. Sherman, November 30, 1872, Sherman Papers, Box 8, Manuscript Division, Library of Congress.

33. John D'Emilio and Estelle B. Freedman, *Intimate Matters: A History of Sexuality in America* (New York: Harper & Row, 1988): 70.

34. Young might have had a motive to be unfriendly to Geddes. On August 29, he complained to Colonel Grierson that Joseph Friedlander, Geddes's good friend, was attempting to trade with soldiers in the field although he, Young, was the only authorized post trader.

35. Bigelow, USMA Diaries.

36. John H. Kellogg, *Ladies Guide in Health and Disease, Girlhood, Maidenhood, Wifehood, Motherhood* (Des Moines, Iowa: W. D. Condit, 1883): 208–9.

37. Orson S. Fowler, *Creative and Sexual Science* (New York: Fowler and Wells, 1875): 891.

38. Carroll Smith-Rosenberg and Charles Rosenberg, "'The Female Animal': Medical and Biological Views of Women in Nineteenth-Century America," *Journal of American History* 60 (September 1973): 340.

39. Peter Gay, *The Education of the Senses,* vol. 1 of *The Bourgeois Experience* (New York: Oxford University Press, 1984): 73.

40. Dee Garrison, "Immoral Fiction in the Late Victorian Library," *American Quarterly* 28 (September 1976): 72.

41. Nathaniel Hawthorne to William D. Ticknor, January 19, 1855, in *The Letters, 1853–1856,* ed. Thomas Woodson et al., *The Centenary Edition of the Works of Nathaniel Hawthorne,* 23 vols. (Columbus: Ohio State University Press, 1962–87), 17: 304.

42. William Perry Fidler, *Augusta Evans Wilson, 1835–1909: A Biography* (University: University Press of Alabama, 1951), is the source of all biographical data on Wilson.

43. Augusta Evans Wilson, *Infelice* (New York: A. L. Burt, 1875): 61.

44. Wilson, *Infelice*: 132.

45. Wilson, *Infelice*: 132–33.

46. Smith-Rosenberg and Rosenberg, "'The Female Animal'": 340.

47. Gay, *The Education of the Senses*: 213.

48. Entry of August 18, 1877, Bigelow Diaries, Box 1, USMA.

49. Wilson, *Infelice*: 128.

50. Wilson, *Infelice*: 134.

51. Wilson, *Infelice*: 134.

52. Wilson, *Infelice*: 387–88.

53. Armes, *Ups and Downs of an Army Officer*: 469. See Marcos Kinevan, *Frontier Cavalryman: Lieutenant John Bigelow with the Buffalo Soldiers in Texas* (El Paso: Texas Western Press, 1988): 116–18, for a full discus-

sion of the Bigelow-Blunt affair; see also entries of March 20 and April 12, 1879, Bigelow Diaries.

Chapter 5

1. Cited in entry of July 3, 1879, Bigelow Diaries, USMA Archive.
2. Geddes to Absalom Baird, letter of April 12, 1880, QQ1387, Box 1927, JAG, RG 153, NARA. QQ1387 is the Geddes court-martial of 1879, along with related documents.
3. QQ1387: Exhibit Qq.
4. The defense called Colonel George L. Andrews, commanding officer of the Twenty-fifth Infantry, because Andrews had been on the retiring board which considered Orleman's case. Andrews denied that Ord had given the board Geddes's deposition, but there is no other explanation for their having it.
5. R. G. Carter, *On the Border with Mackenzie, or Winning West Texas from the Comanches* (Washington, D.C.: Eynon, 1935): 458.
6. Carter, *On the Border with Mackenzie*: 458–59.
7. Carter, *On the Border with Mackenzie*: 481.
8. January 9, 1979, Headquarters, Department of Texas, Letters Sent Vol. 2: No. 35, RG 393, pt. 1, NARA.
9. Medical Certificate for Leave of Absence, San Antonio, March 11, 1879, ACP File of Napoleon Bonaparte McLaughlen, RG 94, NARA.
10. McLaughlen had been ill before, but whether previous illnesses were related to his final decline is not clear. His health may have been undermined by a brief stay in Libby Prison in 1865. By 1872 he was suffering from "chronic rheumatism of all the extremities" and of some internal organs as well. He was given a ninety-day leave. A request to extend this leave described him as suffering from "a neuralgic affection [affliction?] of the bladder and bowels, the result of exposure while on duty with his regiment in Texas." McLaughlen's ACP file.
11. McLaughlen ACP file.
12. Armes, *Ups and Downs of an Army Officer*: 466.
13. Cited in Williams, *Texas' Last Frontier*: 105.
14. Graham Hughes, "The Crime of Incest," *Journal of Criminal Law, Criminology, and Police Science* 55 (1964): 328, describes a study of

incestuous father-daughter relationships in which the daughter participant "was passive and coerced."

15. Entry of March 25, 1879, Bigelow Diaries, 1867–79, USMA Archives.

16. Dr. Taylor to Adjutant General, Department of Texas, Telegram, July 18, 1879, RG 393, pt. 1, Letters Sent, vol. 11: no. 1080, NARA.

17. Entries for July 16, and July 22, 1879, Bigelow Diaries, USMA Archive.

18. He applied for a hearing before a retirement board on August 31, 1878, Records of Fort Stockton, M1189, NARA.

19. Commission, March 23, 1864, 0159 CB 1866*, AGO, RG 94, NARA.

20. All medical records are taken from 0159 CB 1866*.

21. John D. Hall, Medical Records of Fort Stockton: 104.

Chapter 6

1. The two copies of this report in the National Archives, one in the ACP file of Andrew Geddes, the other in court-martial file QQ1387, have pages out of sequence and inconsistently numbered, some on the front side of the sheet, some on the back, some not at all. Obvious hiatuses in several places indicate that some pages are missing.

2. All quotations from Dunn's review are taken from the copy previously referred to in the court-martial file of Andrew J. Geddes, QQ1387, Box 1926, JAG, RG 153, NARA; hereafter called "Review."

3. Dr. T. Gaillard Thomas, *New York Journal of Medicine,* 3d series, 6 (1859): 196–216; cited in unpaged portion of Dunn's review.

4. Dunn enumerates these witnesses: Capt. John H. French, Capt. David Schooley, Capt. M. L. Courtney, Capt. C. A. Gray, Lieut. D. B. Wilson, Lieut. I. W. Tear, Lieut. Harry Read, and Lieut. James Pratt—all of the Twenty-fifth Infantry.

5. Harry Barnard, *Rutherford B. Hayes and His America* (Indianapolis: Bobbs-Merrill, 1954): 291.

6. John W. Burgess, *The Administration of President Hayes* (New York: Charles Scribner's Sons, 1916): 136.

7. Hayes to Lucy Webb Hayes, June 10, 1861, and August 25, 1861; cited in Barnard, *Rutherford B. Hayes and His America*: 216.

8. Col. James B. Fry, "Justice for the Army," *The Army and Navy Journal* 21 (August 25, 1883): 63. Fry is commenting on, and liberally quoting from, an article that appeared in the *New York Herald,* January 21, 1881.

9. Court procedure prohibited identifying members of the court by name. The same person may have been responsible for most or all of the interventions to spare Lillie from testifying, and it may have been Dr. Brown, who made his annoyance with the defense explicit.

10. Research indicates that when daughters reach the age of attracting boyfriends, their incestuous fathers often become violently jealous and controlling, monitoring their behavior to preclude contacts with possible rivals. Tamar Cohan, a researcher on contemporary incest, states: "In many cases, the incestuous father feels that the daughter is his exclusive property" ("The Incestuous Family Revisited," *Social Casework* 64 [1983]: 155; see also Judith Lewis Herman, *Father-Daughter Incest* [Cambridge, Mass.: Harvard University Press, 1981]: 73, 91–92.)

11. Herman, *Father-Daughter Incest,* 87, observes that "many researchers have noted that incest . . . fulfills the offender's hostile and aggressive wishes."

12. David Stout, "An Army as Good as Its People, and Vice Versa," "The News of the Week in Review," *The New York Times,* July 26, 1998: 4; cited from *Broad Arrow, Army and Navy Journal* 19 (April 29, 1882): 890.

13. ACP 4246, Napoleon Bonaparte McLaughlen, AGO, RG 94, NARA.

14. Oliver Knight, *Life and Manners in the Frontier Army* (Norman: University of Oklahoma Press, 1978): 75.

15. Review of court-martial, April 28, 1873, PP3110, JAG, RG 153, NARA.

16. Karin C. Meiselman, *Incest: A Psychological Study of Causes and Effects with Treatment Recommendations* (San Francisco: Jossey-Bass, 1990): 100.

Chapter 7

1. More properly, Peña Colorada, but always written incorrectly in army documents. The camp was located south of the Glass Mountains a few miles southeast of the present Marathon, Texas. Clayton W. Williams, *Texas' Last Frontier: Fort Stockton and the Trans-Pecos 1861–1895,* ed. Ernest Wallace (College Station: Texas A&M University Press, 1982): 233.

2. Letters Sent, Department of Texas, RG 393, pt. 1, vol. 13, NARA.

3. Letter of June 17, 1880, in Box 1926 of QQ1387, RG 153, NARA.

4. Philip Sheridan to Wm. T. Sherman, November 24, 1877; Philip Sheridan to Wm. T. Sherman, December 12, 1879, Sherman Papers, Manuscript Division, Library of Congress.

5. Stanley P. Hirshson, *The White Tecumseh: A Biography of General William T. Sherman* (New York: John Wiley and Sons, 1997): 12.

6. William T. Sherman to Elizabeth Bacon Custer, October 17, 1882; cited in Lawrence Frost, *General Custer's Libbie* (Seattle: Superior Publishing Company, 1975): 254.

7. Two recent biographers of Sherman discuss his relationship with Mary Audenreid and Vinnie Ream: John F. Marszalek, *Sherman: A Soldier's Passion for Order* (New York: The Free Press, 1993); and Michael Fellman, *Citizen Sherman: A Life of William Tecumseh Sherman* (New York: Random House, 1995): 358–70.

8. Sherman to Mary Audenreid, July 11, 1882, Sherman Papers.

9. Peter Gay, *The Education of the Senses,* vol. 1 of *The Bourgeois Experience: Victoria to Freud* (New York: Oxford University Press, 1984): 102.

10. Cited in Fellman, *Citizen Sherman*: 363, 365.

11. See Vinnie Ream Hoxie Collection, Manuscript Division, Library of Congress.

12. Letter of June 17, 1880, to General A. H. Terry, QQ1387.

13. Oliver Knight, *Life and Manners in the Frontier Army* (Norman: University of Oklahoma Press, 1978): 75.

14. According to a document entitled "J. W. Clous, 24th Infantry, Feb. 10, 1880, his opinion in the matter of Affidavit of *Mary Stewart,* accusing Mrs. *W. H. Beck* of adultery with *Joseph Friedlander,* and Mrs. *N. B. McLaughlen* of same offense with Captain *A. Geddes,* 25th Infantry," QQ1387; hereafter called "Clous Report."

15. Entry of May 8, 1879, Bigelow Diaries, USMA Archive.

16. Clous Report.

17. Clous Report.

18. J. C. Nott and George R. Gliddon, *Types of Mankind* (Philadelphia: Lippincott, 1868): 260.

19. Peggy Pascoe, "Race, Gender and Intercultural Relations: The Case of Interracial Marriage," in *Writing the Range: Race, Class, and Culture in the Women's West,* ed. Elizabeth Jameson and Susan Armitage (Norman: University of Oklahoma Press, 1997): 79n.

20. Chicago, March 13, 1880, Headquarters, Military Division of the Missouri, Report, ACP File of Andrew Geddes, RG 94; hereafter called Baird Report. All page numbers cited refer to this book's Appendix B.
21. Baird Report (see Appendix B, p. 231).
22. Baird Report (Appendix B, p. 232).
23. R. E. Drum to E.O.C. Ord, March 2, 1880, QQ1387.
24. Drum to Ord, March 2, 1880, QQ1387.
25. Clous Report.
26. Clous Report.
27. Shirley A. Leckie, ed., *The Colonel's Lady on the Western Frontier: The Correspondence of Alice Kirk Grierson* (Lincoln: University of Nebraska Press, 1989): 120.
28. Entry of June 13, 1878, Journal, January–November 1878, John Bigelow Collection, Union College.
29. Clous Report.
30. Baird Report: 4.
31. Baird Report (Appendix B, p. 235).
32. Baird Report (Appendix B, pp. 235–36).
33. Sherman to Dunn, June 15, 1880, QQ1387.
34. Clous Report.
35. Dunn to Sherman, June 16, 1880, QQ1387.
36. Sherman to Terry, June 17, 1880, QQ1387.
37. Geddes to Baird, April 9, 1880, QQ1387.
38. Geddes to Baird, April 27, 1880. QQ1387.
39. Geddes to Baird, April 27, 1880, QQ1387.
40. Terry to Sherman, September 11, 1880, QQ1387.
41. Sherman to Terry, September 11, 1880, QQ1387.

Chapter 8

1. Fort Stockton, Texas, Medical History of Post, July 1874–June 1886, vol. 362: 18, AGO, RG 94, NARA.
2. No. 1057, Letters Sent, Department of Texas, RG 393, pt. 1, NARA.
3. All citations from the court-martial are taken from the original transcript: QQ2023, The Court-Martial of Captain Andrew Geddes, 25th Infantry, Fort Randall, Dakota Territory, October 1, 1880, JAG, RG 153, NARA. Further quotations from this trial will not be identified with note numbers; all came from the transcript.

4. The defense queried First Lieutenant Henry P. Ritzius on this issue, but he refused to cooperate.

5. Olliver Shannon to Andrew J. Geddes, August 29, 1881, filed with QQ2023, JAG, RG 153, NARA.

6. Andrew Geddes to Adjutant General, May 7, 1882, consolidated ACP file of Andrew Geddes, 6373, AGO, RG 94, NARA.

7. Notation on Geddes's letter dated May 12; letter to Geddes from Adjutant General, May 13, consolidated ACP file 6373.

8. Letter to the President, January 30, 1882, signed by Charles Bentzoni, George L. Andrews, C. L. Hodges, Henry P. Ritzius, Gaines Lawson, H. B. Quimby, and D. B. Wilson, Consolidated ACP File 6373 (see this book's Appendix C, pp. 239–40).

9. He became chief clerk October 1, 1897 (Consolidated APC File 6373). The importance of this job to Geddes may be judged by his entry in the Washington City Directory after his promotion: his name is inscribed in emphatic, larger-than-ordinary letters, and the title "Chief Clerk, Department of Agriculture" appended.

10. Andrew Geddes to A. W. Fulton, July 1, 1898, Chief Clerk's Correspondence, vol. 27 (March 24, 1898–March 17, 1899): 147, Department of Agriculture, RG 16, NARA.

11. Geddes to Hugh R. Belknap, September 21, 1898, Chief Clerk's Correspondence, vol. 27: 236.

12. Medical examination of November 11, 1891, Pension File of Andrew Geddes, certificate 1106737, Letters Received by the Commission Branch of AGO 1863–1870, RG 94, NARA.

13. Report No. 112, January 18, 1900, extract, 56th Congress, *1st Session*: 2–3, in Consolidated ACP File 6373. For the full text, see this book's Appendix C, pp. 240–43.

14. Report No. 112: 1.

15. Shafter to the Secretary of War, December 24, 1897, Consolidated APC File 6373.

16. Report of the Inspector General, May 29, 1890, Catalogue of the Peekskill Academy, 1890–91: 44.

17. Information in a retrospective newspaper article on the Peekskill Academy, n.d., in the file of the Field Library, Peekskill, New York.

18. Orleman to Adjutant General, May 22, 1901, Consolidated Civil War file of L. H. Orleman, 0159 CB 1866*, Letters Received by the Commission Branch of the AGO 1863–1870, RG 94, NARA.

19. Daisy Orleman Robinson to Adjutant General, November 7, 1911, 0159 CB 1866*.

20. Carl Orleman to Adjutant General, 1916, 0159 CB 1866*.

21. Daisy Orleman's obituary in the *New York Times* of March 14, 1942, indicated that she was survived by a brother, Carl, and a sister, Violet.

22. Peekskill Military Academy file, Field Library.

23. Drew Gilpin Faust, *James Henry Hammond and the Old South: A Design for Mastery* (Baton Rouge: Louisiana State University Press, 1982): 290.

24. Obituary of George Paschal, *San Antonio Daily Light,* September 7, 1894.

25. George H. Kalteyer, cited in the *San Antonio Daily Express,* September 8, 1894. In the same article both the Assistant City Attorney and Colonel N. O. Green, who had known Paschal since childhood, described him as a "brilliant" lawyer; *San Antonio Daily Light,* September 7, 1894.

26. Sheridan to Sherman, November 24, 1877, Sherman Papers, 47; Sherman to Sheridan, November 29, 1877, Sherman Papers, Letterbook 1872–78.

27. Armes, July 16, 1879, *Ups and Downs of an Army Officer* (Washington, D.C.: privately printed, 1900): 466.

28. Armes, October 21, 1879, *Ups and Downs*: 458.

29. Armes, November 23, 1879, *Ups and Downs*: 473.

30. Armes, *Ups and Downs*: 481.

31. Marcos Kinevan, *Frontier Cavalryman: Lieutenant John Bigelow with the Buffalo Soldiers in Texas* (El Paso: Texas Western Press, 1998): 228. Armes believed that he had been the victim of a cabal of officers who were out to get him "simply because I happened to have been restored by an act of Congress." He included in this number "General Ord, Col. M. M. Blunt and the Dutchman" (December 31, 1881, *Ups and Downs of an Army Officer*: 496).

32. Letter of January 28, 1886, John Clous ACP File, RG 94, NARA.

33. Kinevan, *Frontier Cavalryman*: 239.

34. Mike Talley, ed., *Texas State Travel Guide* (Austin: Texas Department of Transportation, 1998): 150.

35. See QQ2952, JAG, RG 153, NARA, for the court-martial of Henry Ossian Flipper and collateral documents.

36. *Who Was Who in American History—Military* (Chicago: Marquis Who's Who, 1975): 100.

Epilogue

1. Thomas F. Boyle, " 'Morbid Depression Alternating with Excitement': Sex in Victorian Newspapers," in *Sexuality and Victorian Literature,* ed. Don Richard Cox (Knoxville: University of Tennessee Press, 1984): 212–13.

2. Peter Gay, *The Education of the Senses,* vol. 1 of *The Bourgeois Experience: Victoria to Freud* (New York: Oxford University Press, 1984): 370–71.

3. Leigh B. Bienen, "The Incest Statutes," Appendix, Judith Lewis Herman with Lisa Hirschman, *Father-Daughter Incest* (Cambridge, Mass.: Harvard University Press, 1981): 221–59.

4. Gay, *The Education of the Senses*: 392.

5. Foreword to Joseph Shepher, *Incest: A Biosocial View* (New York: Academic Press, 1983): xi.

6. Lev. 18:6–23, *The Holy Bible: Authorized or King James Version.*

7. Lev. 18:15–16.

8. Judith Herman, *Father-Daughter Incest* (Cambridge, Mass.: Harvard University Press, 1981): 60, 62.

9. Kenneth Neill Cameron, *Shelley: The Golden Years* (Cambridge, Mass.: Harvard University Press, 1974): 398.

10. F. Marion Crawford, "Beatrice Cenci: The True Story of a Misunderstood Tragedy: With New Documents," *The Century Magazine* 75 (November 1907–April 1908): 449–66, refers to original documents for his account of the crime and its circumstances. He observes that in spite of torture, Beatrice never said that her father had sexually abused her, only that he had beaten her on numerous occasions. According to Crawford, her lawyer made the argument without her acquiescence, thus giving rise to the enduring idea that Beatrice was a victim of incest (456).

11. Freud, "The Paths to the Formation of Symptoms," *The Standard Edition of the Complete Psychological Works of Sigmund Freud,* trans. James Strachey, 24 vols. (London: Hogarth Press, 1957), vol. 16: 370.

12. John Henry Wigmore, *Evidence in Trials at Common Law,* rev. James H. Chadbourn, 10 vols. (Boston: Little, Brown, 1970): IIIA, sec. 924a, 736–49.

13. Wigmore, *Evidence,* 3A: 736.

14. Herman, *Father-Daughter Incest*: 11.

15. Herman, *Father-Daughter Incest*: 11.

16. E. Sue Blume, *Secret Survivors: Uncovering Incest and Its Aftereffects in Women* (New York: John Wiley, 1990): xiii.
17. Cited in Anthony S. Wohl, "Sex and the Single Room: Incest Among the Victorian Working Classes," in *The Victorian Family: Structure and Stresses,* ed. Anthony S. Wohl (London: Croom Helm, 1978): 202.
18. Robert Roberts, *The Classic Slum: Salford Life in the First Quarter of the Century* (London: Penguin Books, 1973): 44.
19. Wohl, "Sex and the Single Room": 199, 201.
20. Christine A. Dietz and John L. Craft, in "Family Dynamics of Incest: A New Perspective," *Social Casework: The Journal of Contemporary Social Work* 61 (1980): 602, report that "until recently the discussion of incest has been a greater taboo than its practice."
21. Janis Tyler Johnson, *Mothers of Incest Survivors: Another Side of the Story* (Bloomington: Indiana University Press, 1992): 85. Johnson found that all six of the mothers in her study described a "world of the father" in which "men had the right to do what they wanted."
22. Captain Noel Lustig, "Incest: A Family Group Survival Pattern," *Archives of General Psychiatry* 14 (1966): 39.
23. In Judith Herman's study of 40 women who had had incestuous relationships with their fathers, 17, or 42.5 percent, were oldest daughters, the largest number; 15, or 37.5 percent, were only daughters. (*Father-Daughter Incest*: 69).
24. Herman, *Father-Daughter Incest*: 94: "The phenomenon of the father's 'moving on' to a younger daughter has been observed by many authors, some of whom report even higher proportions of families in which this occurs."
25. Herman, *Father-Daughter Incest*: 78.
26. Dietz and Craft, "Family Dynamics of Incest": 603.
27. Carroll Smith-Rosenberg, *Disorderly Conduct: Visions of Gender in Victorian America* (New York: Alfred A. Knopf, 1985): 188.
28. Cited in Smith-Rosenberg, *Disorderly Conduct*: 336.
29. Herman, *Father-Daughter Incest*: 71.
30. Herman, *Father-Daughter Incest*: 71.
31. Lustig, "Incest: A Family Group Survival Pattern": 33.
32. Lustig, "Incest: A Family Group Survival Pattern": 34.
33. Krzyzanowski recommendation, 0159 CB 1866*, RG 94, NARA.
34. Baird Report (Appendix B, p. 233).

35. Paul H. Gebhard et al., *Sex Offenders: An Analysis of Types* (New York: Harper and Row, and Paul B. Hoeber, 1965): 226–27; Blume, *Secret Survivors*: 35.
36. Karin C. Meiselman, *Incest: A Psychological Study of Causes and Effects with Treatment Recommendations* (San Francisco: Jossey-Bass, 1990): 98.
37. Herman, *Father-Daughter Incest*: 95.
38. Hector Cavillin, "Incestuous Fathers: A Clinical Report," *American Journal of Psychiatry* 122 (1966): 1137.

BIBLIOGRAPHY

Ungentlemanly Acts is based on original military records in the National Archives, primarily the transcripts of the three Geddes courts-martial in the records of the Judge Advocate General, General Courts Martial 1812–1938 (RG 153). In addition, I have consulted records of the Department of Texas (RG 393); carded medical records, Appointment, Commission and Promotion files, and other records of the Adjutant General's Office (RG 94); records of the Office of the Quartermaster General (RG 92); and records of the Department of Agriculture (RG 16).

OTHER MANUSCRIPT SOURCES

Bigelow, John Jr., Diaries. United States Military Academy Archives, West Point, and the John Bigelow Collection, Union College, Schenectady, N.Y.

Dana, Charles A. Papers. Manuscript Division, Library of Congress.

Hoxie, Vinnie Ream. Papers. Manuscript Division, Library of Congress.

Ord, Edward Otho Cresap, 1818–1883, Correspondence and Papers. Bancroft Library, University of California at Berkeley.

Paschal, George Washington. File, San Antonio Public Library, San Antonio, Tex.

Peekskill Academy File. Field Library, Peekskill, N.Y.

Scrapbook (1869). Stowe-Day Library, Hartford, Conn.

Sherman, William T. Papers. Manuscript Division, Library of Congress.

United States Census Manuscripts. National Archives and Records Administration.

CONTEMPORARY NEWSPAPERS AND PERIODICALS

Army Navy Journal

The Atlantic Monthly Magazine

BIBLIOGRAPHY

The Century Magazine
Harper's New Monthly Magazine
The New York Times
New York World
St. Louis Daily Democrat
San Antonio Daily Express
San Antonio Daily Light
The Saturday Review
The Spectator

GOVERNMENT PUBLICATIONS

Secretary of War. Annual Reports. 1875, 1876, 1878, 1879, 1881.

Surgeon-General's Office. *Report on the Hygiene of the United States Army.* 1875.

The War of the Rebellion: A Compilation of the Official Records of the Union and Confederate Armies. 70 vols. Washington, D.C.: Government Printing Office, 1880–1901.

SECONDARY SOURCES

Ammons, Elizabeth, ed. *Critical Essays on Harriet Beecher Stowe.* Boston: G. K. Hall, 1980.

Armes, George A. *Ups and Downs of an Army Officer.* Washington, D.C.: privately printed, 1900.

Barnard, Harry. *Rutherford B. Hayes and His America.* Indianapolis: Bobbs-Merrill, 1954.

Barrett, Arrie. "Western Frontier Forts of Texas 1845–1861." *West Texas Historical Association Year Book* 7 (1931): 115–39.

Barzun, Jacques. *Race: A Study in Superstition,* rev. ed. New York: Harper & Row, 1965.

Baym, Nina. *Woman's Fiction: A Guide to Novels by and about Women in America 1820–70,* 2d ed. Urbana: University of Illinois Press, 1993.

Benét, S. V. *A Treatise on Military Law and the Practice of Courts-Martial,* 6th ed. New York: D. Van Nostrand, 1868.

Bishop, Joseph W. *Justice under Fire: A Study of Military Law.* New York: Charterhouse, 1974.

Blume, E. Sue. *Secret Survivors: Uncovering Incest and Its Aftereffects in Women.* New York: John Wiley, 1990.

Boyle, Thomas F. "Morbid Depression Alternating with Excitement: Sex in Victorian Newspapers." In *Sexuality and Victorian Literature,* ed. Don Richard Cox. Knoxville: University of Tennessee Press, 1984: 212–33.

Brininstool, E. A. "The Rescue of Forsyth's Scouts." In *Collections of the Kansas State Historical Society 1926–1928,* ed. William Elsey Connelley. Vol. 17 (1928): 845–51.

Burgess, John W. *The Administration of President Hayes.* New York: Charles Scribner's Sons, 1916.

Byron, George Gordon. *"Wedlock's the Devil": Byron's Letters and Journals (1814–1815),* vol. 4, ed. Leslie A. Marchand. Cambridge, Mass.: Harvard University Press, 1975.

"The Byron Mystery," *The Saturday Review* (September 4, 1869): 311.

Callahan, James Morton. *American Foreign Policy in Mexican Relations.* New York: Macmillan, 1932.

Cameron, Kenneth Neill. *Shelley: The Golden Years.* Cambridge, Mass.: Harvard University Press, 1974.

Carroll, John M. *The Black Military Experience in the American West.* New York: Liveright, 1971.

Carter, R. G. *On the Border with Mackenzie, or Winning West Texas from the Comanches.* Washington, D.C.: Eynon, 1935.

Casey, Robert J. *The Texas Border and Some Borderliners.* Indianapolis: Bobbs-Merrill, 1950.

Cavillin, Hector. "Incestuous Fathers: A Clinical Report." *American Journal of Psychiatry* 122 (1966): 1132–38.

Chapman, John S. *Byron and the Honourable Augusta Leigh.* New Haven, Conn.: Yale University Press, 1975.

Christian, Garna L. *Black Soldiers in Jim Crow Texas, 1899–1917.* College Station: Texas A&M University Press, 1995.

Cohen, Tamar. "The Incestuous Family Revisited." *Social Casework* 64 (1983): 154–61.

Cook, James H. *Fifty Years on the Old Frontier.* New Haven, Conn.: Yale University Press, 1925.

"Court-Martial of Surgeon Elisha J. Bailey." *The Army and Navy Journal* 7 (August 13, 1870): 817.

Crawford, F. Marion. "Beatrice Cenci: The True Story of a Misunderstood Tragedy: with New Documents." *The Century Magazine* 75 (November 1907–April 1908): 449–66.

Cresap, Bernarr. *Appomattox Warrior: The Story of General E.O.C. Ord.* New York: A. S. Barnes, 1981.

Crozier, Alice. *The Novels of Harriet Beecher Stowe.* New York: Oxford University Press, 1969.

Curtis, George. "From the Editor's Easy Chair at *Harper's*: In Defense of *Lady Byron Vindicated.*" *Harper's New Monthly Magazine* 39 (1869): 767.

D'Emilio, John, and Estelle B. Freedman. *Intimate Matters: A History of Sexuality in America.* New York: Harper and Row, 1988.

Denney, Robert E. *The Civil War Years: A Day-by-Day Chronicle of the Life of a Nation.* New York: Sterling, 1992.

Dietz, Christine A., and John L. Craft. "Family Dynamics of Incest: A New Perspective." *Social Casework: The Journal of Contemporary Social Work* 61 (1980): 602–9.

Dodge, Theodore A. "The Battle of Chancellorsville." *Southern Historical Society Papers* 14 (1886): 276–92.

Downey, Fairfax D. *Indian-Fighting Army.* New York: Charles Scribner's Sons, 1941.

Eisler, Benita. *Byron: Child of Passion, Fool of Fame.* New York: Alfred A. Knopf, 1999.

Elwin, Malcolm. *Lord Byron's Wife.* New York: Harcourt, Brace, and World, 1963.

Faust, Drew Gilpin. *James Henry Hammond and the Old South: A Design for Mastery.* Baton Rouge: Louisiana State University Press, 1982.

Fellman, Michael. *Citizen Sherman: A Life of William Tecumseh Sherman.* New York: Random House, 1995.

Fidler, William P. *Augusta Evans Wilson 1835–1909: A Biography.* University: University of Alabama Press, 1951.

Foner, Jack D. *Blacks and the Military in American History: A New Perspective.* New York: Praeger, 1974.

———. *The United States Soldier Between Two Wars.* New York: Humanities Press, 1970.

Forsyth, George A. *The Story of the Soldier.* New York: Appleton, 1900.

Fowler, Arlen L. *The Black Infantry in the West, 1869–1891.* Norman: University of Oklahoma Press, 1996.

Fowler, Orson S. *Creative and Sexual Science.* New York: Fowler and Wells, 1875.

Francoeur, Robert T. *A Descriptive Dictionary and Atlas of Sexology.* Westport, Conn.: Greenwood Press, 1991.

Freud, Sigmund. *The Standard Edition of the Complete Psychological Works of Sigmund Freud,* trans. James Strachey. London: Hogarth Press, 1957.

Frost, Lawrence. *General Custer's Libbie.* Seattle: Superior Publishing Company, 1975.

Fry, James B. "Justice for the Army." *Army and Navy Journal* 21 (August 25, 1883): 63.

Garrison, Dee. "Immoral Fiction in the Late Victorian Library," *American Quarterly* 28 (1976): 71–89.

Gay, Peter. *The Education of the Senses,* vol. 1 of *The Bourgeois Experience: Victoria to Freud.* New York: Oxford University Press, 1984.

Gebhard, Paul H., et al. *Sex Offenders: An Analysis of Types.* New York: Harper and Row, and Paul B. Hoeber, 1965.

Generous, William T., Jr. *Swords and Scales: The Development of the Uniform Code of Military Justice.* Port Washington, N.Y.: Kennikat Press, 1973.

Glass, Edward L. N. *The History of the Tenth Cavalry, 1866–1921* [1921]. Fort Collins, Colo.: Old Army Press, 1972.

Glenn, Garrard. *The Army and the Law.* New York: Columbia University Press, 1943.

Grayson, George W. *The United States and Mexico: Patterns of Influence.* New York: Praeger, 1984.

Greene, Duane Merritt. *Ladies and Officers of the United States Army.* Chicago: Central Publishing Co., 1880.

Grosskurth, Phyllis. *Byron: The Flawed Angel.* Boston: Houghton Mifflin, 1997.

Haley, James Evetts. *Fort Concho and the Texas Frontier.* San Angelo: San Angelo Standard-Times, 1952.

Haller, John S., Jr., and Robin M. Haller. *The Physician and Sexuality in Victorian America.* Urbana: University of Illinois Press, 1974.

Hamlin, Augustus Choate. *The Battle of Chancellorsville.* Bangor, Me.: n.p., 1896.

Hare-Mustin, Rachel T. "Sex, Lies, and Headaches: The Problem Is Power," *Journal of Feminist Family Therapy* 3 (1991): 39–61.

Harrowitz, Nancy A. *Antisemitism, Misogyny, and the Logic of Cultural Difference: Cesare Lombroso and Matilde Serao.* Lincoln: University of Nebraska Press, 1994.

Hartman, Mary, and Lois W. Banner, eds. *Clio's Consciousness Raised: New Perspectives on the History of Women.* New York: Harper and Row, 1974.

Hawthorne, Nathaniel. *The Centenary Edition of the Works of Nathaniel Hawthorne,* ed. Thomas Woodson et al. 23 vols. Columbus: Ohio State University Press, 1962–94.

Hedrick, Joan D. *Harriet Beecher Stowe: A Life.* New York: Oxford University Press, 1994.

Herman, Judith Lewis, with Lisa Hirschman. *Father-Daughter Incest.* Cambridge, Mass.: Harvard University Press, 1981.

Hirshson, Stanley P. *The White Tecumseh: A Biography of William T. Sherman.* New York: John Wiley and Sons, 1997.

Hoogenboom, Ari. *Rutherford B. Hayes: Warrior and President.* Lawrence: University Press of Kansas, 1995.

Hughes, Graham. "The Crime of Incest." *Journal of Criminal Law, Criminology, and Police Science* 55 (1964): 322–31.

Johnson, Janis Tyler. *Mothers of Incest Survivors: Another Side of the Story.* Bloomington: Indiana University Press, 1992.

Keim, DeB. Randolph. *Sheridan's Troopers on the Border: A Winter Campaign on the Plains* [1870]. London: George Routledge and Sons, 1885.

Kellogg, John H. *Ladies Guide in Health and Disease, Girlhood, Maidenhood, Wifehood, Motherhood.* Des Moines, Iowa: W. D. Condit, 1883.

Kinevan, Marcos. *Frontier Cavalryman: Lieutenant John Bigelow with the Buffalo Soldiers in Texas.* El Paso: Texas Western Press, 1998.

Knight, Oliver. *Life and Manners in the Frontier Army.* Norman: University of Oklahoma Press, 1978.

Lane, Lydia Spencer. *I Married a Soldier, or Old Days in the Old Army* [1893]. Albuquerque: Horn and Wallace, 1964.

Leckie, Shirley A., ed. *The Colonel's Lady on the Western Frontier: The Correspondence of Alice Kirk Grierson.* Lincoln: University of Nebraska Press, 1989.

Leckie, William A. *The Buffalo Soldiers: A Narrative of the Negro Cavalry in the West.* Norman: University of Oklahoma Press, 1967.

Leckie, William A., and Shirley A. Leckie. *Unlikely Warriors: General Benjamin H. Grierson and His Family.* Norman: University of Oklahoma Press, 1984.

Lehmann, Herman. *Nine Years Among the Indians, 1870–1879* [1927], ed. J. Marvin Hunter. Albuquerque: University of New Mexico Press, 1993.

Lombroso, Cesare. *Crime, Its Causes and Remedies,* trans. Henry P. Horton. Boston: Little, Brown, 1918.

———. Introduction by Gina Lombroso Ferrero. In *Criminal Man,* ed. Gina Lombroso Ferrero. New York: G. P. Putnam's Sons, 1911.

Lowell, James Russell. *New Letters of James Russell Lowell,* ed. M. A. DeWolfe Howe. New York: Harper and Brothers, 1932.

Lurie, Jonathan. *Arming Military Justice.* Vol. 1, *The Origins of the United States Court of Military Appeals, 1775–1950.* Princeton, N.J.: Princeton University Press, 1992.

Lustig, Noel. "Incest: A Family Group Survival Pattern." *Archives of General Psychiatry* 14 (1966): 31–40.

McFeely, William S. *Grant: A Biography.* New York: W. W. Norton, 1981.

McMurtry, Larry. *In a Narrow Grave: Essays on Texas.* New York: Simon and Schuster, 1968.

McPherson, James M. *The Negro's Civil War: How American Negroes Felt and Acted During the War for the Union.* Urbana: University of Illinois Press, 1982.

Marszalek, John F. *Sherman: A Soldier's Passion for Order.* New York: Free Press, 1993.

Mason, Michael. *The Making of Victorian Sexuality.* New York: Oxford University Press, 1994.

Meiselman, Karin C. *Incest: A Psychological Study of Causes and Effects with Treatment Recommendations.* San Francisco: Jossey-Bass, 1990.

Mott, Frank Luther. *Golden Multitudes: The Story of Bestsellers in the United States.* New York: Macmillan, 1947.

Myres, Sandra L. "Romance and Reality on the American Frontier: Views of Army Wives." *Western Historical Quarterly* 13 (1982): 409–27.

Nankivel, John H. *History of the Twenty-fifth Regiment, 1869–1926.* Fort Collins, Colo.: Old Army Press, 1972.

Nott, J. C., and George R. Gliddon. *Types of Mankind.* Philadelphia: Lippincott, 1868.

Olmsted, Frederick Law. *A Journey Through Texas: Or, a Saddle-Trip on the Southwestern Frontier.* Austin: University of Texas Press, 1978.

Pascoe, Peggy. "Race, Gender and Intercultural Relations: The Case of Interracial Marriage." In *Writing the Range: Race, Class, and Culture in the Women's West,* ed. Elizabeth Jameson and Susan Armitage. Norman: University of Oklahoma Press, 1997.

Phisterer, Frederick, compiler. *New York in the War of the Rebellion, 1861–1865,* vol. 4. Albany: Weed and Parsons, 1890.

"Phrenology." In *Encyclopaedia Britannica,* 11th ed. New York: Encyclopaedia Britannica Company, 1911.

Pierce, N. H. *The Free State of Menard: A History of the County.* Menard, Tex.: Menard News Press, 1946.

Prucha, Francis Paul. *A Guide to the Military Posts of the United States, 1789–1895.* Madison: State Historical Society of Wisconsin, 1964.

Ridley, Jasper. *Maximilian and Juárez.* New York: Ticknor & Fields, 1992.

Riley, Glenda. *Women and Indians on the Frontier, 1825–1915.* Albuquerque: University of New Mexico Press, 1984.

Rister, Carl Coke. *Border Captives: The Traffic in Prisoners by Southern Plains Indians, 1835–1875.* Norman: University of Oklahoma Press, 1940.

———. *The Southwestern Frontier, 1865–1881: A History of the Coming of the Settlers, Indian Depredations and Massacres, Ranching Activities, Operations of White Desperadoes and Thieves, Government Protection, Building of Railways, and the Disappearance of the Frontier.* New York: Arthur H. Clark, 1928.

Roberts, Robert. *The Classic Slum: Salford Life in the First Quarter of the Century.* New York: Penguin, 1973.

Rodenbough, Theodore F., and William L. Haskin, eds. *The Army of the United States.* New York: Maynard, Merrill, 1896.

Ryan, Mary P. *Womanhood in America: From Colonial Times to the Present.* New York: New Viewpoints, 1975.

Schafer, Stephen. *Theories in Criminology: Past and Present Philosophies of the Crime Problem.* New York: Random House, 1969.

Schubert, Frank N. "Black Soldiers on the White Frontier: Some Factors Influencing Race Relations." *Phylon* 32 (1971): 410–15.

Shepher, Joseph. *Incest: A Biosocial View.* New York: Academic Press, 1983.

Sherman, William T. "Old Times: California from 1848 to 1888." *North American Review* 148 (1889): 269–79.

A Sketch of the History and Duties of the Judge Advocate General's Department, United States Army, Washington, D.C., March 1, 1878, as Prepared at the Request of the Commission (of 1876) on the Reform and Reorganization of the Army, with Additions. Washington, D.C.: T. McGill, 1878.

Smith-Rosenberg, Carroll. *Disorderly Conduct: Visions of Gender in Victorian America.* New York: Knopf, 1985.

———. "Sex as Symbol in Victorian Purity." *American Journal of Sociology* 84 supplement (1978): S212–47.

Smith-Rosenberg, Carroll, and Charles Rosenberg. "The Female Animal: Medical and Biological Views of Women in Nineteenth-Century America." *Journal of American History* 60 (September 1973): 332–56.

Stallard, Patricia Y. *Glittering Misery: Dependents of the Indian Fighting Army.* San Rafael, Calif.: Presidio Press, 1978.

Stout, David. "An Army as Good as Its People, and Vice Versa." *The New York Times,* "News of the Week in Review," July 26, 1998: 4.

Stowe, Harriet Beecher. *Lady Byron Vindicated: A History of the Byron Controversy from Its Beginning in 1816 to the Present Time* [1871]. New York: Haskell House, 1970.

Strickland, Margot. *The Byron Women.* New York: St. Martin's, 1974.

Talley, Mike, ed. *Texas State Travel Guide.* Austin: Texas Department of Transportation, 1998.

Thompson, Erwin N. "The Negro Soldier and His Officers." In *The Black Military Experience in the American West,* ed. John M. Carroll. New York: Liveright, 1971: 259–80.

Utley, Robert M. *Frontier Regulars: The United States Army and the Indian, 1866–1891.* New York: Macmillan, 1973.

Weigley, Russell F. *History of the United States Army.* New York: Macmillan, 1967.

———. *Towards an American Army: Military Thought from Washington to Marshall.* Westport, Conn.: Greenwood Press, 1962.

Welles, Gideon. *Diary of Gideon Welles, Secretary of the Navy under Lincoln and Johnson,* ed. John T. Morse. 3 vols. Boston: Houghton Mifflin, 1911.

Welter, Barbara. "The Cult of True Womanhood, 1820–1860." *American Quarterly* 18 (1966): 151–74.

West, Luther C. *They Call It Justice.* New York: Viking Press, 1977.

Westheimer, Ruth K. *Dr. Ruth's Encyclopedia of Sex.* New York: Continuum, 1994.

Wheeler, Homer W. *Buffalo Days: Forty Years in the Old West,* 2d ed. Indianapolis: Bobbs-Merrill, 1925.

Whitman, S. E. *The Troopers: An Informal History of the Plains Cavalry, 1865–1890.* New York: Hastings House, 1962.

Who Was Who in American History—Military. Chicago: Marquis Who's Who, 1975.

Wigmore, John Henry. *Evidence in Trials at Common Law,* rev. James H. Chadbourn, 10 vols. Boston: Little, Brown, 1970.

Wilbarger, J. W. *Indian Depredations in Texas.* 1889. Vol. 1 in Brasada Reprint Series. Austin: Pemberton Press, 1967.

Williams, Clayton W. *Texas' Last Frontier: Fort Stockton and the Trans-Pecos 1861–1895,* ed. Ernest Wallace. College Station: Texas A&M University Press, 1982.

Wilson, Augusta Evans. *Infelice.* New York: A. L. Burt, 1875.

Wilson, Forrest. *Crusader in Crinoline: The Life of Harriet Beecher Stowe.* Philadelphia: J. B. Lippincott, 1941.

Wilson, James Q., and Richard J. Herrnstein. *Crime and Human Nature.* New York: Simon and Schuster, 1985.

Wohl, Anthony S. "Sex and the Single Room: Incest among the Victorian Working Classes." In *The Victorian Family: Structure and Stresses,* ed. Anthony S. Wohl. London: Croom Helm, 1978: 197–216.

Woolf, Virginia. *Three Guineas.* New York: Harcourt, Brace, 1938.

Wooster, Robert. *Soldiers, Sutlers, and Settlers: Garrison Life on the Texas Frontier.* College Station: Texas A&M University Press, 1987.

Wright, S. J. *San Antonio de Béxar: Historical, Traditional, Legendary.* Austin, Tex.: Morgan Printing Co., n.d.

INDEX

INDEX

Bigelow, Captain John, Jr., 36–37, 81, 93–96, 137, 143, 145, 155, 211–12, 256*nn19, 21*; African-American soldiers commanded by, 57–58, 60; and Beck family, 188; diagrams of Geddes-Orleman quarters prepared by, 95, 106, 108–10; distaste for gossip of, 37, 77*n*, 184; prefers charges against Blunt, 121; as prosecution witness, 93, 95, 148; women's education criticized by, 116–17

Blackwood's Edinburgh Magazine, 18

Bliss, Major Zenas R., 51, 54

Blunt, Colonel Matthew M., 74, 75, 79, 162, 183, 265*n31*; and Beck-Friedlander scandal, 187, 189; McLaughlen replaced by, 121, 127; as prosecution witness, 121–23

Bragg, Braxton, 43

Breneman, C. K., 155–56

Brown, Dr., 136, 261*n9*

Buchanan, W. F., 50–51

Buckney, Wilson, 197

Buell, General Don Carlos, 43

Burbank, Captain, 34

Burnside, General Ambrose E., 42

Burton, John, 35

Bush, Major Joseph, 197

Byron, George Gordon, Lord, 14–20

Byron, Lady (Annabella Milbanke), 14–16, 20–21, 219, 223

Carleton, Colonel James, 59–60

Carpenter, Captain Louis H., 26, 27, 87–88

Carr, General Eugene A., 28, 241

Carter, R. G., 126

Cenci, Beatrice, 216–17, 266*n10*

Cenci, Count Francesco, 216

Chancellorsville, Battle of, 24–26

Chew, Thomas R., 101

Cheyenne Indians, 26

Chopin, Kate, 167

Civil War, 38, 45, 48, 54, 114, 180; African-American soldiers in, 58; Geddes in, 27–28, 30, 32, 200, 240–41; Hayes in, 158; McLaughlen in, 126; Ord in, 41–43; Orleman in, 23–26, 147

Cleary, Peter A., 64–65, 254*n41*

Clous, Judge Advocate John Walter, 12, 69, 142, 144, 149, 209; Armes's antipathy toward, 70–71, 210–11, 265*n31*; Army career of, 69–70, 213; and Bigelow's diagrams of Geddes-Orleman quarters, 95, 109; and defense objections, 73, 90; defense witnesses cross-examined by, 135, 137, 138, 141, 222, 224; in Flipper court-martial, 212–13; prosecution witnesses examined by, 85, 102, 107; rebuttal testimony presented by, 145–46, 148; Sweet affidavit forwarded to, 183, 184

Cohan, Tamar, 261*n10*

Coke, Richard, 47, 209*n*